Insurance Fraud Casebook

PAYING A PREMIUM FOR CRIME

Edited by

Laura Hymes
Joseph T. Wells

WILEY

Published by John Wiley & Sons, Inc., Hoboken, New Jersey.
Published simultaneously in Canada.

For general information on our other products and services or for technical support, please contact our Customer Care Department within the United States at (800) 762-2974, outside the United States at (317) 572-3993 or fax (317) 572-4002.

Wiley publishes in a variety of print and electronic formats and by print-on-demand. Some material included with standard print versions of this book may not be included in e-books or in print-on-demand. If this book refers to media such as a CD or DVD that is not included in the version you purchased, you may download this material at http://booksupport.wiley.com. For more information about Wiley products, visit www.wiley.com.

Library of Congress Cataloging-in-Publication Data

Insurance fraud casebook: paying a premium for crime / edited by Laura Hymes and Joseph T. Wells.
    pages cm
  Includes index.
  ISBN 978-1-118-61771-7 (cloth); ISBN 978-1-118-70093-8 (ebk);
ISBN 978-1-118-70099-0 (ebk); ISBN 978-1-118-70087-7 (ebk)
  1. Insurance crimes–Case studies. 2. Fraud investigation–Case studies. I. Wells, Joseph T.
  HV6768.I544 2013
  364.16'3–dc23
                                                                    2013013593

Printed in the United States of America

10 9 8 7 6 5 4 3 2 1

*To Grampy Hymes, a casebook enthusiast and retired
dentist who has seen insurance fraud from inside the clinic*

Contents

Preface

The idea of *shared risk* is the foundation of all types of insurance. In one of the earliest examples of shared risk, ancient Chinese traders would distribute their cargo throughout many different oceangoing vessels to limit the incurred losses if any single one of them capsized. Later, the Babylonians enacted the first known written laws in the Code of Hammurabi (circa 1750 B.C.), which, among its many provisions, allowed lenders to charge additional costs to cancel loans for which the collateral was lost or stolen.

Early insurance was principally limited to the extreme risks associated with ships and the goods they transported on the high seas. But even in ancient Rome, records exist to show that there were burial societies that paid for funeral costs of their members out of the dues they were assessed. The Achaemenid Empire in ancient Persia (circa 550–330 B.C.) was the first to offer individuals insurance for their general interests. Each year citizens presented the ruler with a gift. If it was worth more than 10,000 gold coins, the gift and the giver were recorded in a ledger. If the gift giver later needed money for an investment, for a child's wedding or another personal venture, the government would give him or her twice the amount of the recorded gift.

By the mid-1400s, marine insurance was highly developed but other forms of insurance were not. Sharing losses, rather than making a profit, was the main goal at the time. However, after the Renaissance in Europe, the insurance industry experienced significant growth and became much more sophisticated.

Other disasters began to be covered by insurance after the Great Fire of London of 1666, which destroyed 13,200 buildings. In 1680, Englishman Nicholas Barbon established the first fire insurance company, known as The Fire Office. Around the same time, Mr. Edward Lloyd of London opened a coffee shop that became a popular hangout for ship owners and merchants. Risk takers also congregated at Lloyd's to provide insurance (for a profit) for shipping concerns. Documents would be prepared, and those providing the insurance would each sign at the bottom, a process that added the term *underwriter* to our lexicon. Lloyds's of London would go on to become one of the largest insurance entities in the world.

More insurance companies sprang up in England and continental Europe after 1711, during the so-called bubble era. Many were downright fraudulent get-rich-quick schemes that sold worthless securities to the public. Others were woefully undercapitalized and could not cover their losses from claims. And no systems had yet been developed to weed out fraudulent claims by the insureds. The resulting chaos of the burgeoning industry took more than a century to right itself.

What we now call *health insurance* probably began in Germany, building on the tradition of welfare programs in Prussia and Saxony that began in the 1840s. By 1880, German Chancellor Otto von Bismarck introduced old-age pensions, accident insurance, medical care and unemployment insurance. The British followed with a system of social insurance in the early 1900s, which was greatly expanded after World War II.

In America, the insurance industry developed slowly, helped along by Benjamin Franklin. In 1752, he founded the Philadelphia Contributionship for the Insurance of Houses from Loss by Fire, which made significant contributions to the prevention field by warning against certain fire hazards and refusing to insure high-risk dwellings. Around the same time, the sale of life insurance commenced in the United States, mostly tied to religious institutions. The Presbyterian Synods in New York and Philadelphia started the Corporation for Relief of Poor and Distressed Widows of Presbyterian Ministers. And within 50 years, nearly two dozen life insurance companies went into business, but most failed.

By the mid-1850s, life insurance companies had started taking hold in the United States. New York Life was formed during this period and is now one of the most prominent. Early life insurance companies had to contend with crooked agents in their employ, a problem that still exists in measure today. It was common then for agents to sign up people they knew to be in bad health for the sole purpose of collecting a commission on the sale; no physical exams were required at the time. But by the late 1800s, employing doctors to use standard criteria for evaluating risks reduced (but did not eliminate) the problem. The other half of the fraud equation was the insurance companies themselves. Many that sprang up were nothing more than Ponzi schemes, which were mathematically predestined to fail.

In the early 20th century, the insurance industry blossomed with profits, and companies sought to expand by offering additional coverage for a variety of risks. One of the first forms of insurance for health was established by Britain in 1911 with the passage of the National Insurance Act. In the United States, a group of Dallas-based teachers formed a partnership with an area hospital in 1929 to provide a set amount of health and sickness coverage in exchange for a set, prepaid fee. This partnership eventually became known as Blue Cross. Meanwhile, physicians developed Blue Shield as an alternative. The two groups eventually merged.

During World War II, wage freezes were instituted throughout companies in America. Group life and health insurance offerings sprang up (at mostly the companies' expense) as corporations, desperate for workers, saw a legal way to attract and keep employees. Such large group policies went to large carriers, which led to a consolidation of the industry, squeezing out smaller entities.

As the healthcare market grew, the U.S. government began encouraging participation, which led to tax-exempt status for employer/employee contributions in 1954. Although some continued to strongly oppose a nationalized healthcare system, Congress enacted Medicare and Medicaid in 1965. Medicare called for compulsory hospital insurance for those over 65; Medicaid provided care for low-income people through a program that combined federal and state resources, the benefits of which vary from state to state depending on per-capita income.

While many counties have nationalized healthcare, the United States remains a patchwork of governmental and private plans. This has resulted in some of the world's most expensive and ineffective health insurance coverage. In 2010, the U.S. Congress passed the Patient Protection and Affordable Care Act (ACA), seeking to extend mandated coverage for nearly 50 million uninsured Americans. The ACA also wants to slow down the growth in the cost of healthcare and improve the patient delivery system. But it has been used as a political football, as a large minority of Americans oppose mandated, universal healthcare. Only time will tell whether it is better or worse than the system (or lack thereof) it replaces.

Fraud in the insurance and healthcare industry has always been a problem. Although there have been many attempts to determine the actual costs, the figures are estimates at best and unsupported guesses at worst. Suffice it to say that fraudulent transactions regarding insurance claims probably exceed those in any other area for a number of reasons.

First is the concept of *diffusion of harm*. This means that fictitious claims are spread across a large number of people. While a person might never steal from a neighbor, committing fraud against a faceless corporation, governmental agency or insurance company is easier to justify. Second, most people just don't like insurance companies. Many argue that they are bloated, rich bureaucracies interested only in their own welfare and not the people they insure. They claim that the insurance companies are there when collecting premiums but absent when it comes to paying claims. This attitude makes insurers an easy target for fraud.

The third reason for large volumes of insurance fraud might relate to the technological processing of claims. Those charged with developing systems to prevent insurance fraud are certainly no smarter than some of those committing it, and internal control systems are designed only to be reasonable, not foolproof. In short, where there is a will, there is usually a way. A fourth reason for insurance fraud, particularly as it relates to health insurance, stems from a patient's instinctual trust of his or her medical provider. Many of us think of our doctors and nurses as benevolent caretakers who have our best interest at heart, but we fail to realize that these providers commit the overwhelming majority of healthcare fraud. Whatever the causes, most experts believe insurance and healthcare fraud is getting worse, not better.

This collection of case studies comes to you directly from members of the ACFE; each case has been investigated and written by anti-fraud experts working directly to combat insurance schemes. The case studies cover a wide array of insurance fraud — from healthcare fraud, to arson, to murder and everything in between — because we want to provide a panoramic view of the problem rather than limit the cases to a narrow sector of the industry. We changed the names of the people and places to protect the anonymity of those involved, but the cases themselves are real. All profits from this publication will be donated to the ACFE Scholarship Foundation to train the next generation of anti-fraud experts.

As legislation develops and the insurance industry evolves, staying abreast of the trends will be essential for the fraud fighters investigating the crimes and the consumers trying to avoid becoming victims. We hope this collection offers you an informative but also entertaining reference, whether you are reading it as an expert or an interested novice.

Laura Hymes, CFE
Dr. Joseph T. Wells, CFE, CPA
Austin, Texas
March 2013

Insurance Fraud Classification System

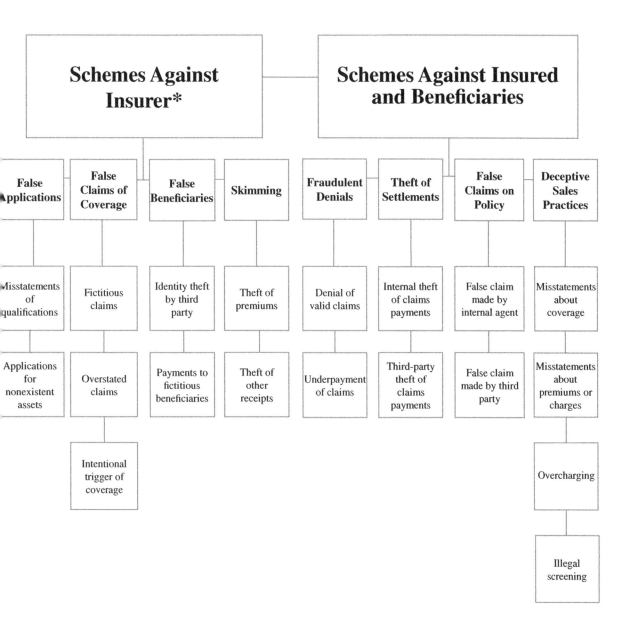

Schemes Against Insurer*				Schemes Against Insured and Beneficiaries			
False Applications	False Claims of Coverage	False Beneficiaries	Skimming	Fraudulent Denials	Theft of Settlements	False Claims on Policy	Deceptive Sales Practices
Misstatements of qualifications	Fictitious claims	Identity theft by third party	Theft of premiums	Denial of valid claims	Internal theft of claims payments	False claim made by internal agent	Misstatements about coverage
Applications for nonexistent assets	Overstated claims	Payments to fictitious beneficiaries	Theft of other receipts	Underpayment of claims	Third-party theft of claims payments	False claim made by third party	Misstatements about premiums or charges
	Intentional trigger of coverage						Overcharging
							Illegal screening

*We include government health care providers in the category of "Insurer." Although these programs are susceptible to frauds by other insurers, such schemes would fall under the "False Claims of Coverage" branch of this tree.

ACFE
Association of Certified Fraud Examiners

Needles in a Paystack

CHARLES PIPER

Susan Shamrock became a doctor because she wanted to provide people with relief from their allergy suffering. Although sticking needles in patients was not her favorite thing to do, Susan knew she was helping them get back to their normal lives. She enjoyed being a physician and helping people.

On the home front, Susan was happily married. She and her husband had two daughters who enjoyed a lifestyle most kids would envy. The girls attended private schools, had the latest electronic gadgets and even received expensive professional golf lessons. The family lived in a big house, and Susan and her spouse drove fancy cars. Dr. Shamrock was highly respected in her community and she gave generously to various local charities.

As the years passed, both Susan and her husband took to gambling at local casinos for entertainment. Eventually, Mr. Shamrock quit his job to pursue professional gambling; by doing so, he could even write off gambling losses on their tax returns. Predictably, Susan's husband lost a lot of their money gambling. But their marriage was good, their kids were happy and Susan's practice was profitable.

A Growing Company

After Susan opened her own allergy clinic, she grew increasingly gratified that she was able to help so many patients; plus the money was good. Business was slow in the beginning, but it didn't take long before patients under her care started coming back for regular treatments. Newer patients followed, and the practice kept growing. Business was so good that she hired employees to schedule appointments, handle accounts payable and receivable and file claim forms with insurance companies and federal and state healthcare programs. She also hired medical assistants and an office manager.

Sometimes Susan became frustrated because a few of her patients didn't respond to treatment regimens. In those instances, her patients not only continued to suffer from their allergies, but they or their insurance companies continued paying for treatment that was not working.

As part of her continuing education, Susan attended various seminars where she learned from other experts in the field. At one training event, the speaker discussed a new allergy treatment that was considered experimental by the Food and Drug Administration (FDA). Susan was intrigued and inspired by the presentation and immediately began offering the treatment as an alternative to her patients who hadn't responded to previous therapy. She even listed the experimental treatment on her website. Several of her patients were willing to try it out of frustration because nothing else worked for them, and they had no financial qualms because their insurance paid for it.

Another New Case on My Desk

I was a federal agent with experience investigating complex fraud schemes (including healthcare provider fraud) when I received a referral in the mail at my office. The note indicated that Dr. Susan Shamrock had possibly miscoded billings for allergy treatments when submitting claims for several of her patients.

The allegation said she provided patients with nonapproved, experimental allergy treatment but listed it on insurance claims as a different, approved treatment. (Allergy treatments not approved by the FDA are not reimbursable by insurance companies or federal healthcare programs.) The referral also mentioned Dr. Shamrock's website description of experimental treatment. Based on her website, there was no denying that Susan was promoting the use of the experimental treatment.

The referral also reported that during a federal audit of a random sampling of billed treatments, Dr. Shamrock was asked to provide supportive documentation for several of the insurance claims she submitted and that the government already had processed and paid. However, Dr. Shamrock ignored or failed to respond to the requests.

Rolling Up Our Sleeves

From experience, I knew that healthcare fraud often affects many insurance carriers and federal healthcare programs — if one program was defrauded by a provider or facility, in all probability other programs and companies were also defrauded. Based on that knowledge, I immediately contacted healthcare fraud investigators I had previously met or worked with and notified them of the referral. Some of those investigators worked for agencies that had their own healthcare programs. I asked the investigators to determine if their agencies received and paid insurance claims from Dr. Susan Shamrock. Only one of the investigators, Agent Andrew Badge, responded positively.

Badge and I had successfully worked together in the past, and, like me, he used to be a street cop before becoming a federal agent. Badge and I met at his office and developed an investigative plan for this case.

Using administrative subpoenas, we separately requested and later obtained copies of numerous patient files and billing records from the doctor's office. Dr. Shamrock took about a month to comply fully with the subpoenas. Waiting this long is not unusual in white-collar investigations, and, in fairness, the doctor had a small office staff and years' worth of records to copy. In addition, they had to do most of the copying after normal business hours when the clinic was closed.

Patient files are often thick and might include: patient contact information (name, address, Social Security number, date of birth, etc.), insurance policy coverage information, claims submitted for payment, records of payment, explanation of benefit forms, dates of treatment, physician notes, lab test results, appointments and so on.

Badge and I worked in different buildings about ten miles from each other so we periodically met for lunch and talked about this case and others. When we finally received the subpoenaed records, we reviewed them at our own offices. We searched for indicators that patients received the experimental treatment, which may have been miscoded and billed as an FDA-approved treatment.

Reviewing the boxes full of patient files was a tedious process. Although I was terrible at dissecting worms and frogs in high-school biology classes, I enjoy dissecting information in fraud cases. The review took several weeks to complete. The first several days were boring because only a couple of files indicated that patients received the experimental treatment. Nevertheless, I carefully reviewed each claim individually.

Although I had never received allergy injections myself, I thought it odd that some of the patients reportedly received shots four or five times a week. I telephoned Agent Badge, told him what I found and added, "I wouldn't go to the doctor's office four or five days a week if they were giving out free lunches — let alone just to get needles stuck in my arm." Badge remarked, "I'd go if they were giving free lunches." We both laughed.

More alarming than what I was finding in the patients' files was what I *wasn't* finding. The files often contained no supportive documentation for any of the billed injections. For example, in one patient's file, the dates on insurance claim forms indicated allergy injections were given to the patient on January 10, 12, 14 and 15. But there was no documentation in the file indicating the patient ever stepped foot inside the doctor's office on any of those dates.

As I continued reviewing patient files, I found repeated instances where there was absolutely no supportive documentation for any of the services billed for.

In addition, when there was documentation, the charts indicated that the patients' next visit would not be for several weeks. The next pages in the patient files often indicated they were last seen on the previously documented dates.

For example, a patient's file might read something like this:

> January 3: Patient John Smith seen today and given an injection. His next office visit will be February 5.

Then the next documentation would read:

> February 5: Patient John Smith last seen on January 3. Patient given an injection. Next visit will be March 7.

In short, the written notes in the patients' files contradicted the insurance claims. The charts were incriminating evidence that the patient had not visited Dr. Shamrock nearly as frequently as the documents indicated.

I alerted Badge to my findings, and he said he had been seeing the same pattern in his files. At this point, I began to understand why Dr. Shamrock refused to comply with the auditors' previous request for treatment records; she didn't have any to give!

Knowing that documents alone do not prove a case, Badge and I began interviews of patients at their homes. Prior to the interviews, I listed questions to help guide me and gave a copy of the list to Badge. Having most of the questions already written down makes it easier to take notes. I emphasized that the draft list of questions was only to be used as a guide and additional questions would be asked as needed. Badge liked the idea of numbering the questions and said he was going to start doing it for his future interviews.

Our first interview was of a former patient named Steve Hardwick. He said he never received more than two or three injections in any given week. But what Hardwick said next was a complete surprise: "I didn't need to go to the doctor's office anyway; Dr. Shamrock just gave me the filled syringes to inject myself."

I asked Steve to elaborate. He said that about once each month, he would show up at Dr. Shamrock's office and she would inject him with an allergy shot. During the same visit, the doctor or her assistant would hand him a month's supply of filled syringes, and he would later inject himself with the antigens two or three times a week.

Hardwick said, "Come with me; I think I have a couple of the syringes in the fridge." We followed him into his kitchen, where he opened his refrigerator and pulled out two filled syringes. Hardwick said, "These are the syringes Dr. Shamrock gave me."

Understandably, Agent Badge and I asked a bunch of follow-up questions. Steve Hardwick said he liked the arrangement because he could inject himself and didn't need to travel back and forth to the doctor's office all the time. But the fact is, he injected himself only two or three times each week, not four or five times like the insurance claims indicated. Plus, the insurance claims specifically listed the location of service as Dr. Shamrock's office.

I studied the claim forms a little closer and observed that all of the injections were reportedly given on weekdays; never on the weekend. I asked Hardwick if he ever injected himself on the weekend and he said, "Sure, lots of times." He said he never had to report his dates of injection to the doctor's office.

I speculated that Dr. Shamrock knew that if she listed Saturday and Sunday treatments on her insurance forms, the insurers would reject the claims (because the doctor's business was closed on the weekends). I also figured that since Dr. Shamrock apparently thought she could get away with allowing patients to inject themselves away from the clinic, she would probably have no qualms about listing the incorrect injection dates on some paperwork.

Agent Badge and I photographed, marked and collected the filled syringes as evidence, and Badge later stored them in his office evidence refrigerator. During the next several weeks, Badge and I conducted more patient interviews. On the days we worked together, we alternated buying each other lunch. It seemed like every time it was my turn to pay, Badge picked a more expensive restaurant to eat at.

During our interviews, Badge and I heard similar stories from Dr. Shamrock's patients. A few people also said they received an experimental allergy treatment. Those patients reported that Dr. Shamrock assured them she would take care of the insurance billings. Since the patients didn't have to pay any money out of pocket, they had no concerns about how much the insurers were billed or how the treatments were coded.

After returning to my office, I contacted one of the government healthcare program integrity officials and was informed that each injection should have been given by a qualified and approved healthcare professional inside the physician's office. The official said the patients should have been monitored by a healthcare professional in case they had adverse reactions to the injections. I was also informed that the government would not have paid those claims had they known the patients injected themselves and that the locations of service were falsely recorded. I telephoned Agent Badge and told him what I had learned. He then called the program integrity officials from his agency and received the same information. Some agencies and insurance companies have different rules, so it was important for us to get clarification from the experts at our respective agencies.

In the days that followed, I attempted to quantify the potential dollar loss based on the patient files and claim forms I reviewed. I began adding up all the dollars for the false claims where there was no supportive documentation or false information. I also included the few instances where the experimental treatments were miscoded. But as I continued reviewing the claim forms, I found something even more alarming.

In addition to billing for injections, Dr. Shamrock billed extremely high prices for "preparing and mixing" the antigens in the syringes. Supposedly, each patient had his or her own unique master serum. Injections were billed at about $50 each, but mixtures were billed for thousands of dollars each!

The real money Dr. Shamrock made came from the falsification in the number of antigen mixtures made. To avoid detection, she billed for lots of injections — and made an extra $50 for each fictitious injection.

I also knew that the insurance regulations required patients to pay copayments when they received treatment. Providers are not permitted to waive the copayments. So circumstantial evidence of fraud was established by the lack of patient billings for copayments. Interestingly, Dr. Shamrock had no qualms submitting false claims to insurance companies, but she never sent her patients false bills for the copayments. I suspect she knew darn well that the patients would have been lining up at the door to complain if she tried to defraud them too.

My next question was: How many syringes could be filled with each mixture? Agent Badge and I issued more administrative subpoenas to Dr. Shamrock's office for the supportive documentation for preparing the mixtures.

Guess what? She didn't have those either. We also asked for the doctor's office appointment and sign-in books and found that the patients who were billed as if treated on certain dates did not have appointments and did not sign in on those dates. The evidence was getting stronger. I started to wonder if there was any legitimate business going on inside the doctor's office.

Badge and I decided we needed to interview some of the doctor's employees. We started by interviewing former employees. Badge and I alternated who would be the lead interviewer while the other took notes. One of the former administrative employees told us, "A few years ago we got into trouble with an insurance company for not having supportive documentation, and I told Dr. Shamrock to stop billing for services that we hadn't provided. But she wouldn't listen to me and we kept on doing it." Badge and I glanced at each other; the case against Dr. Shamrock was getting even stronger.

Agent Badge and I also interviewed Dr. Shamrock's current office manager, Katy Lincoln, at her home on a weeknight. She essentially said the same thing as the former employee. Badge and I decided to try to get additional evidence and asked Katy if she would consent to record a telephone conversation with Dr. Shamrock. She was initially hesitant but finally agreed. Before Katy called Dr. Shamrock, we told her what topics to cover.

In the recorded conversation, Dr. Shamrock said she knew miscoding the treatments was not appropriate. She also admitted she knew the doctor's office was sometimes paid for treatments not provided. But Dr. Shamrock never went so far as to admit that she directed the false claims to be generated.

After returning to my office, I made a copy of the recording, secured the original as evidence and later had a transcript made.

A few days later, Badge and I flipped a coin to determine who would get to interview Dr. Shamrock. I won. Interviewing the doctor was interesting to say the least. I didn't tell her we had a recorded conversation of her admitting knowledge about the false claims because that would have immediately implicated Katy Lincoln as an informant.

When I asked Dr. Shamrock about the missing documentation to support the billings, she blamed an office flood. When I asked why she let patients inject themselves away from the office, she said they preferred it that way. When I asked how she determined the dates that injections were given, she initially said she just guessed but later said the office computer automatically entered the dates. When I asked why she didn't collect copayments from her patients when they were treated, she said her patients couldn't afford to make the copayments.

In short, Dr. Shamrock claimed every mixture and allergy injection billed for was accurate to the best of her knowledge. And when asked why she miscoded the use of experimental allergy treatment to give the appearance that she used an FDA-approved method, Dr. Shamrock said, "That treatment works! It's not my fault that the FDA takes too long to approve good medicine."

Presenting the Facts for Justice

Agent Badge and I brought our collective case to the federal prosecutor's office. In total, the losses were approximately $500,000. The criminal prosecutor declined to accept the case, saying it would have been stronger if Dr. Shamrock said on the recording that she personally directed the false claims to be submitted. Badge and I knew that prosecutors cannot accept every case that comes across their desks, so next we briefed the civil prosecutor, who accepted it without reservation. Using the Federal Civil False Claims Act (Title 31 USC 3729) would potentially allow for treble damages — three times the amount of each false claim.

Dr. Shamrock claimed she did not have the assets to repay. However, she eventually sold a second house and some other property to pay for some of the losses. Rather than debarring or suspending Dr. Shamrock from doing future business with the government, the affected agencies decided to put her on a well-monitored performance and compliance plan, which subjected her to regular audits and other stringent requirements to ensure that this type of activity would not occur in the future.

Lessons Learned

During this case I learned (or relearned) the importance of paying attention to details and of conducting thorough and all-encompassing examinations and investigations. Identifying other affected agencies and working as a team is always important. Each part of every investigation should be well planned and well documented. Conducting thorough interviews and collecting evidence helps make solid cases when wrong-doing does occur.

Fraudsters, as well as most other criminals, usually find ways to rationalize their wrongdoing. In Dr. Shamrock's case, she thought she knew more than the FDA about what was safe for patients. Living beyond one's means is a red flag of possible fraudulent activity — Dr. Shamrock was a prime example of that. Investigators, examiners and auditors should always be on the lookout for billings without supportive documentation when investigating other types of healthcare fraud.

Recommendations to Prevent Future Occurrences

- Thorough and all-encompassing investigations help prove fraud when it occurs and often identify other fraud schemes that were previously unknown.
- In the case of allergy clinics and physicians, examiners should consider analyzing the ratio of antigen mixtures to injections (separately by each patient's name) to determine if the number of mixtures is inflated.
- Analyze the frequency of billed injections (by each patient's name) to determine if the number of injections might be inflated (e.g., billing for five injections a week might be excessive). ·
- Because Dr. Shamrock's patients liked the freedom of injecting them-selves away from the clinic, it is logical to assume that other allergy clinics are also mislabeling the locations of service on their insurance claim forms. Consideration could be given to contacting a random sample of allergy patients who receive injections to determine if any of the injections occur outside the clinic or office.
- The use of experimental treatment (not approved by the FDA) might be a common occurrence, but it becomes a violation of the law when the experimental treatment is miscoded. The most practical way to identify those instances is through periodic audits and reviews of patient treat-ment records (as the auditors did in my case before submitting the referral).
- Interviewing patients is helpful to learn what types of treatments have been (or are being) provided.

Many patients have only few concerns:

- Regaining their health (or relief from their suffering)
- Minimizing their out-of-pocket expenses
- Obtaining the necessary care and treatment conveniently

Most people trust their doctors. When a doctor tells a patient that the treatment will not cost the patient anything, few argue or ask questions. Others who suspect possible insurance fraud might turn a blind eye to it as long as their quality of care is good and they are not personally losing any money. Investigators, examiners and auditors should be mindful that it might be difficult for patients to tell the complete truth about all they know because it could go against their own financial best interests. Some patients may also fear that they could get charged with wrongdoing for false claims submitted by their doctors.

Identifying and proving healthcare fraud includes the use of several different investigative techniques:

- Data and record analysis
- Well-planned and thoroughly conducted interviews
- Collection of evidence

The physical evidence might include:

- Patient files
- Insurance claims forms
- Proof of payments
- Lack of payments (patients not charged copayments)
- Explanation of Benefits forms
- Appointment books
- Sign-in logs
- Patient interviews
- Recorded audio statements
- Previously signed agreements by providers to follow rules and regulations (and perhaps documented training received)
- Previous notices to stop committing the same type of "wrong" in the past
- Other evidence

Proving fraud beyond a reasonable doubt (in a criminal case) or by the preponderance of the evidence (in a civil case) is not an easy task. When conducting investigations and examinations, all possible evidence that can legally be obtained should be pursued and collected. Interviews should be conducted whenever possible, and all facts should be included in written reports.

About the Author

Charles Piper, CFE, CRT, is the owner of Charles Piper's Professional Services located in West Tennessee. He serves as a Certified Fraud Examiner, licensed private investigator and national consultant. Mr. Piper previously served for more than 30 years in law enforcement, including 20 years as a Federal Special Agent and Criminal Investigator.

CHAPTER

2

The Good Doctor and
the Insurance Consultant

MICHAEL KING

Erso Ahmet was an Australian orthopedic surgeon. He was the middle child of a hardworking, middle-class immigrant family, born in the western suburbs of Sydney, New South Wales. Erso's grandfather, a teacher in Palestine, had worked closely with the British forces during World War I, at times passing intelligence on the Ottoman Turk army positions during the battle of Jerusalem. After the war, Erso's grandfather, grandmother and five children (including Erso's father) made their way to Australia, arriving initially in Melbourne in 1919 before moving to Sydney a few months later.

Erso's father, like many immigrants new to Australia, wanted a better life for his children and knew the importance of education. His father owned a furniture business, and the children were expected to help with the business in addition to studying hard at school. Erso lived with his family in the suburbs before moving into town to study with his older brother. Erso attended medical school; his brother studied engineering. While at university, his parents introduced him to Ajda, and a year later the two were married. One year later, the first of their four children was born.

Erso graduated with honors and secured a placement with a large Sydney hospital for his residency internship. While working there, Erso anglicized his name to Edward but often went by Eddie. After working a number of years at the hospital, he went back to school and eventually became a specialized surgeon in orthopedics.

Erso moved into private practice and began to consult on work-related injury claims, including referrals from the state-based Worker's Compensation Agency. He found this work very interesting and learned how minor injuries can have a devastating impact on claimants and their families. However, he found the paperwork and the cap on professional fees a constraint.

On the advice of a colleague who was also a personal friend, Erso decided to undertake plaintiff consultancy. His friend was able to supply him with a reference to a national personal injury solicitor. Initially, work was not as plentiful as he had expected. In a discussion with his friend, he was told that his medical reports read like they were written for the Worker's Compensation Agency and needed to be more "generous and flexible."

The next report that Erso wrote stated that the claimant had suffered "40 percent impairment to spinal function" and "30 percent of the whole body." Erso was uncomfortable because he thought the wording was a little over the top. He waited for the lawyers to contact him and challenge it, but they did not. After the generous report, his reputation grew in the personal injury litigation circle. Referrals began coming in regularly, and soon his calendar was booked two and half years in advance.

A Growing Company

Auswide Insurance Limited has offices in all of Australia's capital cities and had been in business for decades. The company offers general insurance products, including home and contents, vehicle, boat, marine and travel. It also offers injury products, such as compulsory third party, public and product liability and life insurance.

Auswide leadership embarked on an aggressive expansion of operations and acquired a number of leading Australasian insurers, including one that offered workers' compensation insurance. After the various acquisitions, the company began a major software and information technology (IT) revitalization because many of its systems were outdated and incompatible.

As part of the expansion, the company grew its special investigation unit (SIU). Then the investigation areas were reorganized and in some states cut entirely. The SIU's headquarters was located in Brisbane, Queensland. It was managed in two sections: the general insurance arm and injury claim arm.

I was hired as a senior investigator in the injury claims unit and oversaw the expansion of the team from three investigators to nine over the next few years. Most of our investigations were involved with claim fraud arising from motor vehicle injuries. However, we investigated all types of claim fraud. Furthermore, to provide Australia wider coverage and to manage the large number of claims, we used the services of a number of external private investigation firms.

Auswide Insurance Limited is one of Australia's largest insurance companies, employing more than 3,500 staff and with an income of more than 3.1 billion.

On a Hunch

It was early Monday morning in October, and I just sat down at my desk and was once again admiring the pristine views of the Brisbane River as I waited for my computer to boot up when I received a phone call. The caller intro-duced himself as Peter Butler, Investigation Manager of Alpha Insurance. Peter and I had met briefly about a year ago at an anti-fraud conference in Sydney. As at any of these trade events, attendees spent a lot of time network-ing and handing out business cards.

After some small talk, Peter got down to the reason why he called. "I think there is an issue with one of your claimants . . . truthfully I have no idea if it is one of yours! I am doing the ring-around." Peter went on to say "I received a call from an orthopedic surgeon whom we use for our workers' compensation claims. The informant went to a seminar in New Zealand, and one of the speakers was an Australian orthopedic surgeon. The informant told me that the speaker was on a compensation claim arising from a motor accident. I got the impression it was more likely to be gossip; you know what these after-5 drinks are like," Peter said.

I said, "Why go to a seminar and present if you're on a claim?" Thinking a little more about it, I agreed that it was quite strange. I began to shift the various case folders and reports that were stacked on my desk, looking for a pen. "Can you give me the orthopedic surgeon's name?"

"Edward Ahmet," Peter said.

"Thanks, Peter. I'll make some inquiries and have a look at what we got and I will let you know. It may take a few days." After I hung up, I sat at my desk for a few minutes and thought about the odd situation. Initially I thought maybe nothing was wrong. Claimants are capable of working even if they are receiving workers' compensation, providing they have told their doctor and us. Actually, we are happy if they do; it means their health is improving, and we will save money. Then I recalled a story of a claimant who was reporting to be on a total disability claim. One of our investigators was watching television one night and realized that an actor in a television advertisement was the claimant! It would not hurt to check.

I opened up the claims database and reviewed all the active personal injury investigations. I decided to start my search by looking for any doctors. We had three listed, but none by the name of Edward Ahmet.

I called Peter back and I asked if we could speak with the informant. He said he would see what he could do. Peter organized a telephone conference with us and the informant, who was not one of the normal complainants we usually heard from (an ex-spouse, neighbor or coworker who was outraged that the claimant was going to get a big disability payment). Rather, this informant was Dr. Gregory Hugo, a respected orthopedic surgeon. Hugo started by saying "It may be nothing, but I think one of the speakers at the September conference is on a claim. There was talk at the conference about Dr. Ahmet's car accident and that he had been in the hospital a couple of years ago. He seemed fine and displayed no sign of injury. There was also some talk among the conference attendees about him working in Melbourne. He could still be on a compensation claim."

I asked Dr. Hugo if he had a copy of the conference agenda. He said he did and could email it to me. I summarized the information I had and emailed it to Auswide's claims manager, Steven Phillips. I also asked if the claims officers could check their current cases for a claim by Edward Ahmet. Experience taught me to also check on the surname only. I had worked on a number of cases involving Asian claimants who used English first names rather than their own given names. It would not hurt to check.

Paging Dr. Ahmet

Recent mergers with various other insurers resulted in a number of different computer systems that could not "talk" with each other. Indeed, the investigation system was not scheduled to link with the claims data for about three months hence. So it was a long, two-day wait until I received an email from the claims manager with a list of all the claimants by the name of Ahmet. Toward the end of the list was Dr. Erso Ahmet. I thought to myself, this could not be a coincidence!

I emailed the claims officer asking for the case file to be sent through the internal mail. The next day was Friday, and it arrived on my desk at about ten o'clock. I opened the file, which was quite light on detail. The policy had been taken out five years ago. It was what we refer to as a *stapled policy*, which was developed specifically for those in the medical profession. It included income protection, accident injury and business expense coverage. The income protection policy was designed to cover lost wages for a period of five years. Two years after the policy had been taken out, the claimant was involved in a motor vehicle accident that resulted in him making a claim. A quick review indicated the following payouts:

Accident injury policy lump sum	$10,000
Business expense coverage	$20,000
Income protection per month	$15,000

The income protection account stated that as of October, we had paid $540,000 in claim protection over the last few years.

The file also included copies of Dr. Ahmet's income tax returns, which we require because the policy pays 75 percent of the income earned before the accident. The paid benefit is treated as income. On the income tax return, the doctor claimed business income was nil, and his occupation was listed as "orthopedic surgeon." My first thought was the doctor had returned to work and not disclosed his employment. But then the name was not an exact match? Could it have been someone else?

I decided that the most effective way to get to the bottom of it was to call the doctor. I looked up the home phone number on the claim and called it.

It rang several times and when a man answered, he identified himself as Dr. Ahmet. I explained that I worked for Auswide Insurance and needed to clarify a few details on his claim. We had a general chat about the claim and how he was feeling. He said he was still in occasional pain and on medication for it. I asked if he had attended a conference overseas. Without any hesitation he said, "Yes, in New Zealand." To me the doctor sounded like he was happy to talk and he was not guarded in his responses. In short, he was asked by an old friend to speak at the New Zealand conference at the last minute when one of the speakers pulled out. He had not contacted his family doctor because the doctor was on vacation and he did not want to meet the replacement physician. Afterward, the conference had slipped his mind. So when he went back to the doctor the other week, he did not report it. He went on to say that the three-hour flight to Auckland was not nearly as long as the flight to Perth he had to make last year to see a specialist. He also told me he used the name Edward professionally because it was easier for people to remember.

I recall hanging up the telephone and thinking that it sounded reasonable. The story was believable, and the doctor did not deny going to the conference. Still, something did not feel right. I thought about how we had paid more than half a million in claims so far. Was he really working? The comments by Dr. Hugo echoed in my mind; surely he must have had some concerns himself.

I entered Dr. Ahmet's name into a Web browser to see what turned up — only one return with the name of Dr. E. Ahmet and the address and business phone number we had on his claim form. I dialed the number, but it was disconnected. I looked at the business address and noted that it was in a specialist medical center. I called the main line and spoke with a receptionist who told me that Dr. Ahmet no longer worked at the center and had not done so for some time. There were no other listings, and he was still living in Sydney. I also checked the white pages for listings in Melbourne but found nothing. Could Dr. Hugo have been wrong? I decided to issue instructions to one of our private investigators for some surveillance. I found myself actually hoping that I was being overly cautious.

Working Through the Pain

Later I received a phone call from the manager of the private investigation firm, who told me that during the surveillance period, Dr. Ahmet boarded flights for Melbourne on three occasions. The manager asked if I wanted someone in Melbourne to pick up the surveillance of Ahmet when he traveled, and I hesitantly agreed. A lot of the time surveillance is hit and miss, but I wanted to see where this would go.

A few weeks later it was mid-December, and I was looking forward to my annual holidays, when an email arrived from the private investigation company. I opened the attachment and read the cover letter. In brief, the report summarized:

- The subject was observed across a four-week period. During this time, he was observed traveling on seven occasions from his residence to the Sydney domestic airport.
- On each occasion, he was observed boarding a flight to Melbourne.
- On three occasions, he was observed leaving Melbourne airport in a taxi.
- The subject was observed entering the foyer and taking the elevator to Level 27 at 140 William Street in Melbourne on two occasions.
- The investigator made inquiries with the reception staff on Level 27 and determined that a Dr. Edward Ahmet had an office on the floor.

It appeared that Dr. Erso Ahmet was working in Melbourne under the name Edward. I realized a number of things. First, we had never conducted a fraud investigation into an income protection claim — most of our resources were focused on injury claims arising from motor accidents. This could be a very resource-intensive investigation. Second, we had never investigated a doctor, let alone a specialist.

I commenced a review of what I knew with the aim to develop an investigative strategy. The claimant was an orthopedic surgeon who lived in Sydney and possibly worked in Melbourne. I made a wide range of inquiries with specialist practices throughout Melbourne to no avail. I thought perhaps Dr. Ahmet was taking referrals only. I knew that he would have to either write reports for insurers or personal injury solicitors, which would result in a paper trail for me to follow.

I put in a request to our IT department to search for all reports with the name "Ahmet." We had just introduced a policy of scanning reports for personal injury claims, but I was warned that the process was far from guaranteed, as it relied on the claims staff scanning hard-copy reports. I was also told that several departments, including sections of liability claims, had not commenced this practice. Not the most auspicious start to the case.

I returned to work in late January and found out IT finished the report search for "Ahmet"; it found more than 2,000 documents. Then I narrowed the search to medical reports written by "Dr. Edward Ahmet."

We had received the first claimant report written by Dr. Ahmet nearly three years earlier. Since then he had written almost 600 reports for personal injury solicitor firms. I examined each of the accounts and noted they recorded the doctor's business address as 140 William Street in Melbourne and another at Chiefly Tower in Sydney. Until then I was not even aware that Ahmet was working in Sydney. When I compared the dates with Ahmet's own medical claim, I noted that on several dates that he had reported to his doctor that he was still unfit to resume duties, he had in fact done consulting for personal injury solicitors. I began to calculate the fees he had charged for each of his reports. I diligently entered the fees into a spreadsheet and found they totaled $342,511.

Another shock followed soon. The search picked up all of Auswide's documents with the name Ahmet, and while sorting through them, I found an email and service contract dated four months earlier. Dr. Edward Ahmet had been offered a position on our injury claim panel of surgeons in Melbourne! Amazingly, he was now consulting for us on injuries caused by car accidents. During this time, he charged Auswide $15,000 in consulting fees. In one case, we wrote that he suspected that the claimant was exaggerating the limitations!

I totaled up the undisclosed work and benefits paid to date:

Claimant solicitor consultations	$342,511
Auswide Insurance consultations	$15,000
Claim payments	$570,000
Total:	**$927,511**

I entered the details of the investigators' reports, surveillance evidence and each of the 600 reports and other documents into our case management system. Once I had collected the evidence, I organized a meeting with Jill Duggan, manager of Legal Services. Jill said, "This is incredible. . . . He has been working for us." We decided that the next course of action would be to offer the claimant an interview to see if he was willing to explain himself. Jill agreed to be present.

Indisputable Evidence

I called Dr. Ahmet and asked if he could come into our Sydney office next week, and he agreed. On the day of the interview I greeted Dr. Ahmet in the reception area at about 9:30 a.m. and invited him into a conference room. I decided to use this room as it was not as cramped or formal as the interview room. Our interviews are not recorded using audio or video recording equipment; we still managed the interview process the old-fashioned way — writing notes on paper.

Jill greeted Dr. Ahmet, who had arrived alone. I asked if he wanted anyone present. He waved away my concern and said no. Jill and I had conducted interviews together in the past, and, before this one, we had agreed that I would lead it and Jill would take notes. This would allow me to spend my time listening to Dr. Ahmet, asking relevant questions and introducing various exhibits.

I started by asking Dr. Ahmet about his health and how his claim had been managed so far. I then went through the necessary background details, such as name, address, occupation and his signed claim form. I asked him to elaborate on his medical and employment history. I did not want a confrontational interview so I spent time building rapport with him. This was important because, as an insurance investigator, I had no legal power to compel a person to attend or remain in an interview. I needed to foster an environment where he would be willing to tell me his story.

Dr. Ahmet asked if we were checking up on him, and I responded with "Should we be checking up on you?"

He simply gestured to a large number of case folders I had placed on the table behind us. I asked if he wanted to tell us anything before we started, but he said no.

When Jill and I planned the interview, we decided to play the surveillance video first. Normally we use video last, as it often provokes claimants who view surveillance as being spied on. However, since the video did not prove or disprove his injury, we wanted to see where it would take the interview. We played some of the footage taken by our investigators in Sydney.

I asked Dr. Ahmet if he had any comments. He said, "Not really — that suggests I am mobile. I have never said that I am not. It really does not show much at all. I went to the airport, so what?"

I said, "You went to the airport several times in a week."

"So?" he asked.

I then played the video obtained in Melbourne, including the building he entered. After this I stopped the video, and Dr. Ahmet sat in the chair rather quietly. I reached behind me to the table with the folders, which I had already marked one to ten. I opened folder one and turned to the first medical report Dr. Ahmet had submitted to Auswide as a consultant. Dr. Ahmet put on his glasses on and reviewed the report.

I asked "Who is Edward Ahmet?"

He replied, "It is me."

I asked, "You wrote this report?" He said yes.

I turned to the next report and showed him the name.

He said, "Yes, that is mine as well." He went on to ask rather quietly, "Are they all mine?" pointing to the folders behind me.

I said, "All of these folders have reports written by Dr. Edward Ahmet."

He simply said "Oh," and looked down.

Next we went through various reports and other evidence. I asked about the Melbourne work, and Dr. Ahmet became agitated. It was the most emotion he showed during the interview. He said he was not being deceptive; it was easier for him to travel to Melbourne to consult for a day and return home. He said he could see four or more patients in the day and go home. Further, he told his family doctor in May of last year that he would like to return to work but was simply not able to work a full day.

I was familiar with the notes made by his family doctor, who had submitted various medical reports throughout the course of the claim.

I said to Dr. Ahmet that he had been working but failed to mention this to his doctor or us. Dr. Ahmet said, "Not full time . . . it's nowhere near what I did when I worked full time, not even close."

Toward the end of the interview, I asked Dr. Ahmet to confirm that he had been working while on his claim. He said, "Yes, I have been working. I simply could not stand sitting at home. A couple of years ago I was approached to do some consulting for a lawyer and then the work just kind of started to flow in." He went on to ask "Did your investigation start because I was asked to be a panel doctor for your company?"

To my embarrassment, I had to say no. I explained it was because of his presentation at the New Zealand conference. I was curious to find out how he passed the vetting process for our claims area to become a panel doctor for Auswide Insurance Limited. Dr. Ahmet said he submitted all his records, which had his real name, and simply indicated that he was to be referred to as Edward. I was very surprised. No one ever suspected that a claimant would undertake work for us, so we had no internal checks in place. It was that easy.

Before the interview ended, Jill handed Dr. Ahmet a form stating that we would be canceling his insurance policy based on failure to disclose certain facts, namely that he had been working. I advised Dr. Ahmet that we were likely to consider the matter of possible fraud and recovery. He seemed shocked and said there was no way he committed fraud.

Trend Setting

After the interview, Jill and I discussed the matter privately. We considered recovery proceedings and the possibility of running a fraud case as per Australia's Insurance Contract Act. From past experience, we knew it is difficult to prove income protection claim fraud, especially if the injury is not in dispute and the claimant presents well in court. However, this was the first type of fraud we had uncovered involving a medical specialist, and, given the significance, we decided to pursue it.

When the civil trial was about to begin, Dr. Ahmet's lawyer argued that his client had suffered a breakdown and was not fit to undertake a trial. We decided to settle with Ahmet and received partial restitution of $300,000. We were also able to secure our investigation and legal costs.

As a result of this case, a number of other insurers began to review their claims for similar cases, and several frauds were uncovered. In one instance a doctor was convicted and sentenced to jail for three years for committing fraud.

We also took a rare step and approached the state police to pursue criminal fraud charges. In a meeting, Jill and I handed over all our evidence to police, but to my knowledge no progress has been made on a criminal case.

Lessons Learned

I learned a lot from this investigation. Despite years of experience in insurance fraud, something always comes out of left field. That is why the work is so interesting; there are challenges each and every day. When you boil it down, this case demonstrates a fairly simple fraud. The claims staff found no red flags, and hence there was no referral to the fraud investigation team. We just got lucky with an informant.

We learned that focusing on investigating injury claims arising from motor vehicles left us exposed in areas such as income protection insurance. We simply did not allocate significant resources to this area, which allowed fraud to go undetected. As a result, we undertook a business-wide review of life and income protection policies, including training claims officers to handle these cases. This resulted in a number of additional investigations. We also introduced more robust case management software to handle electronic information.

Recommendation to Prevent Future Occurrences

Auswide Insurance Limited introduced a range of risk investigation strategies, including random audits of injury claims. This case provided us the insight to expand our fraud detection program. We determined that relying only on claims staff to identify red flags resulted in the possibility of missing frauds. We did not have a fraud risk search engine to help identify injury claim frauds, so we commenced random audits of live injury claim files. This process also allowed better communication within the company to assist in gathering intelligence and examining risk related to all injury claims.

Furthermore, we learned that our limited focus on injury claim fraud detection had been on blue-collar workers and self-employed individuals, as these types of workers represented the majority of the perceived risk associated with insurance policies. This focus needed to change.

We also made improvements to our background checks into those we engage as contractors, to ensure that they are vetted and have no current or undisclosed claims.

About the Author

Michael King, master's of justice, master's of arts (Justice Administration), bachelor of commerce. Michael has 17 years of fraud investigation experience, four as an insurance and financial fraud investigator with some of Australia's largest insurers and 13 as a compliance officer and fraud investigator for the Commonwealth Treasury. He has published a number of scholarly articles and has also taught within the School of Justice Administration Brisbane North Institute of TAFE and the Australian Security Academy.

CHAPTER 3

Greasing the Wheels in the Oil Business

ABDULRAZAQ AL-MORJAN

When Sarah Mali was 14, she dreamed of working for a company in Saudi Arabia and buying a family house and a farm. Her dream reflected her background — that of a girl from a poor family in a poverty-stricken Arab country.

However, finding a job in Saudi Arabia, where 8 million international expatriates work, is not an easy task, especially for Arab people. Sarah planned to study English at the university to have a competitive advantage to help her realize her dream. When she was 18, she enrolled in a local university in her country. After four years, she received a bachelor's degree in English literature with honors. Afterward, she worked as a high-school English teacher in her home country for two years.

Through the school, Sarah met and subsequently married Sami Ahmed, who was the legal guardian of one of Sarah's students. After a year of marriage, Sarah and Sami moved to the United Arab Emirates (UAE), where she worked for Danh University as a human resource (HR) coordinator.

This move gave Sarah an opportunity to earn an M.B.A. at the university. During her employment, she was an HR generalist working on talent acquisition processes, employees' personnel records, and organizing employee benefits,

Over the next four years, Sarah continued working for the university and also had two children. The family moved to Qatar when her husband found a high-paying job in Tamimi Bank. While in Qatar, Sarah worked part time for Qatri Petrochemical as an HR policy translator. She was responsible for translating HR policy from English to Arabic.

One day Sarah went online and applied for jobs at ten different companies in Saudi Arabia. After two months and after almost giving up hope, she thought her ears were playing tricks on her when she was called by one of these companies, Riyadh Petrochemical Agency, to arrange an employment interview over Skype.

Three months later Sarah's dream finally came true when she received an offer from the company. She was hired as a benefit and compensation specialist. Her role was administering insurance contracts (medical, dental and life) and establishing and maintaining the needed documents for insurance programs.

However, moving to Saudi Arabia would not be easy; her husband did not want to quit his job in Qatar. Their conflict became worse and worse, and they divorced four months after she accepted the job offer.

Sharif Ibrahim was the youngest son of a middle-class family. He had a happy childhood, and his parents were generous with him. They worked in Dubai for 12 years and returned to their home country when Sharif was ten. At 18, Sharif went to a public university and earned a degree in management information systems.

After graduation, he moved to the United Kingdom to improve his English skills, as this language is a golden ticket for Arabs to find a good job with a reasonable salary. During his time in England, he attended and completed a number of computer and management courses. His educational journey was funded by his father.

After six months in the United Kingdom, Sharif received a call from one of his best friends, Hisham Ali, who worked in Saudi Arabia at the time. Hisham had nominated Sharif to work for Niman Company, which had a contract to provide a supplemental workforce to Riyadh Petrochemical.

Upon completing the job application, Sharif accepted the offer to work as an information technology (IT) administrator in the HR department. His role was to maintain HR personnel, benefit and compensation databases as well as create and manage HR user accounts. Sharif knew this opportunity in Saudi Arabia was the first, and a critical, step in his career. Therefore, he wanted to work hard to prove himself.

Two years later, after Sharif began to stand out as an excellent employee, Riyadh Petrochemical transferred him to permanent status rather than as a contractor with Niman.

In light of their backgrounds, it was clear that Sharif and Sarah were intelligent. They put all their efforts into improving the company and gained management's trust. Sarah also had excellent communication skills up to an executive-management level (presentation, papers and briefings).

Riyadh Petrochemical was established by the Kingdom of Saudi Arabia and produced products such as ethylene and polyethylene. Management developed strategic international partnerships to improve its competitive advantage and provide secure positions for the company's 2,000 employees from around the world.

Long-Distance Call for Help

While I was working as an independent fraud investigator and studying for my Ph.D. in England, I often spent long hours conducting experiments in the computer forensic laboratory at the university. Following lab procedures, I always left my cell phone in a locked cabinet outside the laboratory.

One day when I left the lab, I noticed I had a missed call from a friend of mine, Salem, who worked as an HR manager at Riyadh Petrochemical. At first, I was happy, thinking Salem might be calling to offer me a senior position in fraud investigations at his company. However, my hope was diminished when I listened to the message. He said, "When you hear this, please call me back. I need your assistance on a fraud allegation."

When I got home, I immediately called him back. Salem told me, "I received an anonymous email alleging that one of our best employees, Sarah, has been abusing her authority."

I asked Salem to clarify. He said Sarah was accused of submitting counterfeit invoices for reimbursement to Riyadh's medical insurance provider, Perfect Insurance. He added, "I do not believe it. I know how hard Sarah works to provide first-class HR services." Salem was also upset because the anonymous email accused him of trying to bury his employee's wrongdoing to avoid putting himself in a shameful situation with his senior management. He told me he didn't know what he should do.

I assured Salem that as an independent examiner, "my job is not only to prove allegations but also to refute them." I advised him not to prejudge the case because I needed to conduct an impartial investigation. I asked him to send me copies of all the invoices Sarah had submitted for reimbursement to Perfect Insurance along with her personnel file. Once I received them, I spent a long time reviewing them. My preliminary review indicated that all her medical invoices in the past six months had been issued by a clinic called Saffori.

The fact that all her invoices were from one clinic was a red flag for me. In addition, I discovered that Saffori was far from Sarah's residence, and she actually had to drive past two other clinics to reach it. Further investigation revealed that the two closer medical centers would not have cost her anything because they were preferred providers. Sarah would only have had to show her insurance card for no-cost treatment.

I next asked Salem to send me all the Saffori invoices that were submitted by Riyadh's entire workforce. The only invoices Salem found matching that description were from an IT employee named Sharif Ibrahim; he had submitted seven Saffori invoices in the past six months.

At that point, I thought Sarah and Sharif could both be connected to the allegations. They also clearly insisted on visiting this specific center. Two weeks later I traveled to Saudi Arabia, where I met with Salem to discuss an investigation plan for this case.

A Groundbreaking Case

This investigation was challenging for me. It was not only a critical step in my career but also a way to prove how vital internal fraud investigation is for companies in the private sector of Saudi Arabia. In fact, I was conducting the very first one at Riyadh Petrochemical. Therefore, I often worked 70 hours a week, sometimes 18 hours a day. I used numerous investigative skills, tools and resources to conduct this investigation, including transaction analysis, timeline analysis and digital forensics analysis of the suspects' electronic devices and data. I also interviewed witnesses and suspects. Before interviewing anyone, I used transaction analysis to examine Sarah's process for submitting her Saffori invoices for reimbursement. I quickly noticed that all of her invoices were issued and signed by the same Saffori employee, Ahmed, which was another red flag. One of Sarah's job responsibilities was to approve medical reimbursement requests before submitting them to Perfect Insurance, so she simply approved her own invoices and passed them along. At this point, I had three potential fraudsters: Sarah and Sharif working inside Riyadh and the mysterious Ahmed working at Saffori.

Next I met the head of Riyadh Petrochemical's legal team to discuss the case. I also asked for approval to interview the suspects and analyze their business cell phones and emails. Once I received permission, I set up an informal meeting with Sarah. She explained that she liked the doctors and nurses at Saffori and would rather pay the fees in cash and seek reimbursement than go to a preferred provider. She said that according to Riyadh's compensation policy, she had the right to visit any medical center in the Kingdom of Saudi Arabia, so she didn't think she was doing anything wrong. Then, almost as an afterthought, she said that Saffori was the closest medical center to her home. That was the clincher for me — I had already discovered that there were two medical centers closer.

I asked Sarah to give me her company cell phone and handed her a notice from the general counsel stating that I had permission to analyze it. She cooperated and passed me her phone. A turning point in the case came when I examined her phone and realized there were many suspicious, deleted text messages. Out of the 30 total messages I recovered, eight were to someone named Mark at Perfect Insurance, telling him that she had submitted her medical reimbursement requests and asking him to expedite the approval. Always, within hours of these texts, she received approval message from Perfect Insurance. However, based on Perfect's policy, the reimbursement process takes 10 to 15 working days. Clearly, Sarah's requests were receiving special treatment.

I also found that Sarah sent five interesting text messages to Ahmed at Saffori, including one that said "Are you on duty tonight? Can I come by?" Ahmed replied soon after, "Come anytime, your invoice is ready." I ordered a background check on Ahmed.

I decided to review the bids for the medical insurance contract that Sarah had awarded to Perfect Insurance. It quickly became obvious that she favored Perfect Insurance during the bidding process. She gave the company unsupported high ratings while disqualifying other competitors for insufficient reasons. I also learned that Mark was a regional sales manager at Perfect Insurance and Sarah's point of contact during the bidding process.

My review of Riyadh's contract with Perfect Insurance revealed that the cost of a married female's insurance policy was double the cost for a single woman's. I thought that was strange, and I asked Salem to pull an updated list of current and recently resigned employees of all marital statuses. We compared the internal list of married women to Perfect Insurance's list and discovered that a significant number of single women were listed as married on the paperwork.

Another important finding was that Sarah did not remove employees and their dependents from the insurance list when they resigned, even though a part of her job was to update the list weekly. As a result, the contract was inflated by $150,000.

Looking Outside for Suspects

Next I turned my attention to Ahmed. The background check I ran showed that he was the receptionist supervisor at Saffori Medical Clinic, and one of his duties was to issue invoices to customers. Salem suggested that I meet with Saffori's boss, Abdullah, to discuss the situation. He agreed to meet me the following day. During the meeting, I filled him in on the case as I understood it at that point, and Abdullah was visibly upset. He brought Ahmed into his office and asked him to explain the situation.

Ahmed immediately asked Abdullah to forgive him. He admitted that he issued invoices to Sarah in exchange for $50 per invoice, even though she did not visit Saffori or receive medical services. He explained that Sarah was his second cousin and used her position as family to pressure him. He also told us that his salary did not cover his monthly expenses; his mother was sick in his home country, and he was paying for her expensive medical treatments. He was overextended with debt, and, to top it off, Sarah had promised to give him a good job and better salary if he cooperated.

When I reviewed the invoices in question with Ahmed, we realized that seven of them had been issued by someone else; these were Sharif's invoices. I decided it was time for us to talk.

When I met with him, Sharif insisted that his invoices were issued by Saffori after he received treatment there. I pretended to be convinced by Sharif, but as a digital forensic specialist, knowing that Sharif has computer skills, I assumed that he used Photoshop or similar software to create the seven fake invoices. I examined his work computer and found (and recovered) many deleted documents, among of them the seven invoices in question. He had indeed created them in Photoshop.

I reinterviewed Sharif to ask for an explanation, but he continued to insist that the invoices came from Saffori. I confronted him with copies of the invoices I recovered from his computer. He became nervous and said, "I don't know what you're talking about. I don't know where those came from." However, after five minutes, he admitted that he generated the invoices because Sarah had made a deal with him. She would approve and process any reimbursement requests for Sharif's medical expenses and in return Sharif — who was assigned to cover Sarah's workload during her mandatory annual leave — would not remove the resigned employees and dependents from Perfect Insurance's contract list while she was away. He also said that Sarah included him in the fraud because he was having affair with her.

Before I had a chance to interview Sarah again, she resigned and moved back to her home country.

Lack of Accountability

I was able to identify four perpetrators in this case: Sarah and Sharif working inside Riyadh and Ahmed and Mark working externally. Both Sarah and Sharif submitted false insurance claims for reimbursement to Perfect Insurance, totaling $20,970. Sarah received fake invoices from Ahmed at Saffori worth a total of $6,720 and submitted them to Mark, and she processed Sharif's false invoices worth $14,250.

Sarah also inflated Riyadh's annual premium payment to Perfect Insurance by $150,000, using two mechanisms. She manipulated female employees' marital status on file and did not remove employees from the contract when they resigned. She also manipulated the bid process early on, when she awarded the contract to Perfect Insurance.

In the end, Sharif made a full confession in writing and was allowed to resign. Sarah returned home and sent her resignation in to Salem. Perfect Insurance returned the $150,000 to Riyadh Petrochemical.

Lessons Learned

I believe that organizations are usually slow in recognizing the importance and implications of internal frauds. The lack of fraud-control readiness is a serious challenge that faces internal investigators when dealing with such issues. Riyadh Petrochemical's internal auditors did not discover they were paying extra premiums to Perfect Insurance, and Riyadh's senior management blamed them for this fraud. One of my subsequent realizations was that many senior managers do not distinguish between the roles of internal auditors and fraud investigators. In fact, internal auditors do not usually detect fraud, uncover evidence or identify suspects; they focus on enhancing internal controls by examining current procedures and processes. The fraud investigators are the ones tasked with retrieving evidence and identifying wrongdoers.

I learned that many ethical employees observed unusual activities done by Sarah but did not come forward to report their suspicions in a timely manner for two reasons. First, they did not know whom they should tell and how to keep their identities confidential. Second, they feared retaliation, which led me to believe the employees did not trust management or Riyadh Petrochemical's system for handling tips.

Another lesson I learned was that the company lacked checks and balances, which allowed Sarah to perpetrate her fraud. There were no procedures in place to reduce Sarah's authority because she had absolute control over selecting the insurance provider, and no one verified the invoices she submitted to Perfect Insurance.

I closed this case with the lingering impression that management's decision to allow the perpetrators to resign, rather than taking legal or disciplinary action, was ineffective. This decision might encourage the offenders to commit more fraudulent acts, and it created an unethical workplace environment. Additionally, because Sarah technically resigned from Riyadh, backgrounds checks on her by any future employers would come back clean.

I strongly believe that people commit fraud when presented with the opportunity and by abusing their authority, knowing there is a lack of fraud deterrence. It was clear to me that this fraud occurred because Sarah had the opportunity and she was able to rationalize her actions to herself.

Recommendations to Prevent Future Occurrences

To prevent occupational fraud, I believe that government, organizational management and individual employees must share responsibility. We all have a critical role to play, taking into account the need for qualified investigators to take the lead based on their experience. By working together, often we can prevent fraud from happening while creating an ethical environment that can positively impact the entire national economy.

I proposed to Salem that Riyadh Petrochemical should institute an ethical business model (EBM), which comprises formal, informal and technology controls (FIT controls). EBM aims to promote an ethical environment within organizations to enhance the code of conduct and prevent fraudulent activities from occurring.

Formal Controls

Formal controls in EBM include establishing and updating proper organization policies, such as responses to conflicts of interest, codes of conduct and anti-fraud policies and procedures. Companies should also enhance internal controls by clearly defining the roles and responsibilities of each employee. Segregation of duties should also be addressed.

(Continued)

Formal controls should encourage employees to speak up by protecting them from retaliation, for example, by creating a procedure for anonymously reporting fraud and misconduct. Management should be objective, not subjective, by focusing on the content of a complaint, not on identifying a complainant. At the same time, the policy should not only protect whistleblowers but also reward them if they report accurate allegations.

Clearly defined parameters for misconduct and subsequent disciplinary action need to be outlined to staff, and management could consider creating a disciplinary action committee to take an appropriate action against perpetrators. Formal controls should also include background checks on potential new employees and vendors.

Informal Controls

Ethical and brave employees are a key resource for detecting offenses within an organization, and informal controls can cultivate a more diligent workforce. One approach is to stress employee education and awareness while promoting an ethical work environment. Human resources or the compliance department could manage such efforts, including annual training for employees. Also, at Riyadh Petrochemical in particular, I expressed the need for management to earn their employees' trust again. Leaders need to realize their critical roles and responsibilities in the fight against internal corruption, while employees should understand that they are responsible for reporting suspicious behavior when they discover it.

Technology Controls

Technology can help us detect suspicious activities and retrieve evidence while or after transgressions take place. Today, there are many powerful tools that help investigators understand what happened, when it happened and who did it.

- Computer forensics can recover deleted folders, files and emails from a subject's computer.
- Network forensics can collect evidence from network layers and monitor employees' unusual Internet activities, such as stealing intellectual property or leaking bid prices to suppliers.
- Mobile device forensics can monitor employees' text messages and other mobile communications used to leak information to facilitate fraud.

I also believe management should fight illegal behavior in the workplace not by allowing culprits to resign but by terminating them and pressing criminal charges.

About the Author

Abdulrazaq Al-Morjan has an M.S. in information security from London University and was one of the first Saudis to obtain a Ph.D. in the field of fraud and digital forensics from De Montfort University in the United Kingdom. Since joining KAUST in July 2009, he has assisted in the start-up of the internal investigation program and enhanced internal controls. He has conducted hundreds of successful complex investigations, such as frauds, theft of property, theft of intellectual property, cybercrimes and employee and supplier misconduct. Currently Dr. Al-Morjan is working as a specialist in digital forensics and investigations; he also helped the university build an advanced digital forensics laboratory, which saves the university money and allows collecting evidence from complex fraud and cybercrimes.

Living the Dream, Keeping Up the Lie

ANDRIES J. BRUMMER

Christian Lionel Allan was 28 years old, single, good looking, tall and lanky, with short blond hair and a slightly receding hairline. He was fit and in the prime of his life. As the firstborn son, he was named after his father, a man he barely remembered. He took pride in the fact that he was a well-educated, white, young male with above-average intelligence. Coming from a difficult childhood in which money was always an issue, he dreamed of the good life and was not going to waste time getting what he wanted. He had something to prove. He was ambitious and had big plans, but to realize those plans, he needed money and opportunity.

Christian came from a broken family in South Africa and was passed on to family friends, Jeremy and Melinda Burger, at an early age. This left an indelible mark on the young man's mind during his formative years and led to his obsession with being financially self-sufficient. The Burgers were kind-hearted, childless people who welcomed Christian into their home as their own son. They saw to the needs of the young boy and made sure he was properly schooled. Jeremy Burger suffered from epilepsy, and this condition would eventually form the basis of Christian's false disability and income continuation benefits claim.

After finishing high school, Christian obtained his bachelor's degree in mechanical engineering at Blacks University. However, soon afterward, he decided that engineering did not quite fit his lifestyle and future plans, nor did it stimulate him. He entered the import and export business and registered a company by the name of Smoking Hot Tobacco Imports and Exports.

The company dealt in fine cigars (Cuban, Honduran, Dominican and Nicaraguan) and accessories, such as humidors, cases and cutters; e-cigarettes (a new technology offering one the closest experiences to smoking a real cigarette); specialist tobaccos and snuff; pipes (Peterson, Stanwell,

Aldo Morelli, Parker and Savinelli, to name but a few); lighters; and so forth. Christian considered Smoking Hot Tobacco to be his ticket to financial freedom and universal respect as a successful businessman.

At the start of this venture, he took out a policy with Delta Life Insurance, which included the added benefits of disability and income continuation. Around this time, he befriended Dean Hubert Baron, a financial advisor who helped him select and take out the Delta policy. Dean acted as a third-party facilitator. Dean soon convinced Christian to become a financial advisor in his spare time to supplement his income. While studying to become an advisor, Christian learned of the possibilities of financial freedom that his life insurance policy afforded him. He did not have the time or patience to work toward such freedom; he wanted it yesterday. He saw an opportunity and was going to seize it.

Delta Life was established in 1999, and it was the first South African insurance company to separate risk from investment. Due to this unique business approach, the company had a 40 percent share in the independent broker risk market. For such a dynamic and innovative insurance company operating in a cutthroat industry, getting new business on the books was of the utmost importance. This hunger for new clients made the company vulnerable to possible fraudulent claims. The company itself employed approximately 7,000 people and was almost totally system-driven in its business approach.

The Family Illness

Christian's tobacco business was not performing as well as he had expected, and he worried about his dream slipping away. However, rather than sit back and watch his success ebb, he set upon a new plan for financial independence. He contacted Delta Insurance in June and asked to increase his payout benefits in the event that he was unable to work one day. He told the agent on the phone that his business was doing so well he wanted to make sure he would be able to continue living the good life, should anything happen to him. The increase was approved, and Christian's monthly payments increased slightly. On August 22, just over two months after increasing his benefits, Christian submitted an insurance claim for disability and income continuation benefits due to epilepsy; in total, he had had his policy with Delta for just over a year. His claim, if granted, would have given him monthly payments for the rest of his working years — the complete amount would exceed $2.5 million. On the claim, he stated that he suffered from the following symptoms:

- Sudden blackouts
- Constant headaches
- Five to seven epileptic episodes per week

- Difficulty with speech
- Periods of memory loss (e.g., driving his car to an appointment and suddenly not knowing where he was going, losing track of a conversation midway, forgetting words)
- Staring into space
- Sudden bouts of vomiting with no warning signs or nausea
- Tremors
- Uncontrolled twitching of his hands and legs

According to Christian, his symptoms made him unable to focus on running his business efficiently and prevented him from interacting with prospective clients. As per his own admission, his epilepsy also would not allow him to drive, because he was scared of having a seizure behind the wheel.

Following numerous doctors' consultations and tests, Christian was eventually diagnosed with epilepsy in June. It took so long because no doctor wanted to diagnose epilepsy outright, but none of them wanted to exclude it either. Christian was not displaying observable signs of epilepsy, but he was able to describe his symptoms accurately and convincingly. A few medical practitioners had their misgivings and voiced their opinions as such, but nothing was conclusive. Nobody wanted to commit themselves and make their practice vulnerable to malpractice lawsuits.

Watching and Waiting

I worked in the investigation department of Delta Insurance and specialized in surveillance. Christian's claim was referred to me by Jennifer Knowles, his claims assessor, because there were conflicting medical opinions regarding his epilepsy and she wanted to know if he actually displayed any symptoms. This coupled with the fact that he had increased his benefits a few months prior to submitting his claim raised the suspicion. However, Christian was on the warpath because he thought it was taking entirely too long for his claim to be finalized. He was increasing pressure on Jennifer to the point of being downright aggressive and arrogant. She was fed up with his bullying and wanted conclusive evidence one way or the other so she could close the claim. I was tasked with doing surveillance on Christian in November, and I gathered a team of experienced investigators to help me conduct the assignment. It was a bright sunny day on November 17 when we began preliminary surveillance of Christian Lionel Allan's home and the surrounding area. The house was opposite a primary school in a predominantly middle-class suburban area. The house itself was a neat, well-kept, plastered brick dwelling with front porch, a black corrugated-iron roof, a double garage and a carport in front of the garage situated to the left of the main house. The front of the premises was fenced and had an automated sliding gate. The fence itself was partly overgrown with shrubs. At the time we arrived, kids were leaving the school, and the road outside his house was congested with parents and vehicles coming to pick up their children. We were able to take up spots on the street without attracting any attention. The front door leading to Christian's house was open, but there was no sign of anyone moving in or around the house, except for a small black and tan dog walking around the yard. There was a black SUV parked in the garage, but there was no sign of Christian's second vehicle, a champagne-color sedan. We spent the afternoon mapping out the area and deciding on the best vantage points for our continued surveillance.

The next morning we returned to the house. I knew Christian was scheduled for an appointment with a neurologist later that afternoon in Johannesburg, and we wanted to see how he would get to the clinic, because he had asserted that he could not drive. The sedan was parked in the garage behind the SUV; all was quiet in the block. My team and I took up our respective positions, and I was working as the *hotspot* (a term used for the surveillance operative who has sight of the subject or the area where he is expected). We readied ourselves for a long, hot day in the sun. About 45 minutes later there was movement outside the house, and I saw an elderly man and five dogs walking around the garden but no sign of Christian. I made a note that Christian was apparently a dog person.

Later on an elderly woman appeared on the porch and began to sweep. Not long after, the sliding gate opened and the sedan backed out of the driveway and into the road. I felt a sudden rush of adrenaline, and it was all systems go as I alerted the other operatives in the area. It is always exciting when we get the first bit of action on a case. I saw no passengers in the car and as soon as it moved up the road, I followed it to a nearby gas station. The driver got out to fill up the car, and I was able to positively identify Christian. He didn't seem to have any trouble driving by himself, I noted.

From the gas station, Christian made his way to a veterinarian's office, where he parked and got out carrying a small dog. I made a note that he had no hand tremors and seemed in complete control of his pet. I took up position in the immediate vicinity with a view of the vehicle. I took care not to be in Christian's immediate sight when he came out again. Approximately half an hour later he left the vet, got into his car and drove to a nearby shopping center, the Towers. He returned a few minutes later carrying a bag and drove off again, this time to a convenience store. He remained in his car for a few minutes, busy on his cell phone, before getting out and entering the store. Not long after he came out and crossed the road to another shopping complex. I noticed that he was walking briskly and determinedly as he crossed the road. He returned a few minutes later, got into his vehicle and drove off to yet another convenience store. He emerged soon afterward and drove straight home. We took up our positions again and got ready to play the waiting game.

About an hour and a half later, Christian left the house alone and drove away in his sedan again. We followed him to a local municipality office, where he parked and entered the building. Knowing he had an appointment with his neurologist, Dr. Diamond, in about an hour, we decided to drive to the doctor's office and wait for Christian to show up.

Around an hour later, we saw Christian drive up in his sedan, still the only occupant of the vehicle. He parked and made his way inside. As the neurologist's consulting room was open and we ran the risk of being exposed inside, we set up surveillance in a coffee shop in the main building to wait for him to leave. Less than an hour later we were almost caught off guard as Christian suddenly left the building — walking very briskly — long before his appointment was scheduled to end, and drove off. We quickly followed him, but traffic was heavy as it was rush hour and we lost him at an intersection just before the highway. We went back to his house but were unable to confirm if he returned because the garage door was closed and we did not see the sedan. We suspended surveillance for the day, but I recorded that he had driven alone at least three hours that day, had carried a dog with no trouble and walked around by himself without displaying any physical symptoms of epilepsy.

It was a sunny summer's morning on Tuesday, just after 6 a.m., when we returned to Christian's home to resume surveillance. All was quiet and there were no outward signs of movement. The sedan was parked in the garage. We played the waiting game for almost two hours before the sliding gate to the residence opened and my adrenaline started to flow. False alarm! An elderly white male with short gray hair, dressed in a floppy hat, beige shorts and a light blue T-shirt, came out to put the garbage bin on the sidewalk. He returned and closed the gate. A little after 8 a.m. the gate opened again and the same elderly male, now presumed to be Jeremy Burger, came outside with Christian, who was pushing a lawnmower. Christian started mowing the lawn while Jeremy held the electric cord. During this time we saw Christian empty the grass catcher several times. They finished and went back inside. Within a few minutes, Christian returned with a broom to sweep the sidewalk then went back in. At 10:00 a.m. the sedan reversed out of the driveway, and we saw that Christian was driving. An elderly white female was in the front and Mr. Burger was in the back. They stopped at the gas station near the house where Christian filled up the car again.

From here they drove to a residential area in a neighboring town where they parked in front of a house, and all three got out of the car and went into the home. Christian emerged alone a few minutes later. We followed him to a business complex in Edenglen, a town about ten miles away, and saw him go into an office carrying a stack of paperwork. Approximately three hours later he left and drove back to the residential area, where he picked up the Burgers. Due to traffic congestion, we lost them on the drive back to what we presumed to be his house, and decided to resume surveillance the following morning.

The next morning we took up our usual positions and waited; the day promised to be a scorcher. The hours passed by agonizingly slowly until about 10 a.m., when the gate opened and we saw the sedan reversing out of the driveway. Christian was driving and both the Burgers were in the car.

We followed them to a shopping center in town and waited for about 30 minutes while they shopped. After leaving the shopping center, they stopped at a convenience store before heading home. Shortly after they got home, an unknown elderly white male and a young woman driving a small car visited Christian. Luckily it was not a long, hot, tedious wait; after roughly an hour the visitors departed. Christian left alone in his sedan. We followed him for the rest of the day and saw him run various errands, including grocery shopping and picking up a friend at a pawnshop.

On the following Tuesday, I met with Christian's claims assessor, Jennifer, and filled her in on our surveillance efforts to that point. While I was in the room, Jennifer called Christian to obtain further information, and he made the following assertions:

- He last drove a car himself in May, more than six months ago. Now when he was in a car, it was only as a passenger and then only for a maximum of an hour, as he became tired quickly.
  - This was in stark contrast with the information we had gathered from the surveillance.
- He needed to be close to home in the event of a seizure.
- He was driven to his appointment with Dr. Diamond by a friend.
  - Again, our surveillance directly contradicted this. I saw him arrive at the doctor's office alone, having driven himself.
- He goes out of the house only occasionally when visiting doctors or with his parents to visit family.
  - Our surveillance directly contradicted this statement as well.
- He stayed at home every day cleaning, feeding the pets, sleeping and eating. He never had visitors because his condition was so restricting.
  - We had just seen two people visit Christian the previous day.
- His balance was so poor that he would fall when walking and trying to ride a bicycle. His coordination, reflexes and dexterity were poor; he dropped things from his dinner plate, was unable to catch items when they fell and so on. He said that was why he never drove, because he "cannot get the clutch right."
  - Based on the evidence gathered thus far, this was a blatant lie. We saw him driving by himself on several occasions and also mowing the lawn without once losing his balance. We saw him walking without a problem and even hurrying across an intersection at one point. We saw him carrying a dog on one occasion and paperwork on another.
- He never left the house alone — even for a walk — because the risk of having a seizure or injuring himself was too high.

Jennifer thanked him for his time and hung up. She wrote a report of Christian's statements and noted the contradictory evidence for each point. My team and I continued our surveillance for a few more weeks to build up enough evidence to dispute Christian's claim. But in the meantime, Christian had become even more impatient with the claims process and demanded a mediator to assist in the case. Delta agreed and hired a mediator to review the case. The mediator read Christian's claim, our surveillance reports and the document that Jennifer filed after her phone conversation with Christian. After sifting through the evidence, the mediator told Christian that he must submit to a week-long epilepsy-monitoring session to be properly evaluated and to establish the severity of his seizures. Although Jennifer had requested that Christian undergo such an evaluation when he filed his claim with Delta, he had initially refused, stating that we were being unreasonable and trying to waste his time. However, he agreed to this request, perhaps because it came from a third-party mediator.

Jennifer set up an appointment for Christian to stay in a clinic run by Dr. Sanderson, a renowned specialist in the field, and Christian checked himself into the clinic — Mrs. Burger dropped him off for his appointment. Christian was set up in a private room and connected to various monitoring devices. He stayed the full week and was closely observed by the doctor and a team of nurses. Dr. Sanderson's final report conclusively ruled out the possibility that Christian suffered any form of epilepsy. Furthermore, Dr. Sanderson noted that the wires of the monitoring equipment in Christian's room "mysteriously became undone, something that has never before happened," but that "they were reconnected before any valuable information was lost." Our surveillance evidence and Dr. Sanderson's report provided Delta Insurance with enough predication to deny Christian's claim in totality. Faced with all of our observations, he declined to oppose the decision. Jennifer told us she had never been so happy to have a case closed, and Delta saved $2.5 million in fraudulent claim payments.

Lessons Learned

Surveillance is a resource-intensive exercise that requires patience, tenacity and perseverance, along with military precision and vigilance, whether in the corporate or a police environment. Corporate surveillance is even more difficult because we do not have the resources that a police department does. Conversely, following a corporate subject tends to be easier than following a hardened criminal. Whereas police suspects are observant and constantly looking over their shoulders, white-collar criminals are usually unaware of what is going on around them and the possibility that they are being watched. They very rarely notice the operatives following them. In my experience, white-collar criminals think that because they have removed themselves from the "crime scene," no one will suspect them, let alone check up on them. This gives them a false sense of security. And this, coupled with arrogance and ego, leads to their downfall. Criminals like Christian forget that once they lie about their lifestyle, they have to live that lie . . . forever.

Recommendations to Prevent Future Occurrences

In my opinion, insurance fraud will continue to grow in the future. We need to have systems and checks in place to counter this growing problem. As Delta Insurance learned, it will always be problematic to match the needs of growing a business with that of policing it to ensure sustainability. I recommend the following:

1. Be wary of a sudden increase in benefit coverage followed closely by a claim submission.
2. Substantiate client requests with financial documents and a full financial audit.
3. If a claim seems suspicious, request surveillance and a full financial audit to be conducted.

About the Author

Andre Brummer, CFE, was born and raised in Springs, Gauteng, South Africa. He served in the police service for about 13 years, mostly in the detective branch. While in the police service, he married and was blessed with a beautiful son and a daughter. After leaving the police service, he joined the corporate environment doing forensic investigations, specializing in surveillance for the past five years. During this time he finished his national diploma in policing and obtained his CFE accreditation. Currently Mr. Brummer is in the process of finalizing his studies for bachelor of technology in forensics degree at UNISA.

CHAPTER 5

Extinguishing an Arson Fraud

BARRY ZALMA

Gagik Levonian, a career criminal in then-Soviet Armenia, was offered the choice of prison or emigration to the United States. He came to the States as a "refugee" with 300 carats of diamonds, many antique icons, jewelry, Caucasian and Persian rugs and a large bank account in the Cayman Islands. He used what he brought with him to open a wholesale jewelry store and purchased three gas stations.

His obligations to the Soviet Union died with its demise. He became a citizen of the United States, purchased a 4,000-square-foot house in the hills over Los Angeles and became an officer of the Los Angeles Armenian Businessman's Association.

However, Levonian never lost his Armenian patriotism. He hated everything Turkish because of what he called the Armenian genocide carried out by the Turkish government at the beginning of the 20th century. At one point he was approached for a contribution by a representative of an Armenian political party whose purpose was to kill Turkish diplomats. He wanted to donate to the cause, but his wealth was locked in property. Right around this time, he decided to up the insurance on his house and its contents . . . just in case something were to happen.

His insurance agent, Hrant Aratian (a friend of Armenian descent who shared his attitude toward Turks), went to a representative of Goodfaith Insurance Company and acquired a policy for Levonian that insured the house for $2 million, its contents at $1 million and an itemized schedule of antiques and fine art he valued at $970,000. Goodfaith received an application signed by Levonian that represented the values of the property, that he had never had a claim before and that he had never had a policy canceled or nonrenewed. Goodfaith did not inspect the property but — in good faith — accepted Levonian's word.

Two weeks after the Goodfaith policy went into effect, Levonian's house on the hill exploded into flames. A fire department helicopter saw the explosion and quickly dropped water on the property and put out the flames. City arson investigators determined the cause of the fire was arson. The next evening the house caught on fire again and was totally destroyed. The firefighters called it a rekindle, but the arson investigators concluded the second fire was also intentional.

After the second fire, Levonian presented a claim to Goodfaith. The adjuster, Martha Andrews, asked for my assistance as a consultant, investigator and Certified Fraud Examiner (CFE) because she was facing a potential $3 million claim shortly after the policy was issued. I immediately contacted Levonian and made an appointment to meet with him at the fire scene.

Backyard Barbecue

I met with Gagik Levonian at the burned-out hulk of his house. I brought an Armenian-language interpreter (since Levonian's English was limited) and a certified shorthand reporter with me to take a statement from Gagik about the insurance and the loss. I was introduced by the interpreter to a large man who could speak Armenian and Russian fluently and knew some English. He commanded any room he entered. His round, rosy-cheeked face was marred by a large birthmark on his bald head that looked like a map of Texas and a bloated, red nose from overconsumption of Armenian brandy. We sat on rocks outside his swimming pool with a broken sculpture blown into the pool staring back at us. Gagik was drinking from an eight-ounce glass mixed 50/50 with brandy and orange juice at ten in the morning.

"Why are you here?" he asked.

"To help you prove your claim to Goodfaith Insurance Company," I responded.

"You can see the house is destroyed. Where is my check?"

I explained the insurance he had purchased and the process of a claims investigation. I explained that because the fires were intentionally set, Goodfaith was required by law to conduct a thorough investigation and that a detailed statement from him was the beginning of that thorough investigation.

"I paid a lot for this insurance," he said. "My house is burned to nothing. I want my money."

His face began to flush red with anger and brandy. I calmed him down as best I could with the help of the interpreter and finally convinced him to sit back on the rock and answer my questions. I had the shorthand reporter take everything down but did not ask her to issue an oath since this was to be a preliminary statement; I was only getting Gagik's basic background and what he and other members of his family were doing at the time of the fire.

After I finished the statement, I explained to him that Goodfaith would pay to rent a similar $1 million house for his family while we investigated. Satisfied, he left the scene to me and a private fire cause-and-origin investigator whom I had asked Goodfaith to retain. I was concerned about some facts that Gagik gave me that he thought were inconsequential, including:

1. One of the family's Dobermans was at the vet.
2. The second Doberman was with his 18-year-old son and the son's date at a drive-in movie.
3. The Goodfaith policy was the first time he had ever had a schedule of his fine art and antiques.
4. His 14-year-old son was with him and Mrs. Levonian at an Armenian Businessman's Association dinner.
5. The family cat and a coop of rabbits died in the fire.
6. The fire happened after midnight.
7. He had out-of-focus photographs of all the scheduled items, which he provided to me.
8. He accused the fire department arson investigators of theft of diamonds stored in a floor safe in the master bath.
9. His eldest son was at a nightclub the night of the fire and was now visiting his grandmother in Yerevan, Armenia.
10. His prior insurer had canceled insurance because of a claim.

I immediately called Martha and obtained her permission to retain competent coverage counsel and a fine-arts appraiser to review the little debris available as well as to report the claim to the fraud division of California's Department of Insurance.

Expanding the Team

The day after I met with Levonian in his backyard, Martha and I met with attorney Bill Abogador. Bill was an experienced lawyer with more than 20 years' experience dealing with insurance fraud and arson-for-profit cases for Goodfaith and dozens of other insurers.

After introductions Bill asked to see the policy and reviewed it carefully, cover to cover, before saying anything:

"How do you spell *porcelain*?" he asked me.

"P-o-r-c-e-l-a-i-n," I responded, confused.

"Did you notice that the schedule of fine arts in this policy spelled it *procelane*?

"No. Do you think it was a typo?"

"I would have thought so until I saw *Meisen* spelled *Mason* and *Lalique* spelled *Lalik*. Do you have the underwriting file with the appraisal on which this schedule was agreed to by Goodfaith?"

Martha reached into her briefcase and pulled out a copy of the underwriting file, flipped through the pages and opened the copy to the original appraisal.

"Here it is," she said. "Do you know Matthew Krooner, the appraiser?"

"Yes. I represented an insurer with regard to an armed robbery at Krooner's auction house three years ago. We refused the claim when he was arrested and convicted of insurance fraud."

"Oh, my!" exclaimed Martha. "What do we do now?"

"First, Barry should immediately visit the offices of the retail insurance agent and the underwriter and obtain detailed recorded statements concerning the placement of this insurance. I will review the information in the claim file, the transcript of Gagik's statement, the underwriting file, the policy wording and the local law. If, after my review, I find grounds to suspect fraud, I will recommend to Goodfaith that Gagik Levonian be required to submit to an examination under oath. I also recommend that Goodfaith retain the services of an appraiser to review the conclusions of Krooner, who — although he had a problem with receiving and selling stolen property — knew how to spell *porcelain* and *Meisen*. After meeting with an expert, Barry should also interview Krooner."

Martha and I left, and I began following Abogador's instructions including consulting with a fine-arts appraiser.

My first stop was at the office of the retail insurance agent, Hrant Aratian, who sold Levonian his policy. Aratian was cooperative and provided me with copies of photographs he had received from Levonian of each of the items described in the appraisal signed by Krooner. He advised me that Levonian had been his client for five years and that he had written insurance on Levonian's home and his car, his wife's car and the cars operated by two of his sons. They were immigrants from Soviet Armenia who appreciated the American dream and lived well operating gas stations and a jewelry store.

"In the five years you have worked with Levonian, has he ever made a claim to an insurer?

"Yes, he had a water leak in his roof last year, and Strong Hands Insurance paid to repair his house. Two years before, his downhill neighbor sued him because of a mudslide. Strong Hands defended him, but I don't know how the case resolved."

"Why did he move from Strong Hands to Goodfaith?"

"After the second claim, Strong Hands sent out a notice of nonrenewal so I had to find another market to protect him."

"Can I have copies of your files on both the Strong Hands and the Goodfaith policies?"

"Of course, everything I do is open to the insurers with whom I do business."

After the copies were made, I met with Dean Hale, an art appraiser, to review the appraisal and the photographs. Dean and I had worked together on several investigations involving fine art in the past. His office was above a garage in the Hancock Park area of Los Angeles. It was filled with auction catalogs and books on fine arts from the Dark Ages to the day before yesterday.

Dean greeted me with a mug of hot, black coffee and a gleaming white smile escaping from the cover of a thick ginger-colored beard. While I drank my coffee, Dean sat silently reviewing the photographs and the appraisal carefully before speaking.

"Who is this Krooner person?" he asked.

"He's an auctioneer in Sherman Oaks dealing in antiques, artwork and goods with an often-questionable provenance," I replied.

"That makes sense," Dean noted, "because if this man is an appraiser, he was imbibing in some illicit drugs at the time."

"Why do you say that?"

"Because none of the descriptions makes sense, the artists are not well known and all the values seem to have had at least one extra zero added to them. I can't be certain because the photographs are all out of focus, although they appear to depict items similar to those described. Finally, the spelling is atrocious. Do you have any of the remains?"

"No. The fire was almost total, but you and I can visit the scene to see what we can find."

"I'll get my coat and loupe."

Dean and I drove to the scene of the fire. The destruction was almost total, but there were shards of pottery, pieces of glass, metal that had been attached to the icons and small unburned pieces of rugs.

After an hour at the scene, Dean exclaimed: "This is a fraud. The pottery shards are not Meisen as described but Mexican pottery bought at Olvera Street downtown for five dollars, and the Persian carpet remnants are nylon, not wool or silk, and were probably bought in a shop in Chinatown. You need to do a great deal more investigation."

Good Faith Is Easily Exploited

After lunch at a nearby sandwich shop, Dean and I separated, and I headed to the office of the underwriter, Millie Snodgrass.

After a few hours in her office reviewing every document in her file, pointing out to her the spelling errors, I took a recorded statement about her underwriting philosophy since, in California, insurance is a contract of personal indemnity based on the decision of the individual underwriter. Millie had been underwriting personal articles for more than 20 years, was highly experienced and had acted as an underwriter for major insurers and the Lloyd's market in London.

"Millie, how important are the answers to questions on an application to your underwriting decision?"

"They are the most important since we rely on the truthfulness of the prospective insured."

"Don't you check out the insured and the appraisal before you agree to the insurance?"

"Never. It would be too expensive since we only sell 20 percent of the applications on which we make an offer. We have to rely on the good faith of the prospective insured."

"This application states that Levonian had never had a claim before — what effect would it have had on your decision to insure him if you knew he had a roof leak claim paid a month before he signed the application?"

"I probably would have assessed a 10 percent surcharge on the premium."

"What would happen if he told you he had the roof leak and a burglary last year?"

"I would have assessed a 15 percent surcharge on the premium."

"What would happen if he told you he had the roof leak, two burglaries and a liability claim?"

"I would have told him to go elsewhere. I would not touch that risk with a high-value policy like this one."

"And if Levonian told you his last policy was canceled for loss history, what would you have done?"

"I would have been very disappointed, but there is no way I could write a policy with that kind of information. Are any of those things true?"

"Levonian and his insurance agent told me all of those statements are true."

"Heck, if I knew all those things, I would have trashed the application immediately. I only agreed to the policy because the loss and cancelation history was clean, he lived in a low-crime neighborhood, had a detailed appraisal and appeared to be a successful businessman."

"Did you review the appraisal?"

"Yes."

"Do you know Krooner?"

"No."

"Did you notice that the appraisal misspelled the words *porcelain* and *Meisen*?"

"Oh, no! I missed that, didn't I? If I had seen it, I would have asked for a new appraisal before agreeing to the policy."

I had the statement transcribed and asked Millie to sign her responses under penalty of perjury.

I then went to Krooner's office in Sherman Oaks, and he voluntarily agreed to a recorded statement about his work for Levonian.

Lazy Appraisal Work

After pleasantries establishing rapport and making Krooner certain I had nothing to do with a police agency, I showed him a copy of the original appraisal and asked: "Matthew, is that you signature at the bottom of each page of the appraisal?"

"Yes," he responded with a slight tremor in his voice while rubbing his palms on his pants leg.

"When did you last see this document?"

"I've never seen it."

"Perhaps I misheard you — how could you sign it without seeing it?"

"I signed blank appraisal forms. Levonian was in a hurry, said his son was an A student in typing and he would type it if I reduced my fee. I charged him $300 and gave him my notes."

"Read the appraisal; did the son accurately type up your notes?"

"No. It looks like he added a zero on many of the items and called this print an oil painting. This is very disturbing, Barry; he could get me in trouble, and I'm still on probation."

Outcome of the Investigation

I reported the findings of the investigation to Martha and the lawyer Abogador. The claim was eventually denied, Levonian sued and Goodfaith cross-complained to recover the money it advanced for living expenses, along with investigative costs and legal fees.

It took years of trial and appeal for the California Court of Appeals to conclude:

> A contract is extinguished by its rescission. The consequence of rescission is not only the termination of further liability, but also the restoration of the parties to their former positions by requiring each to return whatever consideration has been received. Here, this would require the refund by Goodfaith of any premiums and the repayment by Levonian of any proceeds advanced which they may have received. The policy is "extinguished" from its inception, as though it had never existed.
>
> Levonian, in law, never was insured under a policy of insurance. That status cannot exist in a vacuum, but must necessarily depend upon the existence of a valid policy of insurance. No compelling reason has been suggested to us, nor can we conceive of any, as to why defendants, having obtained the policy upon the basis of material concealment about prior losses and an earlier cancellation should have no rights against Goodfaith.
>
> We therefore hold that upon a rescission of a policy of insurance, based upon a material concealment or misrepresentation, all rights of the insured thereunder (except the right to recover any consideration paid in the purchase of the policy) are extinguished, including the right or standing to prosecute a claim against the insurer for breach of contract and breach of the covenant of good faith and fair dealing.

In the end, Levonian failed to get money to support his terrorist friends, failed to profit from his claims of bad faith and was required to pay $500,000 to Goodfaith to repay funds expended for temporary living expenses and for the investigative and legal fees incurred to defeat his suit.

Lessons Learned

Goodfaith lived up to its name. It did a thorough investigation with the assistance of a claims adjuster, an experienced and knowledgeable CFE and an experienced and knowledgeable lawyer who was also a CFE. Because of management's knowledge of insurance, insurance law and how to conduct a complete investigation, Goodfaith avoided a fraudulent $3 million claim and recovered expenses. Goodfaith's leadership refused to settle and was willing to work for more than five years to defeat this fraudulent arson-for-profit claim.

Recommendations to Prevent Future Occurrences

Goodfaith learned from its mistake in accepting Levonian as an insured. It has, since this case, changed its internal underwriting policy concerning acceptance of high-value scheduled personal property. Now, before a risk like that presented by Levonian is accepted, the underwriters are required to:

- Use a detailed application form and have the insured warrant the absolute truth of the facts stated in the application.
- Read every word in the appraisal for accuracy.
- Obtain information about the experience and expertise of the appraiser.
- Check the claims database for prior loss and cancelation history before accepting the risk.
- Contact the claims department to determine if staff members have any experience with the appraiser or the insured.

Goodfaith management also instituted a company policy that it advertises to its agents, brokers and the public at large that it will never pay a claim it believes to be fraudulent. As a result of the new policy, Goodfaith has seen a major reduction in suspected fraudulent claims.

About the Author

Barry Zalma, Esq., CFE, has practiced law in California for more than 40 years as an insurance coverage and claims-handling lawyer. He now limits his practice to service as an insurance consultant and expert witness specializing in insurance coverage, insurance claims handling, insurance bad faith and insurance fraud almost equally, for insurers and policyholders. He also serves as an arbitrator or mediator for insurance-related disputes.

CHAPTER

Weakest Link in the Chain

ANGELA BISASOR

Tom Harrison was a young man from a humble family background. He lived with his mother and his two younger siblings in a two-bedroom apartment in the inner city. His mother was a fruit vendor in the nearby market. She did her best to care for her children, but it was difficult, even more so since her husband had died. Tom carried a greater burden as the oldest son, and he wanted to help his mother and his siblings afford a better standard of life. Tom graduated from high school but found it difficult to get a job. After months of sending out applications and not getting positive responses, he finally got a small break when a friend managed to get him a temporary job working in the Registry Department of Mutual General Insurance Company Limited sorting mail and registering incoming packages. It was not his dream job, but it was a paycheck for the time being. Tom worked enthusiastically and was always eager to help others, going the extra mile wherever he could. He tried to excel, and his supervisor was impressed at his eagerness to learn the system; she encouraged him as a young man trying to improve his prospects. His coworkers liked him, and he was fortunate to have his former school friend, Jane Burns, there to guide him.

Jane secretly had a crush on Tom throughout high school and was always there to help him in whatever way she could. An apparently tough character on the outside, she had a soft spot for him. Tom knew that she cared for him and was happy to be around her. She often asked about his family and offered advice on different things that he talked to her about. At work, she kept him in the loop of the happenings in the department and the company as a whole, which he appreciated very much.

Mutual General Insurance Company Limited was a medium-size company with more than 200 employees, offering insurance coverage for property and automobiles. It had grown from a small brokerage firm to a network of ten branches. Its head office was located in the city and housed the functional departments of registry, underwriting, claims, human resources, marketing, information technology (IT) and internal audit and compliance. Each department had a policy and procedures manual to guide its operations. These manuals were approved by the audit committee and placed on the intranet for employees to access.

Audit and compliance reviews were done routinely in accordance with the approved work plans for the year. The work plans were designed to ensure that high-risk areas were reviewed over a two-year cycle and other areas over three-years. IT audits were done throughout the year. Based on the findings of the different reviews, recommendations made for improvements were generally brushed aside. The control environment in theory was strong, but, in reality, the checks and balances were not working efficiently, resulting in a somewhat laissez-faire way of doing business. The Registry Department had recently been reviewed, and there were no significant exceptions noted. However, a concern was raised during the audit of individuals' access rights to certain areas in the system where they had no need based on their current job function. Some adjustments were made to user privileges, but it was highlighted that read-only access was not considered a problem and it was required from time to time to know where to direct correspondences and queries. In any case, it was considered an issue for IT to manage.

Despite the weaknesses in the control environment, the company was profitable and a leader in the industry. The incidents of increasing insurance frauds were an industry-wide concern, and Mutual General Insurance was no exception. Management had tightened operations with its intermediaries by implementing systems to facilitate timelier reporting and settlement of outstanding claims. Often it appears that when one loophole closes, many more open, so it was a case of always trying to keep up. There were some good employees who did their best to protect the company's assets, but there were others who were just doing enough to get by and no more. All in all, the company was meeting its objectives and financial targets.

The Unexpected Meeting

I was the sole auditor at Mutual General, and we had a cosourcing arrangement with an accounting firm. Basically, we split the audit assignments, worked together and contributed to the audit report. I had just finished a branch review and was in the process of compiling my report when I got a call from Janice Henderson, the chief compliance officer, asking me to come to her office. I put aside the report, wondering what was happening now. These calls usually meant a special assignment. "If only people would do what they are supposed to do." I sighed under my breath. "If only they would stop strangling the goose that lays the golden egg." That was where my thoughts almost always ended up when I heard about a new case of someone defrauding Mutual General. I had learned to appreciate the source of my income and to defend it, which made my job that much easier in trying to identify weaknesses and strengthen controls to improve the efficiency, effectiveness and economy of operations. I believed that if others could see things the way I did, we would all be heading in the same direction, but the challenge was that not everyone was on the same path . . . and I guess that made my job function so critical to a healthy organization: at least I acted as a deterrent to the weak.

When I entered Janice Henderson's office, there were two police officers sitting in front of her desk. She introduced me to Sergeant Thompson and Corporal Jones from the local police station. After the formalities, they briefed me on what was transpiring. The officers had been summoned to a local bank where a claims check drawn on our company was being presented for encashment under apparently fraudulent circumstances. The officers confiscated a cell phone from the young woman who was trying to cash the check and found a text message that said "The check is ready for collection" sent from an employee at Mutual General. I asked who sent the text, and Sergeant Thompson told it came from Jane Burns, who worked in the Registry Department.

"Was the check genuine or was it fraudulently drawn?" I asked.

"It was a genuine check," replied Janice. "The issue is that the check was collected by a fraudster posing to be the insured."

"I don't understand, because based on my review of the Registry Department just a few months ago, our processes there appeared tight in terms of identifying the collector and ensuring that we are actually giving the right person the right check," I interjected. General Mutual usually mailed claims checks to our customers, but some people preferred to pick up their checks in person at the office. When that occurs, we check their identification and verify that it matches our records for the individual.

Janice explained that the young woman who picked up the claims check had presented what appeared to be a valid ID that matched the information in our system.

"What went wrong then?" I asked. It turns out the woman had presented a fraudulent ID. The picture was that of the person collecting the check — a young woman whose name was Jenny Ginal — but the details matched those of the insured — an older woman named Dorothy Trimble. Very interesting, I thought. "So have we uncovered a case of identification theft?" I inquired.

"It certainly looks that way," replied Sergeant Thompson. "And rarely are these isolated incidents. We are hoping to identify the mastermind behind the operation and take him down. Identification theft is spiraling out of control."

The Interview

Janice summoned Jane Burns to her office. She arrived a few minutes later, looking quite disturbed at this unexpected meeting. I knew Jane from my recent audit of the Registry Department. She had been with Mutual General for more than five years and was well liked by her colleagues. Her supervisor spoke highly of Jane as well, when I asked her to discuss her staff with me. Jane was a young, pretty woman who had a deferential, sweet air about her. I had a hard time imagining her working as part of an identity-theft ring, but I pushed aside my preconceived ideas of her and tried to listen to the interview without bias.

Janice greeted Jane warmly and introduced her to the police officers, and then went on to explain why Jane was there. She informed Jane that a situation arose involving a client who seemed to be connected to her. Janice then handed over the discussion to Sergeant Thompson. He began by asking her not to be alarmed but to cooperate as they tried to ascertain what connections she had with the customer at the bank. Jane was at a total loss and blankly denied knowing who Jenny Ginal was or what they were talking about. She looked genuinely confused.

"So you are stating quite explicitly that you do not know who Jenny Ginal is and that you have never had any reason to contact any one with that name?" asked Sergeant Thompson in a strict tone of voice.

"That is exactly what I am saying," retorted Jane adamantly. She was seemingly less and less like the meek woman I knew.

"Very well then, if that is your statement," said Sergeant Thompson. "Do you by any chance have your cell phone on you?"

"I do not see how that is relevant to this conversation," Jane responded in a feisty voice. She seemed to be getting angrier with every question Sergeant Thompson asked her.

"Your cell phone is what actually linked you to Jenny Ginal," said Sergeant Thompson, watching Jane closely. He seemed to be monitoring her mood changes even more than I was. While Thompson was talking to Jane, I noticed that Corporal Jones was inconspicuously taking notes.

"I do not see how that is possible," replied Jane.

"Perhaps if you let me have a look at your phone, it could solve some of the mystery for us all," said Sergeant Thompson, reaching out his hand in a motion to collect something.

"Why do you want my phone? It is my private phone; it is not a company phone, and it sure was not stolen," she exclaimed.

"You can do this the easy way or the hard way . . . it is your choice," said Sergeant Thompson, evidently starting to get annoyed with Jane's defiance.

"I do not have the phone on me," replied Jane. "I will have to go and get it."

As she turned to go, Sergeant Thompson asked her to hold on just a moment. "Let us just do a quick check."

He nodded to Corporal Jones, who dialed Jane's phone number on Janice's office line. We waited with bated breath and then heard the phone beeping from her pocket. Jane's jaw dropped and it was clear that she was embarrassed. However, more important, it was proof that the text to Jenny Ginal had come from Jane's cell phone.

"I did not remember that I had picked it up off the desk and put it in my pocket," she said in what sounded like an apologetic tone.

Corporal Jones asked Jane for her phone, and she handed it over reluctantly. He clicked through her text messages but said there was no trace of the message to Jenny. Jane was reluctant to provide any further information, so the officers escorted her to the police station, where she was detained for further questioning.

The Interrogation

Both Janice and I decided to accompany Jane to the police station. We were hoping the whole time that Jane would recognize the severity of the situation and tell the police officers whatever she knew about Jenny and the identity theft so they could get on with their investigation. What was she covering up and why? Janice and I speculated in the waiting area, but we did not have much to go on. Sergeant Thompson came out shortly after we all arrived at the station and told us they were going to begin questioning Jane again. He allowed us in the room because any information that Jane provided would likely affect business operations.

Part of me was expecting the Hollywood interrogation scene: a cold, dark room with a small table in the middle; Jane sitting at the table with a spotlight on her; Sergeant Thompson circling her and chain-smoking while grilling her. But no, it was just your run-of-the-mill conference room. Sergeant Thompson and Corporal Jones were sitting across from Jane at the table. Janice and I sat down toward the end so as not to be in the way.

This time Corporal Jones started talking and Sergeant Thompson took notes. Jones began by explaining the implications of the situation to Jane. He made sure she understood that she was being investigated for her involvement in an identity-theft ring and for defrauding Mutual General. The evidence was on her cell phone, which was with a police forensic investigator at the moment. Corporal Jones told Jane that even though she had deleted the text to Jenny, his forensic expert would have no trouble recovering it. He continued this way for a while, thoroughly explaining the case as he understood it, and then offered Jane the opportunity to explain things from her side.

After Corporal Jones' persuasive approach, Jane eventually confessed to having loaned her cell phone to her friend Tom Harrison recently. He told her his phone's battery had died and he needed to send a message urgently. I made a mental note of Tom, and I remembered him from my audit of the

Registry Department. He filled an administrative role in the department and mostly handled the mail. He seemed to be an unlikely suspect to orchestrate a fraud ring.

"Who erased the text message from the phone?" asked Corporal Jones.

"It must have been Tom. I did not see the message and I have no idea what it was all about," declared Jane in a defensive tone. She seemed to be indicating that she would cooperate, but she was not happy about it.

"So, who is this Tom, and what is your relationship with him?" asked Corporal Jones after a moment's thought.

"Why is that important? I told you he is my friend!" exclaimed Jane.

"Young lady, listen to me very carefully. A crime has been committed and you are implicated. It is best if you just try to calm yourself and help us through this investigation as quickly as possible. Both your internal auditor and compliance manager are tired, and I am sure they want to leave in the shortest time possible. I am asking you for your full cooperation," said Corporal Jones in a controlled tone. "Where do you know Tom from?"

"We went to school together," said Jane in a low, hushed voice.

"Are you aware of his involvement in any sort of criminal activity?" asked Corporal Jones.

"No, I am not," retorted Jane, "and I am sure this is all a mistake. I don't know Tom to be a thief and I am sure he is not mixed up with bad company!" By now tears were in her eyes.

"Well, right now, we are following the clues, and at this moment they are all pointing at you."

"I have nothing more to say. I have told you all I know," declared Jane. "I want to leave."

Corporal Jones ended the interrogation session but Jane was remanded to custody.

The Second Interview and Interrogation

The next day, the police came by the office again, and I was summoned to Janice's office, where both Corporal Jones and Sergeant Thompson greeted me warmly. They informed Janice and me that they would like to ask Tom some questions. Janice called Tom and we waited a few minutes before he appeared at the door. The police officers went through the same routine they had done with Jane and asked if Tom knew Jenny Ginal; he said he did not. They went on to ask if he had sent a text message from Jane's phone the previous day, to which he also responded negatively.

"Why, what is this all about?" asked Tom with a questioning look, tilting his head to the right side and gesticulating with his hands.

"Jane said you borrowed her phone and we would like to corroborate this with you," replied Corporal Jones. "So, did you or did you not?"

Tom thought about it a bit then, shrugging his shoulders, said, "If Jane said so I may have. I don't know why she would lie."

"So what number did you text?" quizzed Sergeant Thompson.

"Like I said, I don't remember using her phone to send a message, but if Jane said she lent me her phone, I guess she did."

"We are going to have to take you into the station for questioning. A text was sent to Jenny Ginal's number from Jane's phone and there are implications of wrongdoing on your part," said Corporal Jones. After some formalities, the officers left with Tom for the police station. Janice and I decided not to attend Tom's interrogation.

Jane was released that day but her phone was held as evidence.

Tom, we found out later, was questioned over and over again but did not change his argument that he did not know Jenny Ginal and he did not remember borrowing the phone.

The police asked Jenny Ginal to identify Tom as the person who had communicated with her on Jane's phone, but she could not because they had never met. Jenny was kept in custody but Tom was released because there was no evidence to hold him responsible — it was Jane's word against his.

The Crime Ring Breaks

The police investigation continued over the following two weeks, during which time the officers made several trips to Mutual General's headquarters and in particular the Registry Department to question employees. They were finally able to piece together the full story. Tom was part of an identity-theft ring that had an extensive operation in the area. Tom's role was to collect information on individuals who were owed claims checks from Mutual General. He conveyed their identifying information to someone up the chain, and that person prepared a fake ID, usually a driver's license, with the insured person's information. However, the photograph would be of another fraudster, like Jenny Ginal, who was going to pick up the claims check. Tom would then text when the claims check was ready to be collected.

In this instance, Tom had accessed the payment system to ascertain the details of a payee who was in the queue for checks to be printed that day. He obtained a copy of the payee's driver's license from her records, which he copied and passed on to the mastermind to print the fake license for Jenny. As soon as the check was prepared and received at the registry for distribution, Tom texted Jenny, whose number he was given by the ringleader, that she could pick up the check from Mutual General's office.

Jenny came into the office, presented what appeared to be a valid ID in the name of the payee and had no difficulty collecting the check. The ploy unraveled when the bank teller spotted an anomaly in the age on the ID and the age of the person presenting it. Jenny Ginal appeared to be in her 20s but the age on the ID was 41. The teller excused herself for a moment and went to speak to her supervisor. She returned to the cage quite calmly and tried to keep Jenny engaged in conversation, buying time for her supervisor to alert security and call the police. In a short time, the police arrived and made their way to the cashier window where Jenny was impatiently waiting for the check to be processed. The officers asked her to go with them to an office where they detained her for questioning. Her phone rang while she was with them, and they asked to see the phone. On searching it they found the text from Jane's phone . . . the rest we know.

Based on the outcome of the investigation, Mutual General fired Tom Harrison, and shortly after Jane Burns put in her two weeks' notice. We were lucky that the bank teller had noticed the discrepancy on Jenny's fake ID and stopped the transaction, but I suspected this was not the first time Tom had directed customer payments to members of the crime ring. When we met with Tom before he was fired, our general counsel suggested that if Tom provided the details of his other thefts, we would not file criminal charges. He agreed and wrote down a dozen other names, which I then investigated. I uncovered a total of $18,000 in stolen insurance payments, and asked a customer service representative to follow up with the individuals who were still waiting for the checks to let them know they were being processed.

Lessons Learned

We had conducted reviews of system privileges in the past and recommended that steps be taken to ensure staff members are given access to proprietary systems on a need-to-know basis only. Unfortunately, that had not happened in this case, as Tom was able to access sensitive customer information that he did not need to know to perform his administrative tasks. This case taught me the importance of following up on my recommendations to make sure they have been implemented. It does no good for an auditor to suggest process improvements if no one is responsible for implementing the changes.

Recommendation to Prevent Future Occurrences

I met with Mutual General's IT team to discuss the case and reiterate the importance of limiting system access. We worked together to redefine access to sensitive information, and I feel confident in our ability to reduce the chances of future occurrence. Of course, nothing can guarantee that company information will not be misused in the future, but the process now in place reduces the risk significantly.

About the Author

Angela Marie Bisasor is a fellow of the Institute of Chartered Accountants (FCA), Certified Internal Auditor (CIA) and a Certified Information Systems Auditor (CISA). She is an auditor, chartered accountant, writer and educator.

Ms. Bisasor graduated from the University of the West Indies with a B.S. (Hons) in accounting (1989) and an M.S. degree in computer-based management information systems (2007). Her professional career began at KPMG, where she developed her skills in auditing and accountancy while pursuing ACCA examinations. She has a wide range of experience spanning different industries. Ms. Bisasor upholds integrity and accountability as key values to business success.

CHAPTER

7

Everyone Gets Hurt: A Study in Workers' Compensation Fraud

MICHAEL SPUTO

A man sat at his kitchen table. Spread out before him were bond paper, a utility knife and a glue stick. The laptop, printer and cell phone were fired up. The address of a PO Box was scribbled on a sticky note. From these humble beginnings, a $100 million fraud was born.

Beverly Hills, California, was home to the rich and famous and those who seek riches and fame. Phillip Logan was different from the wannabe starlets who lunched on Rodeo Drive, wishing the paparazzi were interested in what they were doing and fantasizing about being on TMZ. Logan only cared about the riches.

A law school graduate who never passed the bar, Logan bounced around for years as an entrepreneur who could not quite seem to make it work. Eventually, Logan found his calling. Middle age and married, a family man with children who relied on him, Logan used his undergraduate business degree to set up shop as an investment banker — but not the type of investment banker you would find on Wall Street. No, Logan was the type of investment banker who specialized in the murky business of balance sheet enhancement. Logan's specialty was creating shell companies that he could use to find assets to put on the financial statements of his clients' companies for pennies on the dollar. How is it possible to pay thousands of dollars for control of millions of dollars of assets? The short answer is to mix in a bit of fraud and deceit.

Try as he might, Logan could not completely avoid the spotlight as he sought his fortune. Logan and his shell companies were mentioned in various lawsuits and news reports, and not in a good way. Words like *bankruptcy, slumlord, bogus financial documents,* and *defrauding cemetery trust funds* were often mentioned in reports of his business ventures. It was once reported that Logan installed a family pet as president of one of his shell companies.

Fort Lauderdale, Florida, once primarily the winter playground of snowbirds and college students seeking the warmth of the sun and miles of sandy beaches, had evolved into an affluent oceanside community, attracting year-round residents who enjoyed the beautiful weather and low taxes. One of these people was John Davis. In many ways Davis was like any other chief executive officer (CEO) of a public company. Married and in his 50s, Davis certainly looked the part, with his deep tan and silver hair. No one would have guessed that he was not a college graduate and had risen from his start in the hardscrabble trucking industry to become the CEO of a series of public companies. His friends described Davis as a man who got to where he was by relying on instinct and common sense. Almost all of his employees liked his down-to-earth, agreeable nature. With his children grown and out of the house, Davis was ready to settle down in south Florida as CEO of his latest venture, Precision Payroll Services (Precision).

Bundled and Bungled

Precision could best be described as a payroll processing company on steroids. It was a public company with several offices in Florida and clients across the United States. Precision was a professional employer organization, known in the insurance industry as a PEO. Sometimes called employee leasing companies, PEOs combine the employees of separate companies into one large group or pool of employees. In what is described as a co-employee relationship, the PEO assumes responsibility for certain functions, including paying payroll taxes and obtaining workers' compensation insurance. Client companies retain management control over their employees and their daily operations. Client companies write a check to the PEO every week to cover payroll, taxes and benefits. These companies also pay administrative fees, which are where the PEO makes its money.

The theory behind a PEO is that by combining employees from smaller, mom-and-pop businesses into one large group, the PEO can negotiate better rates for certain benefits, including workers' compensation insurance. The reality is that workers' compensation insurance, required by law, is expensive and difficult to obtain. The ability to get it at a reasonable price is the driving force for PEOs to retain clients and charge them for other services — without it, the PEO would soon be out of business.

The reality of many PEOs is far different from the theory. What makes sense on paper sometimes is unwieldy in reality. *Merriam-Webster's Dictionary* defines *unwieldy* as "too big or badly organized to function efficiently." Precision, like many PEOs during their heyday, was exactly that. Handling almost $1 billion in payroll a year at its peak, with hundreds of client companies employing thousands of workers, whose names changed each week as employees were hired and fired, Precision's management soon found that it could not accurately tell on a timely basis how many employees were on the books and how much they were paid. The growing problem Precision faced was that this type of uncertainty just doesn't mix well with the insurance industry.

Upper Darby Insurance (UDI) was a relative newcomer to the insurance industry, getting its start in Baltimore providing property and casualty insurance to GIs returning from World War II. From humble beginnings, UDI had grown to one of the largest insurance companies in North America, providing a full range of products including, of course, workers' compensation insurance. UDI, with a reputation for being fair and running a tight ship, seemed an unlikely match for Precision, which was quickly earning a reputation in the Wild West of the PEO industry as a company that was mostly interested in growing the business and less concerned with running it.

UDI's contract with Precision relied heavily on taking Precision's word about how many employees it had and the payroll amounts to be covered by UDI's workers' comp. Precision reported payroll and employee counts to UDI periodically, and UDI billed Precision based on these numbers. UDI audited the figures only once a year and then adjusted the premium due. When these audits consistently revealed Precision's payroll — and UDI's exposure — to be greater than was reported, UDI began to require more and more collateral, in the form of bank letters of credit (LOCs), to secure unpaid premiums. A bank letter of credit, if authentic, is the next best thing to cash; in the event that Precision defaulted on its premium payments, UDI could cash these LOCs and be made whole. Eventually, UDI held more than $40 million in LOCs from Precision.

As UDI required Precision to provide more and more collateral, Davis and Precision had a problem. Precision did not have the assets to secure bank LOCs in the amounts that UDI required; typically, these letters are secured by providing 100 percent in cash or other collateral to the issuing bank. While reporting gross revenues of almost $1 billion at its peak, Precision actually held little cash of its own — these gross revenues were made up almost wholly of the payroll turned over to Precision, most of which left Precision as soon as it came in, with the bulk of the remaining cash supposed to be put into escrow accounts to pay the Internal Revenue Service (IRS) and state taxing authorities when due. Without collateral, Precision would lose its workers' compensation insurance, and most if not all of its clients would leave, putting the company out of business. Enter Phillip Logan, promising the solution to Precision's collateral problems.

Unlikely Rescuer

Through a series of intermediaries, Logan offered to provide LOCs from well-known U.S. banks for less than five cents on the dollar, which Precision could afford. Precision paid a middleman, who paid Logan, who provided the LOCs submitted by Precision to UDI to secure unpaid premiums. No one, including Davis, asked too many questions about how Logan was able to provide $40 million in LOCs from banks insured by the Federal Deposit Insurance Corporation (FDIC) for less than $4 million. Logan explained to those who asked that he was securing the LOCs with other funds he had under management, and no one cared to look too deeply into the matter. Everyone was happy. Precision had its collateral at an affordable price and could remain in business. Logan had his millions of dollars and could finally be the high roller he always wanted to be. UDI, unaware that Logan was involved and unaware that Precision was paying only pennies on the dollar for the LOCs, verified that the banks providing the letters were FDIC insured and put them in its collateral vault, thinking it was fully secured.

Eventually, UDI came to the conclusion that providing workers' compensation insurance to PEOs was too risky and notified Precision, and its other PEO clients, that it would cease to provide this service. UDI was one of the few reputable insurance companies that provided workers' compensation to PEOs. John Davis could not find another insurance company to replace UDI and had to either think fast and find a solution or close shop.

I, of course, did not know any of this when I reviewed a new insurance fraud case that landed on my desk. There wasn't much to review. The case had been opened based on a complaint from a walk-in — which is exactly what it sounds like: someone walks into their local Federal Bureau of Investigation (FBI) office and tells an agent what is on their mind. According to the complaint, the walk-in said that until she had been recently fired, she had worked at Precision as a clerk. She explained that Precision was a PEO and from what she had observed and overheard while working there, she believed that Precision was issuing certificates of insurance to clients for workers' compensation insurance that did not exist. The complaint did not have much detail, and I made a mental note to go out and interview the person sometime in the next few weeks to see if she had any more information. I was working on several fraud investigations at the same time, and this vague complaint from a fired worker wasn't a high priority for me. I also had never heard of a PEO and knew almost nothing about the workers' compensation industry. This would soon change. At the time, I had been an FBI agent for more than 20 years, most of it spent investigating white-collar crime, and knew that a lucky break in a case never hurts. I was about to get one.

A few nights later, my cell phone rang about 8 p.m., and the caller ID showed that it was the office. The person working the night switchboard had just taken a call from Robert Tyler, a current Precision employee, who was upset at what was happening at work and wanted to talk to someone at the FBI about it. I called Tyler, and after a short conversation, he agreed to meet me and another agent at a local diner the following evening.

Crash Course in Insurance

It was early July, and the diner was almost empty. When my partner and I entered the diner, 15 minutes early, Tyler was already there and waved us over. He explained that he had just finished his workday and had already ordered dinner. After I introduced myself and my partner, I asked Tyler to tell me a little about his background. Tyler explained that he worked in the workers' compensation insurance department at Precision and was very familiar with that specialty, having held several jobs in the workers' compensation insurance over the last few years.

"I contacted the FBI because there are things going on at Precision that are just plain wrong." Tyler explained further. "I can't just stand by and do nothing while Precision's employees do things that hurt innocent companies and workers."

I told Tyler that we would stay as long as it took for him to tell his story, but I needed some background information about PEOs and how they worked in general, and asked him to explain. For about an hour, Tyler answered question after question about PEOs and workers' compensation insurance in general and Precision in particular. This was important; in order to understand what, if anything, Precision was doing wrong, I had to understand how things should be done if everything was being done the right way.

Tyler explained that workers' compensation insurance is regulated by individual states and that all states required most businesses, with few exceptions, to provide this coverage to protect their employees if they are hurt on the job. Insurance companies apply to various states to become "admitted carriers," allowing them to write insurance in that state. In an important part of this process, state agents review assets held by each insurance company to be sure they are solvent and are in a financial position to pay claims. They also periodically review their admitted carriers' operations to make sure everything is in order.

"About a year ago, when UDI stopped writing workers' comp policies for Precision, Davis tried but couldn't find a replacement. All of a sudden, I started seeing workers' comp certificates of coverage being issued in the names of two insurance companies I never heard of: Torchwood Casualty and Benton Coastal Holdings. When I asked Davis about it, he told me not to worry, which made me nervous." Tyler continued, "Now, workers' compensation claims aren't being paid on these supposed policies, and when clients complain about their coverage, they are switched back and forth between Torchwood and Benton. Injured workers aren't getting their replacement wages and medical bills paid, and no one at the top can give us any answers on how to handle those claims."

I asked Tyler if he would be in a position to get copies of some of the Torchwood and Benton insurance certificates that Precision had issued as well as the names of a few of the client companies and injured workers whose claims weren't being paid, and he readily agreed. "Someone has to stop this before more people get hurt," Tyler said, agreeing to meet me again in a few days with the paperwork. Tyler's information corroborated the original complaint of the walk-in, with one difference. Tyler still worked at Precision and was in a better position to provide evidence. He could also be tasked to get information that the walk-in could not. I decided to concentrate on Tyler for the moment.

The next day, I called UDI to see if I could corroborate what Tyler told me about UDI ending its business relationship with Precision and to get more information about how things worked when an admitted carrier wrote workers' compensation insurance for a PEO. After a few phone calls, I received a call back from UDI's head of security, John Saunders, who split my single investigation into two directions.

Tracking the Letters of Credit

Saunders explained that UDI had stopped its relationship with Precision and was owed millions of dollars for unpaid insurance premiums. When payment didn't come, UDI tried to draw down on some of the bank LOCs that Precision provided as collateral. Saunders continued, "When we submitted the LOCs to Fowler National Bank, they said they were fraudulent and wouldn't pay. We hired a private investigator to try to get to the bottom of it, and he thinks the fake LOCs were provided by a guy named Phillip Logan in California." Saunders said UDI was probably going to sue Precision for the unpaid premiums and that UDI would cooperate fully with the FBI. Saunders agreed to overnight me copies of the fraudulent LOCs so I could start my own investigation.

Once I received the LOCs, I looked at them closely. They appeared to be written on bank letterhead, and provided a bank branch address in California and a phone number. They were signed by a bank officer named George Tenor. I did a quick Internet search and couldn't tie the address or phone number to any Fowler National branch. A quick call to bank security confirmed that no one named George Tenor worked at Fowler National, and the address and telephone number were not associated with any Fowler National branch.

Since I knew the key to finding out who was behind these fake LOCs was finding who was behind the address and telephone number on them, I prepared a summary of what I knew and sent a memo to our Los Angeles office. No matter where you go in the United States, there is an FBI office that covers that area. Sometimes parts of an investigation can be done over the telephone, but something like this needed to be done by an FBI agent in person. I sent my lead to the Los Angeles office, asking an agent to investigate the address and telephone number. I also passed along UDI's suspicion that Phillip Logan might be involved. The more information I could give the local agent, the better.

While waiting to hear back from L.A., I refocused my attention on Tyler's allegation. The following week, Tyler called to say he had some documents to show me, and we met again at the diner after he got off work. As I sat down, he handed me a folder of documents and said, "I think this will help." The folder contained copies of insurance certificates issued by Precision to several client companies, showing that their employees were insured by Torchwood and Benton. Tyler told me that these were some of the companies whose injured workers' claims weren't being paid. Tyler explained that Precision kept all the files on the "problem claims" related to Torchwood and Benton in a specific area of their Fort Lauderdale office.

Now the real work could begin. Tyler's information was invaluable, but I could not rely on it by itself. What if Tyler had a grudge against the company's leadership and made up the paperwork? Just because someone says something, it doesn't mean it is true. I needed to thoroughly investigate his information to see what I could prove.

I contacted the Florida Department of Insurance (FDOI) and spoke to an agent who confirmed that insurance companies writing workers' compensation insurance in Florida had to be approved by the FDOI. The agent confirmed that Torchwood and Benton were not approved. Using the information on the insurance certificates Tyler provided, I contacted some of Precision's clients who were paying for workers' compensation insurance but had employees' claims go unpaid for extended periods of time. They sent me copies of their insurance certificates, which matched those that Tyler provided. I was able to tie one of the addresses on a Torchwood document to Precision's address, which made it appear to me that Torchwood might be related to Precision.

Torchwood appeared to be nothing more than a shell company. Other than the address, I could find no evidence of its existence or operations. Benton did appear to actually exist; however, it was the subject of several lawsuits. From these lawsuits, it looked like Benton was providing some sort of unapproved alternative to workers' compensation insurance. A quick check with the FDOI found that this was not permitted, and the client companies I contacted said they were told they had standard workers' compensation insurance, not an alternative.

This information, coupled with what Tyler told me about the location of records at the Precision office, gave me enough probable cause to try to get a search warrant. I could get records that would help me identify the extent of the fraud and more potential victims who could provide evidence. Additionally, a warrant would put Davis and other Precision executives on notice that they were under investigation and, I hoped, stop the fraudulent activity. If I notified anyone at Precision before getting the search warrant, evidence could be moved or destroyed.

It All Comes Together

In August, the agent in Los Angeles sent me the results of his investigation. A physical inspection of the address on the fraudulent LOCs showed it was a PO Box rented by Phillip Logan. The agent tried to interview Logan, but he refused to talk. Logan got an attorney, and, after some negotiating, Logan and his attorney agreed to meet with me and the prosecutor on the case.

In September, Logan flew to Miami and met with us, with his attorney present. Logan said that in the course of his balance sheet enhancement business, he learned that Precision needed some bank LOCs to use as collateral. Logan agreed to provide these for a 3 percent fee. Upon further questioning, Logan admitted to creating the fake LOCs and receiving more than $1 million from Precision in exchange. Logan said he started by getting a PO Box, which he rented in the name of Fowler National, and a disposable cell phone. He then found Fowler National letterhead on the Internet and printed it out. Using sample LOCs he already had, Logan created the text of the LOCs to meet Precision's specific needs. He made up the name of a bank officer and used the disposable cell phone and PO Box as the contact information, in case anyone tried to verify the LOCs. After printing a LOC on high-quality bond paper, Logan cut out the Fowler letterhead and glued it to the LOC. It was that simple.

I could now redirect my efforts to the workers' compensation insurance fraud. By December, I was able to establish probable cause and obtain a search warrant for Precision's offices. We obtained files that allowed us to fully identify all of the victim companies and injured workers who did not get the insurance they paid for. Several Precision employees approached me while I was executing the search warrant and agreed to cooperate with the FBI. Over the next year, they provided information regarding this and several other fraud schemes.

Eventually, as the evidence mounted and one subordinate after another pleaded guilty, John Davis decided to take responsibility for his actions. Davis told me that when Precision lost its workers' compensation insurance agreement with UDI, he tried to find replacement coverage but could not. Due to the size of Precision's payroll, no insurance company would take the risk. Eventually, after trying to find alternatives, Davis decided that Precision would self-insure the risk by charging clients for insurance, keeping the premiums and paying the claims. This explained why Benton and Precision shared an address at one point. His plan worked for a while, but as claims increased, Precision was unable to pay them. Davis also admitted that Precision did not turn over all of the payroll taxes it collected to the IRS as required and spent the money instead. Davis denied knowing that the LOCs were fraudulent.

John Davis pleaded guilty to conspiracy to commit wire fraud and to a charge of willfully failing to pay taxes. He was sentenced to 60 months in federal prison. Phillip Logan pleaded guilty in federal court to a charge of conspiracy to commit wire fraud for his role in providing the fake LOCs and was sentenced to 57 months in federal prison.

Including Davis and Logan, a total of six individuals pleaded guilty in federal court to their involvement in the fraud. All received prison sentences and were ordered to pay varying amounts of restitution. Total losses in this case to UDI, the IRS, and various Precision clients and their workers exceeded $100 million.

Lessons Learned

During this investigation, I had to rely on industry experts to explain the subject matter. To understand the fraud, I had to learn how the insurance industry worked. The value of an insider's vantage point was very helpful as well — Tyler was crucial in getting the investigation rolling.

I also had to concentrate on not having tunnel vision. Even though I started to investigate a specific claim, several other schemes arose in the process. It was helpful to divide the investigation into several smaller segments that could be concluded individually.

Recommendations to Prevent Future Occurrences

I had two major recommendations that could have minimized the fraud and the associated losses:

1. Large-dollar-amount collateral should be independently verified before being accepted. Just as in an audit, verification should not rely on the address and phone number on the LOC. If UDI had tried to independently verify the LOCs when they were first received, they would have found they were fraudulent and could have minimized potential losses.
2. Companies should take an active role in understanding their insurance and how it works. If any of Precision's clients had contacted their state insurance regulator to check on the insurance companies, they would have learned that their insurance was invalid since it was not placed with an authorized carrier, preventing losses down the road.

About the Author

Special Agent Michael Sputo, CFE, has investigated white-collar crime for the Federal Bureau of Investigation since 1987. He graduated magna cum laude from Boston College with a B.S. degree in accounting and worked as an auditor for Price Waterhouse prior to his employment with the FBI. SA Sputo has been a Certified Fraud Examiner since 2007.[*]

---

[*]Any opinions expressed in this chapter are the author's and not those of the FBI.

CHAPTER

The Hazards of Doing Business with Friends

BILL MALONEY

Jack Fellows was a man who could fool anyone, even those closest to him. He was married with two children, but he had never been very savvy with his career moves and he had a checkered employment past. However, he hit the jackpot when his longtime friend, Phil Careselli, took it upon himself to help out his buddy.

Phil was also happily married and had three children, two of them in college. He was a successful business owner, and he wanted to use his position to help those he cared about. When he was just out college, Phil was hired as a claims processor for a large, well-respected insurance company in the Midwest. He put in five years with the company, earning promotions and gaining valuable insight into the insurance business. Shortly after he got married, he took another big plunge and opened his own company, Careselli Insurance Agency. He started in a small office with one assistant. Over time, Phil's hard work and dedication grew the company to five branches in several cities. His flagship office employed 12 people, and each regional office had four to five staff members. The company offered a range of insurance products, but its main trade was in policies for other business enterprises.

While Phil enjoyed professional success, he watched his close friend Jack struggle to hold down a series of sales jobs and listened to his stories about unfair bosses and how nobody respected his ideas and abilities. Phil knew some of Jack's rants had to be bluster — after all, his string of "bad bosses" was pretty long — but Phil had known Jack for almost two decades; he was a good guy. Phil thought if he could just give Jack the break he so desperately seemed to need, Jack could turn things around for himself and his family.

Phil offered to hire Jack and train him to be the manager at Careselli's main office. Jack jumped at the chance to work with his friend and to oversee the small staff. He boasted to his wife that he was going to be "the boss of people" and wouldn't have to stress about pleasing his own tyrant of a boss anymore. Phil spent months explaining to Jack the day-to-day operations of his company, the insurance industry as a whole, the accounting and finance processes and the roles of other employees. At the end of his intensive training, Jack was given the title and responsibilities of office manager. He happily began to oversee the staff and manage the daily operations. After a few months, Phil was pleased with Jack's performance and gave him free rein to run the office as he needed. Jack had an engaging personality and earned the trust of the staff easily. He managed Careselli Insurance Agency without any apparent problems

Before hiring Jack, Phil had divided the daily tasks among his staff based on their individual strengths and how they benefited the system of opening new accounts and managing claims. This meant that several people could be working on a single policy at various points, each addressing different concerns. This placed the general oversight of accounts on Phil and Jack, and enabled Jack to take advantage of his position. Phil was a true entrepreneur who kept himself busy expanding his business endeavors and branching out into related fields, such as real estate and mortgage financing, and getting more clients. Phil totally trusted his friend — his mentee — to maintain the insurance office side of the operation.

In addition to management responsibilities, Phil gave Jack authority to broker third-party financing to fund corporate insurance policies — and Jack alone controlled this function. He was able to create financing accounts but divert the funds without the knowledge of Phil or other office staff members. It was common for companies to need pricey insurance that they could not afford to pay for up front. In these situations, Jack would arrange financing for them through his preferred vendor, Grandview Financiers. The clients received the insurance they needed, Grandview had a steady stream of new accounts and Jack earned a small commission on each contract. It was a win-win situation.

It Started with a Single Call

A fluke of memory served to bring Phil back into the thick of his business operations. One day an agent at Grandview Financiers couldn't remember Jack's direct phone number, his contact at Careselli, so he simply looked up the office number and called Phil, assuming the owner of the company would be able to assist him. He had a question about one of Careselli's accounts that had gone into default and needed answers. However, after explaining the situation to Phil, he received confused silence. After a moment Phil said, "What were those account details again?" The agent got the impression Phil had no idea what was going on with the account and decided to remind Phil about the many other default accounts that Careselli had with Grandview. Phil said he would look into the matter and call the agent back.

Certain that there was some misunderstanding, Phil began pulling files related to the various financing contracts that had gone into default and discovered that they were all for straw insurance policies — someone had requested financing from Grandview for policies that Careselli didn't sell. Phil was able to trace some of the funds from Grandview to the personal bank accounts of Jack and his wife. Still in a state of disbelief, Phil confronted Jack about what he had discovered.

Jack assured Phil that it was an error and that he would take care of it. He explained that the checks written to him were for a company loan that he intended to pay back. However, Jack could come up with only a portion of the money, and Grandview was becoming more assertive. The story didn't make sense to Phil, and when managers at Grandview threatened to start legal proceedings and go to the state insurance commission, Phil decided he had to fire Jack, contact the police and file a complaint of employee theft, which was referred to me.

Understanding the Industry

I was an investigator at the local police department where Phil filed his complaint, and I received the intake officer's initial report. After reading through the details, I contacted Phil for a meeting. I asked him to come to my office, and he readily agreed. I conducted a fact-finding interview with Phil and learned the structure of his various offices and particularly the headquarters where Jack worked. I asked about the staff and job functions. Phil explained how the office was set up, what the various duties of his employees were and what Jack's responsibilities were within the business. After finding out how the accounting and bookkeeping was done and how Grandview had been used, we discussed Jack's alleged theft and the evidence needed and gathered so far to support the allegation.

After my meeting with Phil, I contacted the state insurance commissioner's office, informed them of the complaint and requested an investigator from their office be assigned to assist. I also contacted the National Insurance Crime Bureau (NICB) to have an investigator from its office help with the case. This proved to be a mistake made so early in the investigation, and one that I won't make again. The investigation stalled several times while I waited for the other agencies to take action. I had requested several documents from them, but — although they had regulative authority to obtain the items I requested — because of the civil nature of their organizations, they had different procedures than law enforcement when faced with noncooperative parties. Long story short, I never received the files I requested.

Phil did provide me with the paperwork for the policies funded through Grandview. In addition to the theft of funds from Grandview, we also found that Jack had misappropriated checks from Careselli. Jack did not have check-signing authority, so he simply forged Phil's signature on checks that he made out to himself. Being the office manager, with little oversight, it was easy for him to take, sign and hide the forged check. When Phil went through the books after the theft was discovered, it was no problem for him to find the checks that Jack had forged. I obtained copies of the fraudulent checks and forgery affidavits for each one. A review of the company checkbook revealed that Jack had written checks to or for his personal benefit worth more than $150,000.

A few days later, Phil called and told me that Jack was contacting some of his customers and asking them to switch from Careselli Insurance Agency to a new agency that Jack was starting on his own. One of the customers who informed Phil of this development said that Jack was also sending an online advertisement to potential clients that appeared to be affiliated with Careselli Insurance, but the contact number was to Jack's personal cell phone. Phil knew immediately what the customer was referring to; when Jack was still employed at Careselli Insurance, Phil had asked him to set up an online ad to attract new clients for the company. Phil didn't think anything of it when Jack suggested that, since he was the office manager and would field most of the calls anyway, he should put his cell phone number on the website. That way Jack could take calls from potential clients even when he was out of the office. It looked like Jack left the ad up after he was fired and was now using it to try to start his own business venture. Phil asked me if I could do anything about it, so I decided to use this as my reason to contact Jack and have him explain his side of the story.

In my years of experience as a police investigator, I've learned that it is essential to gather as much information as possible before contacting a suspect and setting up a meeting. It is very important to learn about the subject of the interview and to thoroughly understand the fraud at issue. Having this knowledge prior to the interview gives the interviewer a distinct advantage over the subject for developing rapport, detecting deception and formulating interview strategies from the answers provided compared to the information already known. Before I called Jack, Phil and I recapped the various ways Jack committed the fraud, and Phil gave me a full account of Jack's background.

What Jack Did Not Know

I called Jack the following day and asked him about the online ad he posted. He told me that he had forgotten all about it, and when he left Careselli's he didn't think to take it down. He promised to take care of it right away. I asked Jack to come to police headquarters for an interview about what was going on between him and Phil, and he agreed. He came to my office that afternoon and gave his side of the story. He explained that it was a misunderstanding and insisted that he had not done anything illegal. He initially thought that he was there to explain the advertisement and the disagreement he had with Phil. He said that was surprised the police had been contacted and were involved in the matter.

I asked him about how Careselli's office was run and what he did there, and this led to a discussion of how Grandview was involved in the business. He explained how Grandview financed various accounts several times and in different ways so that I could understand how this was just a misunderstanding. My feigned confusion led him to provide more and more details on how everything was done. From there I was able to have him talk about how financing procedures were normally handled, and then he was left to explain why deviations from normal practices had been made in some instances. He hesitated for a moment and seemed confused about how we ended up on the topic.

Jack was unaware of what paperwork I had or how much I had discussed with Phil Careselli. I had called him in to talk to me so soon after he and Phil had parted ways that he assumed I had not discovered what really happened. After we discussed the business details, I started presenting various documents concerning the loans he established with Grandview for his straw companies and asked for explanations. It became apparent to Jack that I had a lot more evidence and knew much more about what happened than he assumed. I had a clear paper trail showing that Jack set up fake accounts with Grandview to finance fraudulent fake policies and then diverted the funds to his private bank account.

In addition, I had discovered that some of that funding had been used to finance a "preferred customer's" commercial insurance policy at no cost to the client. Essentially, Jack was giving someone insurance for free but taking financing from Grandview. I asked him about this client, but he said he didn't know what I was referring to and clammed up.

Jack left my office but agreed to come back after I gathered more paperwork and investigated further. I considered this initial interview a success and was eager to learn what I could about Jack's special customer. Why would he put himself at risk by funding a third-party policy? What was he getting out of the deal? He was open about everything else I asked, and his silence on this issue was intriguing. I dug into my files and conducted lengthy online research. I discovered the client, Express Midwest Freight, was a trucking company owned and operated by a man named Jacob Gilkey. From archived news stories and police records, it looked like Gilkey was a man no one would want to cross. He had several convictions for assault and was reported to control a gang of "employees" who used their sway to further the interests of Gilkey and Express Midwest Freight. I started to understand why Jack shut up so quickly when I brought up the topic.

It Does Not End with a Confession

I interviewed Jack again a week later, and he brought his attorney. Jack provided a written confession through his attorney and explained which accounts he had fraudulently created and how he did it. When I raised the question of Express Midwest Freight's policy, Jack became quiet again, and his lawyer said they did not want to discuss the matter. Jack said he was scared to talk about it. I assured him that I knew about Gilkey's history and could understand Jack's hesitation, but I told him that the paper trail was going to show what happened and who was involved, whether Jack gave me his account or not.

When Jack realized that I knew the full scheme, he confessed to financing the policy for Express Midwest Freight. He explained that Gilkey had approached him because the trucking company had outstanding debts to its insurer worth more than $75,000, due to problems with a workers' compensation claim. Gilkey told Jack that he needed a new insurer and wanted to go with Careselli Insurance Agency, but he demanded that Jack first pay off his outstanding debt. Feeling threatened, Jack arranged for a straw account with Grandview for the money Gilkey needed. Jack insisted that other than the commission for writing this fraudulent policy, he did not receive money from the transaction.

He said that he also wrote a new policy for Gilkey — financed by Grandview — and received another commission. Jack said that almost immediately Gilkey failed to make payments on the loan, so Jack fabricated additional insurance policies and financed them to make payments on behalf of the trucking company. He was afraid to approach Gilkey about the money and was trying to take care of the situation himself. Jack said at that point he figured if he was generating funds for Gilkey, why not do it for himself? But when Grandview started catching errors in the supporting paperwork for these straw accounts and looking into them, Jack tried to get money together to pay back his theft. He said he paid back more than $100,000 before it all came to a head.

Plea Deal

As a result of this case, I was able to secure a promissory note from Jacob Gilkey to repay Grandview Financiers for the amount of his loan; however, Gilkey has already defaulted on the note.

Phil Careselli filed a dishonest employee insurance claim with his insurance provider. Careselli's policy paid out for the loss to the business on the amount insured per incident, but his policy was insured for a maximum of $50,000 per incident. I contacted Careselli's insurance provider to obtain its investigative report and learned that it had determined that, although Jack Fellows was responsible for $250,000 to $300,000 of loss to Careselli Insurance Agency, it was obligated only for $50,000. Phil was out $200,000 to $250,000.

The case is still open with the agencies I contacted at the start of my investigation, but my criminal case was resolved. Jack accepted full responsibility and agreed to a plea deal that included probation and full restitution to Careselli Insurance Agency.

Lessons Learned

Coordinating with several outside regulatory agencies to act at once is difficult. Due to the different regulatory and administrative procedures and the varying enforcement actions that each agency takes, it was impossible to get an across-the-board prosecution on everything simultaneously in this case.

I found that the regulatory agencies had administrative procedures that were very time consuming and that the companies dealing with them did not always cooperate in providing requested documentation. When that happened, the agencies handled the delays administratively rather than pursuing it as a regulatory violation. I found it hard to have to wait for something to be completed in the regulatory agencies' investigations only to find that the company they were requesting information from would not cooperate and I was not going to get the requested information.

I would suggest, if possible, that you notify external agencies of an investigation that you are working on but then handle your own jurisdiction investigation and file charges without worrying where the other parties are in their case. Of course, I would then forward my referrals to the other agencies for them to conduct their investigations and take whatever action as they see fit. However, coordination is sometimes more hassle that it is worth.

Recommendations to Prevent Future Occurrences

My insight into Phil's experience taught me about how *not* to run a company. It is never a good idea to allow one person to have control of the checkbook and oversight of accounts. Other than the owner, Jack was the only other person who had access to Careselli Insurance Agency's bank accounts and could issue checks. Phil, after training and guiding his friend in the insurance business, left the day-to-day operation of his agency to Jack while he pursued other business opportunities. Unless a problem was brought to his attention, he trusted that that his company was operating smoothly. Phil should have monitored the bank accounts more closely and not blindly trusted his manager, regardless of their friendship. If he was too busy to actively monitor the accounting processes, oversight should have been separated and assigned to other staff members who reported to him.

It is important to have checks and balances in place, including requiring that a separate employee verify all checks before they are sent out, and assign another individual to balance the accounts. If there had been a co-signer or

(Continued)

someone else handling the books at Careselli Insurance, Jack would not have gotten away with cutting himself checks worth $150,000.

Do not allow one person to arrange the financing of new accounts and open and manage accounts without proper oversight in place. Jack set everything up with Grandview and was the self-appointed point of contact. This enabled him to set up the straw accounts, receive the financing and deposit and divert the funds. If the various duties associated with Grandview were segregated, it would have much more difficult for Jack to accomplish his scheme.

Another issue stemming from Phil's blind trust in Jack was that when the finance company came to him with the problem, Phil initially believed in and trusted Jack when he said he would take care of it rather than acknowledging that there was a problem. This gave Jack time to try to cover his tracks. Phil told me that in almost any other facet of his business, this wouldn't have happened — he would have trusted his instincts if they told him something was wrong. He said that in this particular case, because Jack was his close friend and mentee, he subconsciously put Jack beyond reproach. This enabled Jack to prolong the scheme, and it could have been a lot worse if Grandview had not been persistent in resolving the matter quickly. This forced Phil to check further and uncover the fraud.

About the Author

Detective Bill Maloney, CFE, works in the Norwalk Police Detective Division of Fraud Investigations. He has 32 years of police experience, 24 of them as a detective. He is a Certified Fraud Examiner and is certified in all the National White Collar Crime Center's (NW3C) fraud courses. He is a CT P.O.S.T. Police Academy Certified Training Instructor and has specialized training in fraud investigation, interview and interrogation schools, FBI hostage negotiation training, photography and videographer for crime scene processing, National Fire Academy's arson investigation course and composite artist schools. Bill's proudest achievement is being father to and raising a son, Michael, and two daughters, Meghan and Kelly, during a 30-year-marriage to his wife, Vicki.

CHAPTER

There's Gold in Them Thar Malls!

CARL KNUDSON

Thomas Bourne's credentials were impeccable. He and his conglomer-ate, Emerge Markets, owned and operated ten large malls throughout the United States, plus several others in foreign countries. Thomas had a degree in finance and an M.B.A. and had spent his professional career developing an impressive network of connections. He was in his mid-40s, married with two beautiful daughters whom he showered with love and affection, and his trophy wife, Greta, was a major stockholder in his business. The Bournes lived in a $3 million townhome in upscale Beverly Hills, California, and trav-eled extensively throughout Europe.

However, Thomas had a dark side: He was arrogant, dismissive and short-tempered with his office staff and often launched into obscenity-laced tirades. The turmoil in the property management arm of his company was constant. It was the classic hostile work environment.

When It Rains, It Pours

World Wide Insurance Inc. (World Wide) received a claim from Thomas Bourne two months after a storm had purportedly caused severe damage to the Border Towne Mall, located in a small community 60 miles east of Los Angeles, California. Border Towne was one of the many malls owned and operated by Emerge Markets. The timing of Bourne's claim was strange in that the policy on the mall, written by one of World Wide's Los Angeles con-sultants, had only been in effect for a few months before the storm caused substantial damage to the 400,000-square-foot structure, including the roof, plus interior water damage and mold accumulation.

The insurance claim came with a very detailed report and numerous photographs from Lawrence Tolson Insurance Adjusters, Inc., an estab-lished firm based in Mobile, Alabama. The report detailed substantial roof repairs by contractors, ongoing mold remediation by specialists, external damage to mall fascia and signage surrounding the property, plus an outrageous claim for loss of business. The claim also included copies of invoices and checks paid by Border Towne Mall to insurance adjusters and construction companies that were brought in to do emergency repairs on the mall a few days after the storm hit. So what was the problem? At the time, nothing seemed amiss.

Jillian Krauss, World Wide's in-house adjuster, processed the claim on the Border Towne Mall and authorized preliminary payments to reimburse the up-front costs paid by Bourne to mall contractors based on the documents provided. Jillian had a law enforcement background and had a couple of years under her belt at World Wide, but she was soon to discover one of the largest insurance frauds in the company's history. However, she couldn't know it at the time, or that the insurance fraud targeting World Wide had already been perpetrated against many of the company's global competitors.

Divide and Conquer

One of the time-tested markers of a sophisticated fraudster is the concept of divide and conquer — keep the guardians of accounting records and business records divided so no single individual understands the complete flow of the finances. It was clear that Thomas Bourne understood this tactic well and intentionally created an atmosphere of fear in the office. Each and every day, he presented the accounting staff with incoherent to-do lists, which kept them from focusing on their daily duties. This constant chaos led to last-second scrambling to reconcile the mall's monthly banking activity and prepare the required quarterly reports for the lenders.

It seemed like just when the staff became an efficient team despite Bourne's best efforts to create dissension, he would fire the office manager, or the manager would quit, and the whole process started anew. In retrospect, it was a red flag that Bourne had fired the office manager and accounting staff just after he filed the first claim with World Wide.

Just the Tip of the Iceberg

A year after Bourne submitted his claim for damages to the Border Towne Mall, Jillian Krauss received a sizable loss claim from the Prairie Harvest Mall in Omaha, Nebraska. As with the Border Towne claim, Krauss noticed that the signatures on Prairie Harvest's policy were barely dry before the mall suffered damages from "a heavy wind and rain storm." The specific damage even mirrored the damage claimed by Border Towne. Then Krauss saw that the claim certification document was signed by Thomas Bourne and that he had used the same adjusters and construction companies in Nebraska that he used in California. These contractors had already received hundreds of thousands of dollars in up-front fees for emergency repairs to Prairie Harvest. The total losses claimed were $15 million, including $7 million for lost business.

Krauss queried Bourne's name online and discovered, to her chagrin. that one of World Wide's major competitors had recently filed a lawsuit against one of Bourne's malls in Illinois for insurance fraud. The lawsuit allegations related to purported false claims from storm and wind damage. The codefendants named in the lawsuit were the same subcontractors that Bourne used in the two claims with World Wide.

Krauss immediately notified World Wide's general counsel and detailed what she believed to be a pattern of fraudulent claim submissions by Thomas Bourne related to the "severe storms" that had damaged the malls. Krauss also searched local and national weather databases to determine whether any such storms had actually occurred on the dates in question and learned, with a sickening feeling in her stomach, that they had not.

Whistleblower, Beware

Allen Linn was a 20-year veteran bookkeeper with government and corporate experience who responded to a job posting on an accounting temps website. Linn was interviewed and screened by Ronald Jepson, the new office manager at Border Towne Mall; Jepson had only been on the job for about a month and was building a new office staff, including the bookkeeping position. Linn received a tour of the office and was able to review the accounting programs that recorded and tracked the mall's financial affairs. The accounting system was a customized product that included a function to scan all of the deposits, deposit items, payables and invoices, culminating in the monthly bank reconciliation. Linn was also given a tour of the file room where the accounting backup programs and some paper boxes of documents were stored.

Later that day, he was interviewed by Thomas Bourne, who struck Linn as a little condescending but overall on the up-and-up. The salary was not the best, but the office was close to home and he had already retired from one job. A few days later, Linn was notified by Jepson that Bourne had authorized his hire and they wanted him to start as soon as possible.

The first couple of weeks went well, and Linn was catching up on inputting the latest receipts and payables for the mall. The office staff seemed competent and responded well to his suggestions regarding the bookkeeping processes and procedures. He reconciled the bank account and prepared a preliminary profit and loss statement for the first quarter. He made a mental note that the mall had only one bank account at a nationally known institution. Linn then prepared a balance sheet and noted some interesting receivables from other businesses owned by Bourne, including malls in Colorado, Nebraska, South Dakota, Illinois and California.

"That's odd," Linn thought to himself when he opened the daily mail and found a sizable check from a company called World Wide Insurance. The memo section of the check indicated that the funds were being paid on a claim filed previous to his employment at Border Towne Mall. Linn scanned and processed the check through the accounting system but wasn't sure how to categorize the payment, and there wasn't an insurance-pending file in the office.

Later that day, he called Jepson to ask what to do with the check but was told to talk to Bourne directly. Linn again thought something weird was happening; why couldn't Jepson explain an insurance claim? When Linn called Bourne, he received a rude and antagonistic response that it wasn't his business and he shouldn't have opened the mail. Linn wasn't the kind of guy to pick a fight, especially since he was fairly new, but he explained to Bourne that the deposit had to be accounted for in some fashion. Bourne told Linn that he would take care of it himself.

A few weeks later, a letter arrived from a World Wide Insurance claims adjuster requesting additional information on the checks paid by Border Towne Mall to the contractors for the emergency repairs. Linn opened the letter because it looked like normal mail, but he saw copies of checks from a Border Towne Mall bank account — not the account he was familiar with. It was a regional bank in Los Angeles and had no offices in the immediate area. Linn could tell that the some of the copied checks had not been processed through a bank because they did not have MICR coding at the bottom of the checks.

Linn signed onto Border Towne's accounting system and brought up the checking account to verify that the checks had cleared. However, he could not find the account listed on the books. Linn felt a dull pain in the pit of his stomach; this was beginning to look like a real problem. He queried last year's balance sheet data to see if the bank account had been listed, but it wasn't there either.

Maybe there was an explanation, but the office staff was as new as he was, so he asked Jepson if he could speak with him privately. The meeting did not go well; Jepson told him that he knew nothing about the accounting or insurance claims before his tenure and that Linn should ask Bourne for the information.

Linn's subsequent meeting was an utter disaster. Bourne accused Linn of spying into his private affairs and threatened to fire him on the spot, but he didn't. Bourne informed Linn that the final accounting for the mall was done by an accounting firm that prepared the financials and tax returns, but he refused to explain why the missing bank account was not in the accounting system. Bourne advised Linn that he was handling the insurance claim and that the check from World Wide should not have been deposited into the mall's bank account. Bourne berated Linn for opening the mail and told him that he was never to open the mail again.

Over the next few weeks, Linn's relationship with Bourne became increasingly strained, to the point that Linn decided to work at home for a few days and contemplate his future at the Border Towne Mall. Linn was a proud man and honest to a fault, so the situation with the insurance claim and the mystery bank account wore on his conscience. After much soul-searching, Linn decided to do the right thing and turn in Bourne to law enforcement officials. Of course, being familiar with qui tam claims Linn saw an opportunity to make a few bucks for his effort. He downloaded Border Towne's entire general ledger onto a thumb drive that he kept in his briefcase to substantiate what he believed to be insurance fraud and possibly tax evasion.

Complications Begin to Mount

Linn arranged for a meeting with the Federal Bureau of Investigation (FBI) at the local agency and provided the data stored on the thumb drive to the agents. The agents seemed impressed and assured him that they would check out the allegations and get back to him, so Linn continued to work at the Border Towne Mall.

It wasn't long after this that Linn was contacted by Gerald Riley, an attorney working for World Wide Insurance. Riley told Linn he was investigating allegations of fraudulent insurance claims related to the Border Towne Mall and another mall located in Nebraska. Linn agreed to meet with Riley at a nearby diner and brought along his thumb drive just in case the attorney was interested in the data.

The meeting went well and Riley was interested in Linn's documentation, but he was even more interested in having Linn's cooperation because he was still employed at Border Towne. Linn agreed to cooperate but asked for an advance on the anticipated recovery from the lawsuit. Riley agreed to Linn's request.

Riley downloaded the several gigabytes of data from Linn's thumb drive and began issuing subpoenas to banks and lending institutions based in part on Linn's information. World Wide Insurance hired a local forensic accounting firm to help Riley analyze the records. As the last step in the information-gathering process, Riley subpoenaed the business records of Border Towne Mall and contractors who had allegedly provided repairs to the damaged mall.

Delay, Delay and Delay!

Soon after Border Towne's records were subpoenaed, Bourne learned that Linn was cooperating with World Wide Insurance and had supplied Riley with extensive documentation relating to Border Towne's finances. Within days of learning that Linn had taken copied and shared business files, Bourne and his attorney filed motions of attorney–client privilege to prevent the use of any and all of the Border Towne records.

Bourne's counsel reviewed the documents and provided an assessment log for the court to determine whether any of them should have been made available to World Wide Insurance's management and attorneys. The court ruled preliminarily that almost all of the accounting and tax records provided by Linn were in fact privileged. Next, Border Towne's and the contractors' attorneys filed motions to prevent the production the subpoenaed bank records.

World Wide Insurance's legal fees were escalating at a dizzying pace, not to mention the fees of the forensic accounting firm brought in to analyze the financial records. After two years of dispute, the case was stalled due to legal gymnastics. World Wide's management team made a tactical decision to hire a bigger and more experienced law firm to continue the battle.

Our Team Enters the Fray

World Wide's leaders hired the law firm of Albert, Jennings & Luck, which specialized in fraud cases. Elaine Luck, senior litigation counsel, was leading the new charge. Elaine had hired me as an external examiner on cases before (I run a local, private anti-fraud investigations practice), so I was pleased to get her phone call one afternoon, asking me to help review financial information in this new case. Elaine gave me access to a database with more than 200,000 records, but there was no index to help me wade through everything. My initial analysis of the enormous amount of financial discovery showed that it was, on balance, virtually useless. Bourne's attorneys clearly did a data dump of irrelevant information in all the files they were forced to provide, and they turned over many documents that were not requested in the subpoenas. No one at the original forensic accounting firm had seemed to notice.

In large-scale civil fraud cases, a common litigation strategy — known euphemistically as baffle 'em with BS — is employed to frustrate and divert the attention of opposing counsel and their consultants. This strategy makes it so important to be on top of the discovery stage of an investigation. It was clear that Border Towne's counsel was well trained in the baffle tactic and equally clear that World Wide's initial lawyers and consultants were ill equipped to handle it.

I was also given spreadsheets from the previous forensic accountants with thousands of entries, including bank account data from more than 50 sources. The spreadsheet was overly detailed and confusing, with hundreds of duplicates of the same transactions from 15 related financial institutions. I resorted the data in the spreadsheets and eliminated duplicates to come up with a general picture of the financial data. My analysis showed that during the relevant time period, Bourne took out more than $5 million from the various related bank accounts.

Next I reviewed World Wide's records related to the claims for damages to the two malls. In particular, I was interested in the banking documents provided to substantiate the amounts paid to contractors for the "emergency" repairs. I was amazed to find that Gerald Riley's review of these important bank accounts was incomplete; there were still missing bank statements and canceled checks for the relevant period of time. I immediately advised Elaine Luck that we needed to issue a follow-up subpoena to the relevant banks.

I turned my attention to the Border Towne Mall's general ledger, but it was not a treasure trove of actionable information. Instead, I realized that what was *not* in the ledger was more telling that what was recorded. In cash accounts, I found only one bank account, but it was not the account from which funds had been paid to the contractors for emergency work. I tried to find a record of another bank account in the jumble of information Border Towne provided us but to no avail.

I next reviewed a series of financial institution documents related to the purchase and refinancing of the Border Towne Mall, hoping to find tax returns or an appraisal for the $35 million property. Again, I was frustrated by the lack of useful information; there were no financial statements — audited or otherwise — that could verify the stated value of the mall. Moreover, there was no indication that Gerald Riley realized he was missing these critical documents.

An Outcome, Not a Resolution

World Wide's corporate leaders were anxious about the substantial costs that this case had already racked up and the potential fees they would amass if they continued pursuing it. After I had been on the case for a few months, Elaine called to tell me World Wide decided to put the case on hold; in my experience, that means management has given up and decided to cut its losses. A month later, Elaine called to tell me she and Bourne's attorneys came to a settlement in which World Wide would not pursue restitution for the Border Towne reimbursements but denied the claim for Prairie Harvest.

Lessons Learned

All projects have a certain shelf life, as this case clearly demonstrated. Intervening events alter the course of our work and influence how issues are ultimately resolved. In civil litigation, the client's bankroll is often an issue, and at some point "throwing good money after bad" becomes a reason to settle the litigation.

I also learned some of the concerns that attend a whistleblower case. For World Wide Insurance, Allen Linn's information was invaluable — until the chain-of-custody issues arose.

Recommendations to Prevent Future Occurrences

Attention to detail is essential to the successful resolution of a fraud case, and some recommendations include:

- Start an index log and a chain-of-custody record of evidence. This simple task at the beginning of an engagement will help in each subsequent step, including a court battle if it comes to that.
- Understand that in complex white-collar crime cases, such as insurance fraud, there are documents and evidence that must exist. Examiners need to know what evidence they are missing before they can try to find it.
- Evidence can come from the victim, the defendant's accounting documents, financial institutions that provide funding to the defendant, other third parties, public records, bankruptcy files or government agencies. Knowing where to look for evidence is invaluable.

In my experience, most civil cases do not run their course to a trial of the facts. At any time, the litigants can make a tactical decision not to continue the litigation and settle the dispute where both sides declare the contest a draw. If that happens, the examiner who has exhausted all sources of evidence can provide the client more leverage in negotiations.

About the Author

Carl Knudson, CFE, has more than 37 years of fraud investigative experience at the highest level of government and in the private sector. He has been a private investigator and Certified Fraud Examiner since 1995. As a special agent for the Internal Revenue Service (IRS), Mr. Knudson investigated complex white-collar crimes. Upon retiring from the IRS, he was hired as a director in the Dispute Analysis and Investigative practice at Price Waterhouse. Mr. Knudson started his own business in 2000 and specializes in forensic accounting and fraud investigations for his private and government clients.

Damsel in Diamonds

MICHAEL SKRYPEK

Only 21 years old, newlywed Vicki Barnes relocated to Virginia with her husband, Tanner. Their relationship was explosive and at times violent on the part of both spouses. Just a few years into the marriage and two children later, Vicki and Tanner separated. It was an unforgiving separation leading to a bitter divorce, and Tanner fled the state, never to return.

Following numerous other spiraling relationships, heart-wrenching breakups and living paycheck to paycheck, Vicki met Robert Bickett. A steady and hardworking man, he openly accepted and embraced Vicki's children as his own. Robert soon proposed marriage, and the beautiful but exhausted Vicki eagerly accepted. She was worn down from ten years of countless temporary, dead-end jobs and personal relationships. Since Robert earned a generous income, he insisted Vicki be a stay-at-home mom. Robert told Vicki she was never to worry about money again. Soon, the Bicketts doubled the number of children in their household with two of their own.

As the years progressed and her youngest child became a teenager, Vicki wanted excitement and new challenges beyond child care and housekeeping. During one of her shopping sprees, Vicki stopped at her favorite store, Viceroy Jewelers. Through the years, Vicki had become a well-known and well-liked customer at Viceroy. She appeared to have a bottomless bank account, selecting numerous items for purchase during each visit. During one, Vicki inquired about the posted employment opportunity for a sales associate. As store manager Marie Torres explained the job expectations and benefits, Vicki's eyes flashed with excitement. After years of service to her husband and children, Vicki wanted to get away from domestic duties and start what she hoped would be a long-term career. Vicki was hired.

Attractive and flirtatious by nature, Vicki quickly became a rising sales force in the business; she had a predominant male clientele base. Many of Vicki's clients returned for repeat jewelry purchases, and others just stopped by to talk, some with gifts and dinner invitations for Vicki. As time progressed, she became entangled in several extramarital affairs with her male clients.

It wasn't long before the Bicketts' marriage became strained due to failing commitment from both partners. Vicki and Robert separated and had numerous unsuccessful attempts to reengage the relationship in the following years.

Viceroy Jewelers

Viceroy Jewelers was one of the largest jewelers in North America. It originated as a family business on the northeastern coast of the United States in the early 1900s. During the next 100 years, the company evolved into a publicly traded corporation while expanding across North America, owning and operating more than 1,800 retail unit locations. The corporation's continued expansion was a direct result of revenue reinvestments to perpetuate product acquisition and licensing, personnel recruitment and training, technology development and business planning. Viceroy owned and operated its own credit center, distribution center, e-commerce business and insurance service groups, in addition to the ownership of multiple retail divisions.

The Viceroy Jewelers' retail unit where Vicki worked was in an economically depressed, blue-collar area. The store employed a store manager, office manager and six to eight sales associates. It was one of 14 stores overseen by an area manager, who was supervised, along with five other area managers, by a territorial vice president. Although surrounded by competitors in its midsize metropolitan area, the business unit generated approximately $1.5 million annually from sales of jewelry merchandise, jewelry repairs and insurance replacement services. The corporation had recently experienced a decline in sales due to softening national and global economic conditions. Numerous locations had been closed across the continent, corporate and field personnel were reduced and the focus shifted to expense reduction and control.

One Thing Leads to Another

I had been employed with Viceroy Jewelers for approximately ten years at the time of this investigation. I covered nine states with direct fraud examination responsibilities encompassing more than 200 retail units. My responsibilities included conducting property and financial crime investigations, mostly dealing with employee theft. As a senior investigator, I also supervised seven others who collectively covered the remaining 1,500-plus retail units across North America. We used computer-based exception reporting that generally occupied the morning hours of our workdays, compiling, sorting and analyzing data relating to all aspects of business performance.

In addition to computer-based exception reporting, we also used profit and loss statement analysis and various related audit-based computer reporting programs. Unannounced visits to field locations and business unit compliance auditing as well as frequent communications with our operations counterparts were vital and of great value to ensure business control and quick response to problems.

Last fall, a review of payroll exception reports indicated possible noncompliance with payroll entry and reporting policies at the Viceroy Jewelers located in Walter, Virginia. Further investigation and review of the store's electronic access opening and closing records, compared to payroll records, indicated possible payroll fraud. The amount of potential fraud appeared to be minimal at best. Further research of computer-based exception reports did not reveal any major profit and loss exceptions but did reveal some minor areas of concern for slightly increasing costs relating to insurance product replacements.

The store was only about an hour from my office, so I decided to go by for a visit.

When I walked into the Viceroy store, I greeted the employees and told them I was there for a compliance audit and business survey. I mentioned I would also need to talk with everyone and that I appreciated their time and assistance. Naturally, when someone from corporate visits a store — especially someone from corporate who conducts audits and investigations — the employees become a little nervous. During an investigation, that nervousness usually diminishes in honest employees during both nonspecific and specific questioning. When the nervousness increases during questioning, that usually is a warning sign of the need for increased attention.

After I reviewed the audit documents, I began meeting with individual staff members. I remembered from past store visits that the associates were usually upbeat and did not talk about each other negatively. The staff had appeared to be a close-knit family, with a positive attitude shared by associates and directed toward one another. But not this time.

It was obvious that tension had developed in the store; in particular, it appeared as though everyone had something negative to imply or suggest about Vicki Bickett. When I asked about the payroll adjustments, almost everyone voiced mild suspicions that Vicki fraudulently adjusted her recorded hours, yet no one had bothered to use the corporate anonymous tip reporting line or to call me directly with any concerns.

No one produced conclusive examples of wrongdoing relating to the alleged payroll fraud, yet when I attempted to drill down on particulars, many associates became increasingly nervous and evasive.

I eventually interviewed Vicki, and she denied any intentional wrongdoing. She said her payroll adjustments were due to her lack of understanding about the payroll system and procedures.

I investigated the store's payroll accounts further and found many other "errors," some by the same associates who accused Vicki of wrongdoing. I concluded my audit the following day and arranged to meet with the store manager, Marie Torres. I informed her of my findings and concerns about Vicki and other employees. When I finished, Marie almost seemed disappointed that I had not discovered conclusive evidence of wrongdoing by Vicki. I wondered how Vicki, who at one time seemed to be a well-liked and respected member of the team, had become a target of her boss and coworkers. Perhaps I was misreading the situation and there was just a little tension between competing sales associates, since Vicki had become popular with customers and her sales performance continually improved.

But why would Marie not diffuse the tension and pull the team back together, as she had done in the past when minor eruptions of personalities and tension occurred?

I shared my concerns with Marie and advised her of my intent to requestion some associates to calm my curiosity. At that point, Marie admitted she had more information to share with me. She said she and several of the sales staff suspected Vicki Bickett of perpetrating an insurance fraud against the Viceroy Jewelers corporate insurance department. Marie stated that she and several of her employees had talked about their suspicions and hoped there would be a way to get rid of Vicki without confronting her directly or reporting it to the corporate office.

The Truth Comes Out

Marie said she and her coworkers had recently seen Vicki wearing a $6,250 diamond ring that Vicki had claimed was stolen from her residence five years before. Apparently she had purchased the diamond ring from the Viceroy Jewelers location approximately six years ago. Vicki had worn the diamond every day since the purchase, until she came in one day and said that it had been stolen, along with other jewelry, from her home while she was sleeping the night before. Vicki said she had called the police and filed a report prior to going to work that day.

Marie told me the story seemed strange to her at the time, but the involvement of the police reassured her that Vicki was being honest. When Vicki originally purchased the ring, she also took out a theft insurance agreement, and Marie allowed Vicki to process her own claim through the corporate office. She had been fully reimbursed.

I said Vicki could have purchased a replacement ring with the insurance payment, but Marie said that was not the case. She clearly remembered Vicki using her insurance payment to purchase other new jewelry at the store. I pulled the insurance documents from store files and asked Marie not to discuss the matter with any associates. Then I concluded my visit and returned directly to my office.

Solving the Paperwork Puzzle

That same day, I called our insurance department and spoke with claims processor Nora Jacobs. She reviewed the notes in the file and said the claim originally had been denied based on insufficient requirements to process it. Nora said additional paperwork, including a police report of loss, had been received, signed by Robert Bickett. I decided to research online and discovered the insurance claim was filed after the Bicketts' rather hostile divorce. Why would Robert help Vicki with an insurance claim when they were no longer together?

I reviewed the electronic sales database for Vicki and her family and found a record of her original purchase but no replacement purchase of the same ring. Then I pulled up a description and photos of the ring in question and emailed the information to Marie Torres. She confirmed it was the same ring Vicki had begun wearing again recently.

That same week, I received claim files from Nora. Robert Bickett's signature on the claim paperwork strongly resembled Vicki's handwriting. I also learned that Robert had left the area and was not in contact with Vicki following their tumultuous separation and divorce.

I traveled to Vicki's local police department and requested a copy of the police report she had filed years earlier. The report showed that Vicki gave the police a written statement, claiming that she awoke in the middle of the night and noticed the jewelry missing from her dresser across the bedroom. She wrote that she got out of bed, searched her bedroom for the jewelry without success and returned to bed without looking anywhere else. Vicki filed the police report the next day. There was no indication of forced entry or the presence of anyone else in the residence that night. Vicki's statement to the police claimed the stolen jewelry included the diamond ring in question, an additional diamond band and a gold bracelet, totaling $8,250 in losses.

I continued my online research and found that Vicki had multiple civil actions against her for nonpayment for financial goods and services, including collection processes by three different financial institutions. I also uncovered the Bicketts' divorce record, a domestic violence charge and conviction against Vicki for a past altercation with Robert, along with bankruptcy and foreclosure filings. At this point, there were no absolutes, although investigative experience indicated there was a good chance that Vicki had committed insurance fraud to avoid or delay what appeared to be imminent financial ruin.

I called Marie again to ask if there were further developments. She told me that Vicki didn't wear the ring to work every day but seemed to wear it often on her weekend shifts. During my last visit to the store, I had retrieved digital video surveillance images, but the footage was inconclusive as to the specific jewelry Vicki had worn on previous shifts.

I told Marie I had prepared my investigation and planned on interviewing Vicki the following week. Again, I told Marie not to discuss any aspect of the investigation with the staff. I concluded the call by asking Marie to contact me immediately if she saw Vicki wearing the diamond ring during a shift prior to my visit to the store. I told Marie I would most likely see her next week but could not pinpoint a date since I had numerous other scheduled appointments and meetings.

Duty Calls

That Saturday Marie called me to let me know Vicki had just arrived at work and was wearing the diamond ring. I told my wife I needed to take care of an urgent work matter and canceled our Saturday afternoon plans. I put on a suit, grabbed the case file and my computer bag and aimed the car toward Walter, Virginia. About an hour later I walked into the store. I immediately noticed Vicki, dressed to the nines, laughing with a male client at a diamond showcase. As I walked past Marie, I quietly inquired if she had adequate floor coverage for me to talk with Vicki. Marie barely lifted her head and nodded affirmatively. I continued walking and stood near Vicki at an adjacent showcase. I had my head down as though I were looking into a neighboring showcase, but my eyes were focused on the diamond ring on Vicki's hand. It was an exact match to the pictures I had in my computer bag.

When Vicki concluded her conversation with the customer, she looked in my direction and seemed surprised to see me. I smiled and immediately outstretched my arm to shake the hand that displayed the sparkling diamond ring. She greeted me through a painted smile and was obviously uncomfortable. I said, "Vicki, great to see you; by the way, that is a beautiful diamond ring," as I pointed to her finger. She dropped her head, glanced at her hand and timidly thanked me. I told Vicki I had to speak with her in private and asked if I could buy her a cup of coffee. She quietly agreed but said she had to retrieve her purse locked in the back office. I quickly replied that there was no need and that I was buying the coffee. I motioned with an outstretched arm toward the exit and told her it was pretty important we talk in private immediately. She walked around the showcase and we left the store together. As we walked toward the neighboring coffee shop in the mall, she told me she did not want coffee and inquired as to the reason for our private conversation. I told her we would talk in detail momentarily. I selected a table in a quiet area of the food court and we sat down.

As I began talking, I noticed Vicki had moved her hand from the table to her lap, out of my sight. As I continued explaining why I was there, Vicki's hand reappeared on the table, but the ring was missing from her finger. I presented paperwork and narrowed my interview focus. At one point in the interview, she raised her voice and appeared to be rallying in her mind for an upcoming strong denial. I remained professional, constant and persistent, and talked through her words. As I continued my interview, she began to slouch in her chair, her chin and head dropped downward and tears began to stream down her face. I continued to question her until we eventually reached the point when she acknowledged her wrongdoing.

At that time, Vicki retrieved the ring from her lap and placed it on the table. I took a picture of the ring with my cell phone and placed it back on the center of the table, between us. I recapped various aspects of the investigation and my understanding of the chain of events. She remained somewhat quiet, occasionally glancing upward and making brief eye contact with me to silently acknowledge the accuracy of my statements with a nod of her head. She eventually talked me through the $6,250 insurance fraud she had perpetrated against Viceroy from start to finish. Vicki continued and detailed the additional $8,250 insurance fraud against Westlynn Insurance, her homeowners' insurance company, for the same diamond ring in question, another diamond band and a gold bracelet. Vicki admitted the jewelry was never stolen. She admitted she had forged Robert's signature on various documents and filed a false police report and false insurance claims.

Vicki also admitted to several hundred dollars of fraudulent payroll adjustments for herself and to hundreds of dollars of repair service fraud. She explained how she retrieved actual information from customer-service agreements and used those accounts to perform jewelry repair work on jewelry she, her family and select customers owned free of charge.

When the time was right, I slid a blank legal pad with two black pens on it across the table toward Vicki. I asked her if she had been truthful to me about everything we discussed and asked if she had anything else to share with me at that time. Vicki said there was nothing more to tell me, so I asked her to recap our entire discussion in writing.

Over my years of investigation, I've realized that writing can be cathartic for the soul. Vicki seemed to feel the same way, as she filled each line and turned countless sheets of paper on the pad as she hurriedly began to write on the next fresh sheet. It was almost like she was worried she might lose her thoughts. When she finished writing, I asked her if she wanted to voluntarily surrender the diamond ring to me at that time. Vicki pushed the ring toward my side of the table and said, "It's yours. It belongs to the company. I know what I did was wrong." I asked her to write one last voluntary statement, explaining why she wanted to surrender the ring. She agreed and wrote yet another statement detailing her feelings and desires to give the ring back to the company, in my care. I concluded our interview and told Vicki we needed to tell Marie about our conversation. Vicki agreed and we walked back to the store together.

Once back at the store, Marie, Vicki and I met in the private office and I recapped Vicki's admissions. I asked Vicki to confirm my account, and she did so while apologizing to Marie. We suspended Vicki's employment at that time, obtained her keys, provided her with her belongings and escorted her from the store. The diamond ring was cataloged, sealed in an envelope with my signature and a time stamp and secured in the safe as evidence.

The following Monday, I reviewed the investigation with my boss, our corporate insurance group, human resources and legal. Vicki was contacted by her area manger later that same day and informed that her employment was terminated.

Police Involvement

Later that week, the local police department reviewed my case file and Detective Benny Michaels, whom I had worked with on a previous case, referred me to the neighboring town where Vicki lived, since that was where the falsification of the original police report occurred. Detective Michaels helped me schedule an appointment with Detective Dave Vasek for the following day.

Detective Vasek seemed pleasantly surprised with the thoroughness of the investigation and seemed eager to continue where I had left off. He contacted Westlynn Insurance Company and obtained additional documentation relating to Vicki's claim.

Vasek contacted Vicki the following day and requested she meet him at the police station for an interview. Vicki quickly consented and was there within the hour. Vasek reviewed the entire investigation with Vicki and asked her supplemental questions. However, Vicki refused to answer any questions without an attorney. She asked to leave, and Vasek told her she was free to do so.

After she left the police station, Vasek drove to the prosecutor's office and signed a criminal complaint against Vicki. He then drove directly to Vicki's home, reintroduced himself and arrested her on the spot. She was charged with one felony count of falsification and two felony counts of insurance fraud. Vicki's new fiancé, Tim Bitwell, later posted a $7,500 bond, and Vicki was released from custody.

Months later, just before the preliminary hearing at the courthouse, I met with Detective Vasek, Prosecutor Ted Ryan, Defense Attorney Jim Painter and two representatives from the Westlynn Insurance Company. During the meeting, the Westlynn representatives made several demands and said if they received immediate restitution, the company would consent to reduced charges against Vicki, who remained silent throughout the meeting. Detective Vasek looked at me several times as Painter, Ryan and the insurance representatives negotiated the case. Vasek was cut off several times when he tried to comment. I remained silent and leafed through my case file. Finally the lawyers and insurance agents reached an agreement that seemed to make everyone happy except me and Viceroy.

Painter said Vicki would send a restitution check to the Westlynn Insurance Company within days. In turn, the charges and possible sentences against Vicki would be reduced. Apparently, since I had recovered the diamond ring, all was good in their eyes. Painter talked quickly and was eager to share the plea agreement with the judge. Both lawyers began to gather paperwork, assuming the meeting was over. I stood up, collected my paperwork into the case file and said, "Guys, no deal. I want to continue with the original charges and, if need be, forsake the restitution. After all, there is always civil court following Vicki's sentencing."

Painter, visibly angered, began to question my authority and intentions. I glanced at Vasek who sat quietly with a smile on his face, looked back at Painter and Ryan and said, "It's great these folks from Westlynn showed up after the good detective and I solved the case for them, but if there is a restitution line, Viceroy will be at the head of it and everyone else can get in line behind me." I went on to explain that the recovered ring would not suffice as restitution because Viceroy was not a pawn shop. We did not sell stolen or worn merchandise to unsuspecting customers. In my eyes, the ring was worthless, other than securing it as evidence for Vicki's prosecution. Painter seemed outraged. I then suggested to Ryan that we should pursue the original charges and mentioned if he was questioned by the judge as to why a plea agreement was not reached, I had absolutely no problem addressing the court with my concerns.

Ryan and Painter stepped away from the table and briefly conversed before including Vicki. Ryan asked to adjourn the meeting for an hour, and as we all walked out to the lobby, Ryan, Painter and Vicki walked over to Vicki's fiancé, Tim Bitwell, who was waiting in the lobby.

About 50 minutes later, Vicki and Tim returned and sat across the lobby from Vasek and me. Ryan entered the lobby moments later and our meeting reconvened. As Painter sat at the table with his head down, not making eye contact with me, Ryan slid a certified check for $6,250 across the table to me. He also passed a check for $8,250 to the Westlynn representatives. Ryan asked if I had any objections to a plea agreement for reduced charges against Vicki at that point. I said, "No sir, not at all." The police would later release the ring to Tim, at the prosecutor's direction. The case was quickly concluded without trial.

Detective Vasek later informed me that Tim Bitwell had visited two banks during that hourlong break from the courthouse. He exhausted some personal accounts and tapped into his retirement savings to help Vicki out of the mess in which she had put herself. I later learned that shortly after her court-appointed probation ended, Vicki broke up with Tim to pursue another man.

I guess history does repeat itself.

Vicki also landed a job in another jewelry company in a neighboring county, but her employment was short-lived. Perhaps she was terminated for theft? Maybe management completed a background check, detected her criminal history and acted before she could? I hope it was the latter.

Lessons Learned

I think any successful investigator knows that it isn't just how you ask a question but how many different ways and times you ask the same question to the same and different people. At the onset of this case, I felt as though something were missing from the staff responses. The case might have gone undetected if I hadn't asked the same questions to different employees, in different ways, multiple times.

I've often said in my personal and professional life that when demands and emergencies start to feel too burdensome, just remember, emergencies are rarely convenient.

When one occurs, we have to readjust, refocus and sometimes tap into our personal time and patience to help others and do the right thing. I can't think of once when I planned an emergency, but I know how to handle one when it arises: with patience, understanding and persistence.

Recommendations to Prevent Future Occurrences

Fraud can never be eliminated completely in any corporate environment, but the following recommendations would have most likely deterred Vicki's fraud from occurring, or at least detected it sooner:

1. Implement corporate control procedures to cross-reference insurance claims with corporate personnel records of employee names, residential addresses and purchases, to flag possible fraud.
2. Include our fraud hotline in ongoing and frequent store trainings to increase the perception of detection. Reinforce with all employees that the program is available and can be used at any time by any employee.
3. Monitor insurance claims with required coapproval by the store manager and office manager at the field level. Immediately question and report suspicious employee claims to the corporate office for further review and inspection.
4. Implement ongoing procedural and ethics training for personnel. Frequently inspect those areas of the business during visits by operations supervisors, corporate personnel and onsite management. Act efficiently for any noncompliant results via timely reporting, investigation, training and detailed documentation of events.

About the Author

Michael Skrypek, CFE, has 25 years of experience conducting and supervising financial and property misappropriation examinations throughout the United States and Canada. Mr. Skrypek, a Certified Fraud Examiner, is currently a member of the board of directors for a local Association of Certified Fraud Examiners chapter.

Operation Give and Go

EDWARD P. BUTTIMORE

It came in to the Newark Police dispatcher as a frantic 911 call. The caller said he had just been the victim of a carjacking at the intersection of William and Halsey Streets by a man armed with a gun. Units from Newark Police Department were immediately dispatched to the scene, given the serious nature of the call. When police arrived, the victim excitedly described in detail the armed and dangerous carjacker, how he stuck the gun in the victim's face, how he took his car.

A witness also volunteered that he had seen the whole thing, confirming the car owner's story. Despite a diligent search, the Newark Police could not find the owner's car or the carjacker. Later, the owner, a computer programmer for a major corporation, filed a theft claim with his insurance carrier for the total theft loss, and the carrier paid more than $16,000 on the claim.

Only there was no carjacking, and the owner was no victim at all. He was a thief, who faked the entire carjacking scenario with a friend in order to file a fraudulent insurance claim. How did the authorities know? Because the car had been in the possession of state investigators from the New Jersey Attorney General's Office for six full days at the time the owner reported the carjacking. The car had been purchased from a street-level middleman during Operation Give and Go, a proactive undercover initiative by the New Jersey Attorney General's Office to confront the growing problem of owner give-ups and stolen automobiles in northern New Jersey.

To conduct the investigation, undercover state investigators gained access to street-level middlemen who traffic in owner give-ups, where owners literally give up their vehicles to someone else with the understanding the vehicle will "disappear," allowing the owners to file a false theft claim and fraudulently collect insurance benefits for the alleged loss. To lend an air of legitimacy to the operation, state investigators rented a garage in Jersey City, completely outfitted with tools and auto parts, where middlemen could bring cars to undercover investigators. Unbeknownst to the would-be insurance cheats, however, the garage was also fully equipped with concealed audio and video recorders to memorialize all activity at the shop. As a result of this initiative, investigators conducting Operation Give and Go recovered 46 luxury cars and SUVs with a total value of $1 million. The following June, 18 criminal indictments were handed up by the state grand jury charging 28 defendants on charges that they planned or participated in owner-involved automobile thefts in order to collect more than $1 million in bogus insurance claims.

But why did the New Jersey Attorney General's Office want to make such a significant eight-month undercover effort and dedicate so much manpower and money to an individual street crime normally left to local police? The answer to that question materialized in two places, in the boardroom of one of the largest automobile insurance carriers in New Jersey and under the gold dome of the New Jersey Statehouse inside the governor's office. It was created by a sense of urgency, and this is how it started.

It was a bright sunny day as Ed Carroll, the new governor of New Jersey, settled in to his oversize burgundy leather chair in his new office. Everything looks sunny when you're the new governor and it's the first few weeks of your administration. Until the phone rings with the first problem of the day, that is — and this was going to be a big one. "Governor, Mr. Farmstead is here to see you," the governor's secretary said. "Send him right in," the new governor confidently said, anticipating his first meeting with the president and chief executive of one of the largest car insurance providers in New Jersey. Automobile insurance in New Jersey had been a problem and a hot issue of many campaigns for public office for as long as drivers and voters could remember. With 8 million people and 4 million drivers, New Jersey is also the most densely populated state in the nation. New Jersey drivers not only have a propensity for bumping into each other's vehicles, they're also pretty creative about the insurance claims they file. For as long as anyone can remember, New Jersey has had the highest automobile insurance rates in the nation. A driver in New Jersey under the age of 25 will likely pay about $3,000 a year for auto insurance, provided they have a clean driving record. A young person with a poor driving record could pay closer to $5,000 per year. A family with three or four drivers will pay a lot of money to auto insurance companies in the state. But the new governor was determined to change all that. He even campaigned on the issue and promised to lower automobile insurance costs for everyone. And today was the day he was going to start . . . or so he thought.

"Good morning, Tom, thanks for coming down," the governor said as he stood to meet his guest with a hearty handshake and a big smile.

"Thank you, Governor," a more melancholy Tom Farmstead responded.

The new governor started right in to his pitch, "Now listen, Tom; automobile insurance costs in New Jersey are crazy. We're number one in the nation with the highest rates by far. When I ran for governor, I promised the citizens of New Jersey I would do something about it, and I want to start today and I need your help."

Farmstead began to shake his head slowly. "I'm not going to be able to help you, Governor."

"Why not?" Carroll asked in obvious bewilderment.

"Because we're pulling out of New Jersey. It's just not profitable for us anymore, and it doesn't make business sense to stay."

The governor was stunned. He was literally speechless for five seconds, but it seemed like an eternity. "What do you mean you're pulling out of New Jersey? You can't do that. You insure 800,000 drivers here. That's 20 percent of all the drivers in the state," he said in utter disbelief.

"I'm sorry, Governor. The decision has been made," Farmstead said matter-of-factly.

The governor got up from his chair and began walking around his office, looking at the floor, not knowing what to say or even think. The thought of 800,000 drivers trying to secure auto insurance at the same time and the likelihood of price gouging by the other insurance companies ran through his head. A look of desperate panic came over his face. "Tom, what do I have to do to get you to stay?" begged Carroll.

Farmstead looked away and began to shake his head slowly again. "There are lots of issues. It's the give-ups and the false claims. We're losing too much money," he said.

"What do you mean?" the governor asked in anxious anticipation there might be a chance he could turn this meeting around.

"We're putting out too much money to settle false auto theft claims when car owners are falsely reporting their cars stolen to get out from under their monthly lease or loan payments," Farmstead said.

"What do you need me to do?" the governor eagerly asked.

"Stop it!" barked Farmstead, who then got up to leave.

"I will, just give me some time," assured the governor. As Farmstead opened the door of the office to leave, the governor shouted past him to his secretary, "Gail! Get me the attorney general on the phone right away."

Designing a Sting

I headed the auto fraud north unit of the New Jersey Attorney General's Office Criminal Division. I had a squad of 12 diverse, college-educated and very talented criminal state investigators. Our mission was to focus more on auto insurance fraud investigations rather than auto theft cases. Our geographic area of investigation was the northern half of New Jersey, which included most of the urban areas where much of the auto insurance fraud was committed. Orders came down from the eighth floor — where the attorney general was located — that we had been selected to design and carry out an undercover auto fraud operation somewhere in northern New Jersey that would target owner give-ups. The goal was to make a significant case that would draw front-page media attention to act as a deterrent to others throughout the state who were contemplating giving up their cars to file false insurance claims.

We needed a retail commercial garage as our cover for the sting. It would be the location where would-be insurance cheats or their co-conspirator middlemen would bring the cars they wanted to disappear. It had to be in an easily accessible area. We wanted it to seem that we were in an auto-service business, but we didn't want to attract legitimate members of the public as consumers. That was going to be tricky, but we came up with an idea.

We selected Jersey City as the location for our undercover garage. It was located in Hudson County between Bergen and Essex Counties and one of the most densely populated areas of the country. We found a commercial garage for rent on Tonnelle Avenue, an old, battered industrial highway with trucking companies, body shops and mechanic shops. In the front was a two-room office and around back was a garage large enough for 14 cars. We agreed on setting up a wholesale auto detailing business as our cover story. It meant we detailed cars for resale, but our only clients were retail auto dealers. This way we wouldn't attract any walk-in business from individual customers. And so was born Santos Wholesale Auto Detailers. The electronic surveillance unit (ESU) of the attorney general's office installed covert cameras for us, one in the garage and one in the office. The undercover state investigators would wear the audio recorders on their bodies for quality recordings.

Our cover story for the illicit business was that if anybody needed to make a car disappear, we had contacts at Port Newark and Port Elizabeth who could, in only three days, have a car placed in a large container at the port and shipped to South America, where it would be sold and could never be traced. Car owners could then falsely report their cars stolen and not have to worry that it might be recovered by local police. Basically, we said if you give us your car, we'll make it go away. That's how we came up with the name Operation Give and Go, which is also the name of a basic play in basketball.

Staffing our undercover operation was the next step and certainly an important one. State Investigator José Santos (his undercover name) was the perfect candidate to be the lead investigator, and we were lucky to have him on staff. José was in his mid-30s, good looking with an engaging smile and personality. Bilingual in Portuguese, he could put people at ease and make them feel comfortable, even when they were committing crimes. The big bonus was he had grown up working in his family's auto body shop business so he could both walk the walk and talk the talk when it came to cars. That proved very helpful throughout the investigation.

Next we needed props to make the garage and office look like all the other rundown businesses on Tonnelle Avenue. We secured a number of beat-up desks, chairs and file cabinets for the office, and then I asked my investigators to locate abandoned car parts and bring them to the garage and spread them around. They spent the next couple of weeks picking up abandoned and damaged fenders, bumpers, hubcaps, wheels, tires and even car seats. We had a couple of undercover cars that we brought into the garage and took apart slightly to give the appearance of being worked on. We brought in buffing machines for waxing cars, vacuums, cleaning fluids and lots of rags. In undercover work, a picture is worth 1,000 words. We had to look like the business we were purportedly in to avoid suspicion, and we did.

Next was spreading the word of our existence and willingness to engage in making cars disappear. Now, this was not something we could advertise in the local newspaper. Getting the word out was slow at first, but things picked up pretty quick. Through a network of undercover investigators, informants and underground middlemen, we spread the word of our illicit business. We were now ready to start accepting give-up automobiles.

The First Deal

When we were ready to go, it took about a week and a half before one of our undercover investigators, Juan, got a phone call from Raul, a would-be insurance cheater, that he had a car he wanted us to make disappear so the owner could file a phony insurance claim. Raul was told by Juan to bring the car to the Tonnelle garage, go around back and Juan would introduce Raul to José Santos. We were pretty excited to collect our first car and see if we could gather all the necessary evidence during the illicit transfer of the vehicle.

Operation Give and Go used five undercover investigators. In addition to José, who would deal with the insurance cheaters turning over the vehicles, we also had Ted, a young, up-and-coming detective who would run the electronic surveillance cameras from a small locked room in the garage. Mike was our six-foot, 300-pound enforcer, if need be. It was always comforting to know Mike was onsite in case things went south in a hurry. He dressed in dirty work clothes and was always working on a car when a luxury vehicle came in. We also pulled Jaret on the team, another young, aggressive investigator. He was very knowledgeable about cars and had previously worked for an insurance company investigating false auto claims. And finally we had Juan. In my 25 years in law enforcement, I hadn't met an investigator who was more talented at undercover work than he. In our office, Juan was used in undercover cases to buy drugs, guns, fictitious Department of Motor Vehicle (DMV) documents, participate in health-care claims frauds and so on. Juan was in his mid-30s, about five foot eight, in great physical shape, had a shaved head and was bilingual in Spanish.

When he dressed down to get into the needed undercover role, he looked like a street thug. If you were walking down the street with your wife or girlfriend and Juan was walking toward you, you would seriously consider crossing the street to avoid him. He was that intimidating. In reality, he had his master's degree, was a part-time professor of criminal justice at a local state college and worked part time at a fitness gym as a personal trainer. He was also an incredibly nice guy.

At about 2:00 p.m. on a warm July afternoon, in drove our first give-up car. It was a late-model Infiniti driven by Raul, who was accompanied by an unknown friend. One of the first things we hoped to do in each of the car transactions was to identify with whom we were dealing. To prosecute some-one for a crime, it's helpful to know who they are and where they live, so when it's time to round up all the defendants, you know where to find them. Unlike normal business transactions, such as walking into a car dealership and introducing yourself by name and shaking hands with the salesperson and manager, illicit transactions among criminals don't follow social proto-cols. Criminals don't like to identify themselves and certainly never use their last names. And if you ask for their last name, they immediately become suspicious of you.

Law enforcement officials often identify people by the license plate of the car they are driving. That wouldn't work in this case, as we knew the car was not registered to either of man. We knew Raul's identity, but his friend's was going to be a little more difficult to get.

Raul hopped out of the Infiniti and the covert cameras started rolling. *"Que pasa, mi amigo?"* Raul shouted to Juan with a big smile as they walked toward each other in the oversized garage and shook hands. "I like this place. You're on a main drag, but you're tucked around back so no one can see who's coming and going. This is great," Raul said approvingly. Juan introduced Raul to José Santos, but Raul's friend just gave a head nod and a "how ya doin'," clearly not interested in a formal introduction.

José, wearing an audio recorder, immediately went to work. "What do you got here? This? This looks sweet," Santos said as he walked around the Infiniti smiling.

"Yeah, man, it's only a year old and the guy just doesn't want it anymore," Raul explained.

Nodding his head, José said, "Well, we charge $400 to make it disappear, and you got to give us the keys and three days before the owner can call the police to report it stolen. I got a hook down at the port and this car will be on a ship to South America by Thursday."

"No, no, man," Raul said, his face turning more serious. "I'm looking to get some money for this. I need at least $800."

José walked around the car like a prospective buyer at a car dealership. After the appropriate hesitation period, he relented and said, "I can go $600 but that's all."

"Come on, man, this ride is worth 40 Gs, you can do better than that," Raul pleaded.

"All I got is $600 today. We can do the deal now," José stated. After a moment of silence he added, "Cash." That was the magic word to Raul who said okay. "I got the money upstairs in my office. Follow me," José said, and all four of them then headed to the office.

Ted, working the cameras, stopped the garage camera and started the office camera. José pulled out a bank envelope from his desk and invited Raul and his friend to sit in the two chairs in front of the desk. Juan had already sat in the chair at another empty desk. The office covert camera was pointed directly at the two chairs in front of José's desk. José counted out the $600 as Raul and his friend watched carefully. We made sure to have $20 and $50 bills instead of $100 bills simply to make the counting take longer and have more proof on film. José handed Raul the cash and said, "Double check that to make sure that's $600." So now the covert camera is filming Raul counting out on the desk the $600 himself. Assistant prosecutors like that type of evidence. The meeting ended with happy handshakes and José's invitation that Raul return anytime with other give-ups ups, but always to call first to make sure José had cash on hand. In reality, José wanted Raul to call first so we could be prepared for his arrival.

On a Roll

In the next few weeks, about two give-ups a week began to roll in, and we continued gathering the evidence we would need for a successful prosecution. Whether we received a give-up car directly from an owner or from a middleman, we told each it would take three days to get the car on a ship to South America and not to report the car stolen for three days because we didn't want to be stopped by local police driving a "stolen" car. Raul agreed and complimented José for good thinking. The real reason we instructed them to wait three days was if they gave us the car on Monday and then filed a false police report on Thursday, it made the case stronger for us since we had possession of the car over those three days. We also required the keys to the car so we could move it to the port. We told the owners and middlemen we would return the keys to them in three days because their insurance company would ask for both sets of keys to verify a car was stolen. Many of the keys we received came with keyless remotes. With these, we opened each remote's case, inserted a small piece of paper with the date and case number, photographed it, closed it back up and returned the remote and key to the owner. The owners would surrender the keyless remotes to their insurance companies. Much later in the investigation, when we contacted the insurance companies, they would give us the keyless remotes they received from the owners. We opened them up and photographed the piece of identifying paper we had inserted earlier. This was additional evidence of intentional fraud.

Some owners actually paid us a few hundred dollars to make their $40,000 car disappear. Many of the middlemen who brought us cars were charging the owners a fee and also wanted to get money from us for the car. In one instance, we bought a $60,000 Jaguar for $800. José knew to haggle with the middleman who brought the car in, all on videotape in the garage. Just as with Raul, when they agreed on a price, José would bring the person up to his office for the cash. The covert camera in the office would get an even closer video of the defendant's face. In each transaction, José would count out the cash, hand it to the fraudster and tell him to double check it. The prosecutors assigned to the case were very pleased with a video containing defendants bringing in cars they admitted were not stolen but were going to be reported stolen and the counting out their ill-gotten gains.

Over the next several months, our undercover garage received 46 luxury cars, including Cadillacs, BMWs, Mercedes, Jaguars and fully loaded SUVs. We turned away anything that was not high end. The owners we ultimately identified were successful Wall Streeters, well-to-do suburbanites and working-class city dwellers. One Cadillac owner was struggling with the $780 monthly lease payment. Another owner had a perfectly good luxury car under a three-year lease, but he fell in love with a newer-model car and wanted out of his current lease. Some owners had damaged their cars but wanted to avoid the costly deductible on the repairs, so they just turned the cars over to us and reported them stolen. There were owners who, due to the economic downturn, simply could no longer afford the high payments on their luxury cars. Others faced thousands of dollars in penalties from their leasing companies for exceeding strict mileage restrictions. And then there were owners who wanted to defraud an insurance company and make a few bucks.

Unexpected Consequences

One of the requirements we had put out there when we announced we were accepting give-up cars was that the owner or middleman would have to give us the keys. So as the luxury cars came in to our undercover shop with the keys in the ignition, we assumed they were give-ups because the middleman had the keys. We quickly learned how resourceful the middlemen were and how wrong our assumption was.

First we had a BMW brought to us that we later learned was actually stolen using the jump-in technique. This happens when a car owner stops at a local convenience store for a cup of coffee and leaves the car running in front of store; the car thief easily jumps in the car and drives away. A variation of this can happen on cold mornings when a driver starts a car in the driveway to warm it up, goes back inside to finish getting ready for work only to come back out to an empty driveway.

The second tactic was the key swap. This is when two car thieves go to a car dealership for a test drive of a luxury car. After the test drive, one of the thieves distracts the salesperson and the other thief switches keys and hands the salesperson a generic key for that type of vehicle. Later that day, the thieves return to the dealership and drive the new car off the lot with the real key.

We found out about these specific car theft instances months later when we contacted the insurance companies and found out the cars were reported stolen on the day we received the cars, hours before we received them.

The landlord to our garage on Tonnelle Avenue also posed a bit of a challenge. We never identified ourselves as undercover law enforcement officers to him for obvious reasons. He spent his workday just a block down the street from us in his own garage. The first week we were there, we changed the locks on the garage and office entrance. About a week later, the landlord, who had to fix our nonworking bathroom, changed the locks back during the day so he could gain access. Mike, our "enforcer," wanted to confront the landlord. I said no, let him finish the plumbing and just change the locks again.

Identifying accomplices continued to be a challenge. If a middleman brought us a car and had someone else with him, one of our other undercover investigators would try to engage the accomplice in a conversation about a possible future illicit deal in hopes we could later identify that person.

Successful Sting

After eight months undercover, the attorney general's office obtained 22 criminal indictments against 38 individuals on charges of insurance fraud worth $790,000. In all, we took in 46 luxury cars worth just over $1 million.

We learned the identity of the unknown middlemen who worked with Raul in three different ways. We ran the license plates of each accompanying car, which was the most successful option because Raul always needed a second car to leave the garage. Other times José was able to find a reason to get the middleman's cell phone number, which we could then trace to the owner. And finally, we relied on informants to identify the middlemen for us if they could.

The 38 defendants were charged variously with conspiracy, theft by deception, receiving stolen property, tampering with public records, false swearing, altering of motor vehicle identification numbers and simulating a motor vehicle insurance fraud. Depending on each individual's criminal history, if any, defendants received sentences ranging from probation to up to five years in prison. Where appropriate, restitution to the insurance carriers was ordered.

We also helped Governor Carroll convince Tom Farmstead to continue offering auto insurance to New Jerseyites.

Lessons Learned

When conducting an undercover sting, such as Operation Give and Go, there are two primary concerns. We had to be careful to avoid entrapment, which we were — no defendant successfully brought that defense. We also had to be careful that the sting did not cause a mini-crime wave. We targeted give-up cars, not stolen cars. We quickly learned that some of the cars brought to us were being stolen just for the purpose of selling them to us. When we knew or suspected a car had been stolen rather than given up, we refused it. This put the people who brought us the stolen car in a difficult position, as they had to leave the garage in a stolen vehicle.

We also learned of the varied backgrounds and motivating economic situations of the people who voluntarily gave up their cars. Some were greedy while others had just fallen on bad times. We learned there was no typical person who voluntarily gave up his or her car to commit insurance fraud.

Recommendations to Prevent Future Occurrences

Law enforcement officials do not have the time to understand why otherwise law-abiding people commit criminal acts. Police and prosecutors must simply investigate and prosecute offenders. In New Jersey, the theft or attempted theft of less than $75,000 in value has a presumption of nonincarceration upon sentencing if convicted. Although our operation had a positive (but perhaps temporary) effect on Tom Farmstead's decision, New Jersey continues to have the highest automobile insurance rates in the country, and owner give-ups contribute to that. New Jersey addressed the problem of widespread health-care fraud by lowering the dollar amount that could land an offender in jail. I recommend giving the same consideration to any auto-related crime that affects insurance costs. We need to change the behavior of criminals whose illicit conduct impact auto insurance rates.

About the Author

Edward P. Buttimore, CFE, CPM, is a former 25-year, career supervising state investigator and administrator of criminal investigations for the New Jersey State Attorney General's Office. He investigated major frauds, insurance fraud, auto fraud, DMV document fraud, healthcare claims fraud, organized crime and corruption. He also designed and directed numerous special undercover initiatives of statewide significance.

CHAPTER 12

An Inspection Is Worth a Thousand Photos

ED MADGE

Unlike most antique car buffs, William Honaker didn't take his old Fords to auto shows. Few people even knew he owned them — but somehow someone kept stealing them, he said. Eleven times, in fact, in five months he had different antique cars stolen. William owned and operated an automobile parts business near Fort Lauderdale, Florida, and had a nice rambling home that looked as if it had been moved from a hacienda in Arizona. The Honaker house covered about a half-acre in a large suburban area of Sunlight Ranches near Fort Lauderdale. He owned and drove a brand-new Cadillac but collected antique Fords. William was married and had two children, a boy and a girl, ages nine and 11, who attended a private school near his home. Overall, he thought he had done very well for a high-school dropout.

To their neighbors, the Honakers seemed like the typical suburban family. William left for work every morning around seven and dropped off his children at school on the way. Joan, William's wife, picked up the children and brought them home in the afternoon before going to her job as a nurse in a nearby hospital.

William had very few close friends, and most of his social network consisted of acquaintances he met through work. William also fancied himself as a country western artist, and he had cut an album featuring military blues tunes. He used the name Billy Appleton to record the album in Nashville. But this Billy had a dark side.

One of William's acquaintances was a car salesman named James Santini, who had a nasty cocaine habit. William also spent time (unbeknownst to his wife) with his girlfriend, Mary Osceola, a Seminole Indian who lived on the reservation west of Fort Lauderdale. Mary was divorced from her husband, Jimmy, a police officer in a large municipality in southern Broward County.

One other acquaintance, Roy Gordon, was a guitar player in the band that did the background music on Billy's album. Roy lived in a small duplex in Fort Lauderdale and commuted to Nashville to play with some of the city's biggest artists. This diverse quartet began collaborating on a side project, but it wasn't a musical endeavor.

Billy and his ragtag group started working with small, independent insurance agencies in close proximity to one another in Pennsylvania and New Jersey. The agencies specialized in antique automobile insurance and accepted insurance applications by mail. Billy tested the water with these insurers by receiving coverage for his real Fords but then quickly branched out.

Start Your Engines

I sat at my desk in the criminal investigations division of Florida's public safety department, absentmindedly staring out the window. It was Friday afternoon and the weather outlook was promising a great weekend for South Florida, warm with low humidity and beautiful blue skies. Of course, it was October, the beginning of tourist season. It was also the time of year when fishing was really fantastic off the southeast coast — prefect for hitting the Gulf Stream and picking up those elusive dolphin and wahoo that I knew would be just waiting to jump on my line. Well, I could dream, couldn't I?

A phone call jarred me from these musings and back to my role as a lead investigator for the state. After I hung up the telephone, I picked up my pad of notes and headed for Lieutenant Goodell's office. At least this would keep me from sitting behind my desk shuffling through incoming paperwork for a while. I was tired of looking at the gray cloth walls of my cubicle with all of the photographs and bulletins. Those incoming cases were the standard fare I reviewed every day before assigning them to one of the investigators in the financial crime unit.

I knocked on the frame of Goodell's door because the door was partially open. He answered my knock with a low, monotone voice that sounded like he wasn't having a very good day. I said, "Got a minute?" as I entered and he said, "Have a seat; for you I have the time, but these end-of-month stats are driving me up the wall. Whatcha got?" he asked. Goodell, a very sharp administrator with a keen nose for interesting cases, was all ears. I told him about the phone call I had just received from Betty Allen and John Bundy at Bundy Insurance Company. Betty, John's secretary, had brought to Bundy's attention two documents that looked as if they were typed on the same typewriter. One was an application for a 1939 Ford convertible coupe insured by a party named William Honaker. The Hub Group had insured that vehicle and had subsequently received a claim that the vehicle was stolen. The other was an application from James Santini for a 1940 Ford Convertible Super Deluxe.

Lieutenant Goodell asked a few pretty routine questions: the jurisdiction of the alleged crime, how many hours I would need to complete the case, and so on. I told him it looked like something I could wrap up in a few weeks. Little did I know how wrong I would turn out to be. When I finished my cursory briefing, Goodell gave me the green light to use whatever resources I needed, with a closing caveat of "Be careful; it's a real jungle out there." I returned to my cubicle.

When I reached my desk, I decided to call the Hub Group in Tampa, Florida, which insured one of Honaker's vehicles. While I was speaking with April, the representative, she asked me to hold for a minute while she checked something. When she returned to the phone, she told me that she had remembered another recent claim on an antique Ford and wanted to check it. In August the Hub Group had insured a 1941 Ford convertible for Mary Osceola. The agency that had referred the policy to them had requested an inspection of the vehicle. I asked if this was a normal course of business for them, and she said it wasn't in the case of antique automobiles. But before the Hub Group could arrange a vehicle inspection, the car was reported stolen. Because of Florida's insurance "good faith" law, the Hub Group was going to have to pay the claim within 30 days of receipt. Hub's management was waiting for Mary to be deposed by an attorney in Fort Lauderdale before paying the claim. I asked April to send me copies of the supporting documents that Mary submitted to them and let me know when and where the deposition was to take place.

Now all I needed were the documents, a background check on Mary and William, and an analysis from the crime lab. This should be a piece of cake, I thought, and take me away from the mundane forgery cases that that cluttered my desk. Based on the information I received from Betty Allen and John Bundy, it didn't need much manpower. The original documents were being sent overnight Express Mail, so I should get them on Monday.

When I returned to the office on Monday after a peaceful weekend of fishing, I checked with Bill, the mail room clerk, to see if the package had arrived. He was sorting through the mail that had arrived over the weekend and said he would call my office if he found my package. I arrived at the office around 8:30 a.m. and met with Wanda, my secretary, who had a handful of new cases for me to review. It's remarkable how the reports just keep piling up. This area was what we in law enforcement referred to as Fraud Lauderdale. We also knew that fraudsters worked here in the winter rather than in Buffalo. We couldn't be the only ones in the country with such a case overload, could we?

At about 8:50, Bill called from the mail room and said, "I've got your package; come on down and pick it up." I did not wait for the elevator at this time of the morning; employees tied it up coming to work. I hit the stairs and in a flash was standing at the mail room counter. Bill handed me the package and I headed to the copy room on the way to my office, opened the package and made two copies of the documents Betty sent. One of them was an application for insurance for a 1940 Ford Super Deluxe Convertible bearing the owner's name of William Honaker. The other was an application for insurance for a 1940 Ford Super Deluxe Convertible and the owner was listed as James Santini. Both applications were typed and bore different serial numbers for the vehicles. The owners lived approximately 23 miles apart, one in a suburb of Fort Lauderdale and the other in a different municipality. I headed to the analysis department to ask my colleague Janice to conduct background checks on Honaker, Santini and Mary Osceola.

When I got to my desk, I made a call to the crime lab and spoke with Greg Sanders. He was the in-house expert on forged documents and was often an expert witness in court. I explained the documents to him, all type-written with the exception of signatures. Greg recommended that I send the documents to the state lab in Tampa, and he gave me the name of Steve Upland, a specialist in typewritten specimens. I called Steve and explained the documents to him. He assured me that he would be able to determine from the original documents whether they were both authored on the same typewriter. Steve said, "I can tell what brand of typewriter typed the documents." I asked him to handle the documents with gloves because my lab would want to perform tests for fingerprints too.

Rather than mail the documents to Tampa, I decided to deliver them to save time and maintain chain of custody. I made a property receipt with a case number attached to the package. The case classification was kept as a "Police Information," since we had no real evidence of fraud.

Bringing on a Navigator

I drove to Tampa on Tuesday morning and delivered the documents to Upland for examination. I returned to my office in Fort Lauderdale and gave Lieutenant Goodell an update on my progress. I called the state department of insurance to see if they would be interested in a joint investigation, and the woman I spoke with agreed to send an agent to help tomorrow.

I arrived at the office on Wednesday morning and had message to call Paul Wilson at the department of insurance. I returned his call and we arranged to meet at 10:00 a.m. at my office. When I went down to meet him at the reception desk, I immediately noticed that he had a striking likeness of Clark Gable, right down to the pencil-thin mustache. He was impeccably dressed in a three-piece suit, was over six feet tall and had close-cropped dark hair sprinkled with gray. We went to my desk where I showed him copies of the documents I had so far. He looked through them and without hesitation said, "I think they were both done on the same machine." I said, "I think so too, but it is not going to be that easy." He wrote the names of the two applicants on his notepad and borrowed my phone to call his office and have them run the names through their databases.

Ten minutes later while we were getting coffee in the cafeteria his cell phone rang. "It's my office," he said, and stepped in the hallway to take the call. When he returned he said, "This is going to be one helluva case." Paul's databases showed several other insurance applications — all typewritten and within the past eight months — submitted for antique automobile insurance to several different insurers. I called state attorneys and briefed John Jenkins, an investigator. He said he would see if he could find an empty office space that Paul and I use at their facility. John's reasoning was legal documents would be more accessible there. In the meantime, Paul and I decided it was time to "put some boots on the ground" and begin surveillance of our three suspects.

On Thursday and Friday, after checking with Lieutenant Goodell, I moved my files and equipment to an empty conference room in the state attorney's office that John had reserved for me. It was an ideal location for continuing the investigation. Paul and I were only steps from the office of the section chief, Lenny Kent, an experienced financial crimes prosecutor; Kent and his staff gave us a hearty welcome.

I returned to my office and assigned investigator John Mallony the task of reviewing incoming cases while I handled this one. I visited the analyst department and picked up additional information obtained by Janice on Honaker and Santini. I took the weekend off but couldn't shake the thought of our next moves in the investigation. Janice had put a lot of information together on the subjects' criminal backgrounds. The package contained known associates of Santini and Honaker as well as property information. I looked it over during the weekend and made some notes. I'd brief Paul on Monday at the office. Janice had found no information on Mary Osceola.

Monday morning I arrived at the office early and laid out some of the association matrices that Janice had put together on the conference table. When Paul arrived, he walked around the conference table and added some more documents he had picked up at his office. The paperwork showed several other insurance companies had received applications on antique Fords in South Florida in the past eight months.

Since both of the initial applications we had were typed, we concentrated on the other ones that were also typed — they all looked like they were done on the same machine as the documents submitted to the lab. We had copies, but we needed the originals for lab comparison, so we spent the next two months assembling the originals to send to Steve Upland. Additionally, each application came with a photograph of the car being insured.

We began surveillance of Honaker's home and business and Santini's home. We were unable to conduct surveillance of Osceola because she lived on an Indian reservation, which is federal land. We had nothing to tie the suspects to each other, but we hoped the surveillance would provide the evidence we needed.

The surveillance team recorded the license plates of cars coming and going from all the locations and sent them to Janice to analyze. I made contact with the Antique Ford Motor Club of South Florida and requested their assistance. Paul contacted other insurance companies known to specialize in antique and collectible cars and asked for information on insurance applications for cars fitting our profile.

An analysis of the applications we uncovered showed Honaker using several aliases to insure a total of 12 antique cars manufactured from 1939 to 1948. The applications began in November of the previous year and continued through October, when my investigation began. Starting in March in the current year and continuing through December, Honaker and his team began reporting the vehicles stolen to the insurance companies. Traditionally these types of policies have low premiums and high payoffs because collectors' vehicles are rarely stolen.

Becoming Car Buffs

During this investigation, Paul and I learned more than we ever thought we'd know about antique cars. For example, Fords circa 1940 are extremely difficult to steal without keys or a flatbed wrecker because they have a large, round steel locking device on the steering wheel that makes it impossible to turn the wheel without the keys in the ignition.

I contacted a local antique car collector, Larry Lawson, who belonged to the Antique Ford Motor Club of South Florida. I asked if Honaker, Santini or Osceola were members of the club, but Larry told me no. He asked what kind of cars they owned, and I told him about the 1939, 1940, 1941 and 1948 Fords listed on the various insurance applications. He said, "The '39, '40 and '48 are quite common and I thought I knew everyone in the area who owns those. The '41, now that's another story, very rare, because of the war, there weren't that many made and no one around here has one — I'd know it. I haven't seen one of those bullnose cars in quite a while, even at car shows." Things were coming together now, at least in my mind. It looked like we were dealing with "paper" cars being insured.

John Bundy called to tell me that he had just refused to insure a 1940 Ford that Santini had applied for. I told him we had contacted all of the antique automobile insurers and told them to flag Santini, Honaker and Osceola in their files and let us know if future applications or claims were filed.

In addition to the surveillance we were running on Honaker and Santini, we began to subpoena bank and telephone records. Janice began tracing the numbers in Honaker's business phone. Bank records showed Honaker's business was in financial distress.

Steve Upland called and told me that the first two applications we had submitted had been typed on the same machine — an Olympia manual typewriter. He said if we recovered a typewriter, he could let us know if it was the same one used on the documents. I told Upland we would send the other applications to him for typewriter identification. Next we had the original applications sent to another lab for fingerprinting. Three days later we received the results, and they were in our favor. Honaker's and Santini's fingerprints were on Santini's application. The second application only had Honaker's prints.

April, the representative at the Hub Group whom I spoke to at the beginning of the case, called to tell me that Mary Osceola's deposition had been scheduled and gave me the details. Paul and I decided to arrange surveillance outside the building because we were not allowed into the deposition, and we joined the experts in the parking lot. We saw Honaker arrive in his Cadillac with Osceola in the passenger seat. She exited the car and went into the building while Honaker waited in his vehicle. So far, so good for establishing that connection. Mary returned to the Cadillac and Honaker drove off. I later learned from April that during the deposition, Mary stated that she was a member of the Antique Ford Motor Club, which was later disproved. I called Osceola's ex-husband — a police officer in a large municipality in our county — and asked if Mary owned a collectible 1941 Ford car. James laughed and said, "She can't afford the gas cap for that kind of automobile; are you kidding?"

While this was going on, we had an analyst tracing calls from Honaker's phone records and discovered that he was in contact with three particularly interesting numbers: Lowell Bohling in Walker, Iowa; Snuffy's Antique Cars in Cedar Rapids, Iowa; and Nils Johansen of Karlstad, Minnesota. Bank records showed Honaker was making car payments to a bank in Cedar Rapids on a 1948 Ford automobile. Investigation revealed that Lowell Bohling had purchased the car unrestored, restored it and sold it to Snuffy's. According to Bernice Keenan, the title clerk for Snuffy's, the car was sold to Honaker and he was making payments to the bank. Records showed that even after Honaker had reported the car stolen, he continued to make payments to the bank. Once he collected the insurance premium on the car, he negotiated another deal for a 1940 Ford Super Deluxe Convertible. The vehicle was bought in the same manner as the 1948 and shipped to Honaker's business. Snuffy's had the negative films of all of the vehicles they had sold on file, and I asked him to send me photos of the cars. When they arrived I recognized that all the photos Honaker, Santini and Osceola submitted with insurance applications were taken at Snuffy's. Additionally, the supporting documents that had been submitted came from Nils Johansen, who sold "old car memorabilia" from junked cars. The photographs were sent to Honaker as a potential investor in those vehicles. The only photograph that was not taken at Snuffy's was that of the 1941 Ford insured and reported stolen by Osceola.

Seeing What's Behind the Photos

Gordon Kelly, the owner of Gordon Kelly's Insurance Agency in New Jersey, contacted Paul and said he received an application from James Santini for a 1940 Ford Super Deluxe with serial number 18-5645689; Santini also sent a photograph of the vehicle — it was the same one that Bundy declined to insure. Gordon Kelly referred the application to National Collectors Insurance, and they requested an inspection of the car before issuing the coverage. As soon as I saw the photograph I realized it was taken at the home of Larry Lawson, the head of the Antique Motor Club of South Florida. I contacted Larry and he told me the car belonged to Billy Appleton, who had taken the picture while visiting Larry on the pretext of joining the club. Larry had not seen or heard from Appleton since then.

National Collectors contacted Paul when the inspection had been scheduled, and he asked the adjuster, Lisa Papkolaskis, to meet us. She also agreed to ask Santini for additional photos of the car before the inspection, and he submitted a few different ones. We could tell that they were all taken in front of Honaker's home. So that we could get a better read on Santini, Lisa agreed to take Marilyn Williams, a detective on my team, with her as a "trainee" learning how to do inspections.

I set up surveillance of Honaker's house and Santini's apartment for the night before and the day of the inspection. During the evening, Shane Clement, head of surveillance, called to tell me that Honaker had moved the 1940 Super Deluxe to an underground garage at Santini's apartment.

The following morning we briefed Lisa and Marilyn on what to ask Santini, and then I checked with tech support; they were on location ready for the inspection team to arrive. Marilyn was equipped with a body transmitter to record the entire transaction. When they arrived at Santini's, Lisa requested that he move the car out of the garage to the open parking lot because they needed more light. He did so but had trouble locating the key on his very large key ring. Lisa asked Santini where the serial number was located, but he said he did not know. She quickly saw that it had been removed.

After Lisa and Marilyn left, the surveillance team saw Honaker arrive at Santini's apartment and drive the Ford back to his home while Santini followed in Honaker's Cadillac. When they arrived at Honaker's, the surveillance crew there saw another antique vehicle in his garage. We were at this point five months into our "short" investigation and had probable cause for arrest and search warrants.

One More for the Road

I received another call from John Bundy, who said he had an application for a 1947 Ford convertible with documents and photographs submitted by Roy Gordon of Fort Lauderdale. I drove by the address and saw no such vehicle, so I contacted Gordon directly. After identifying myself, I showed him a photograph of the 1947 Ford. He immediately said, "That's not my car; I've never seen it. Billy Appleton asked me to sign an application for insurance on it because he couldn't insure any more antiques in his name." Gordon gave me a sworn affidavit attesting to this fact and cooperated fully in the case.

I obtained arrest and search warrants the following day and sent out teams to make simultaneous arrests. Paul and I served two search warrants on Honaker's home and business and arrested Honaker at his business while serving the first search warrant. He cooperated fully and told us where we would find his files on the antique vehicles. When we served the search warrant at his residence, two antique Fords were confiscated, both with the serial numbers removed — the 1940 that he had driven to the inspection and a 1948 convertible — and an old Olympia typewriter, like the one used to type the applications. Other files and paperwork were taken as evidence of other "vehicles" he was ready to insure under aliases. If Honaker had filed all of the applications he had prepared and been paid the premiums, he would have collected more than $2 million in payoffs.

Only two cars belonged to the fraudsters; the rest were insured based on fraudulent paperwork and photographs of vehicles owned by others (later all identified) or by Snuffy's. Roy Gordon became a state witness for the prosecution. Honaker, Santini and Osceola were charged with 134 various felonies, and, before trial, they each pleaded guilty to the charges. All three received 25 years of probation and were ordered to reimburse the insurance companies and the sheriff's office for the expense of the investigation.

Lessons Learned

Paul and I both learned that through total cooperation between agencies, an investigation can be brought to a successful conclusion. My quick-and-easy case turned out to be more than a mere diversion from forgery cases on my desk, and I'm happy that it did. We had the opportunity to stop a large fraud ring that was continuing to expand and include new perpetrators. There is a sense of satisfaction that comes with knowing you helped end a problem before it became much, much worse. And perhaps even more important, I learned that a fishing boat is an excellent place to mull over the details of a case and come up with new plans to investigate.

Recommendations to Prevent Future Occurrences

As this case proved, if insurers do not demand to see cars in person before they are insured, individuals can provide "proof" of ownership and the type of car relatively easily. Dealers are willing to send photos to potential clients, and those photos are sent to insurers. It's also easy to claim that a car is held at a separate address to assert ownership. Due diligence is essential when insuring any asset.

About the Author

Ed Madge is a CFE, regent emeritus of the ACFE and retired detective sergeant from South Florida. He was the first law enforcement recipient of the CFE of the year award in 2002. Mr. Madge is currently a police science/criminal justice faculty instructor at Nashville State Community College in Cookeville, Tennessee, and an ardent supporter of the ACFE.

CHAPTER

13

The Danger of Trusting Too Much

JOE BONK

Henry Olson — Hank, as he was known in the office — was originally assigned to work at Blizzard Insurance through a temp agency to help out during a busy time. Hank worked hard and had a positive attitude, and he seemed to like the work. When a position in the claims department at Blizzard opened up 18 months later, Hank applied for it and was hired. He kept several pictures of his wife and kids on his desk and seemed to be a dedicated family man. When having lunch with coworkers, he spoke of weekend visits to the soccer field or baseball diamond to watch his children play and of the importance of family. Oddly, Hank became quiet when the conversation turned to former jobs. He chastised those who lived in the past and would often say, "The future is so bright, I gotta wear shades!"

Blizzard Insurance had claim offices in many cities, including one in Hank's adopted hometown. With excellent brand recognition and superior customer service, Blizzard was the first choice of many consumers.

I wanted to work for a successful company and Blizzard fit the bill. I was asked to lead the team of ten that monitored payments issued by our claims employees. Given the volume of payments, the enormity of the process was a little overwhelming at first. Fortunately, my team was up to the challenge. The staff members got along well, and everyone readily shared their knowledge; we were always willing to help each other. My subordinates were located all over the country, but we kept in constant contact to share observations and learn from each other. We had different skill sets, which was helpful considering the specialization within the Blizzard Insurance's claims offices.

As I reviewed the processes in place, I was surprised at the manual nature of the monitoring procedures. During our first team meeting, we identified the need to improve our use of technology. We embarked on a long-term strategy to improve our efficiency by leveraging computers to help us identify unusual transactions. The core of this improvement was a database containing all payments issued by our claims department.

Blizzard Insurance's leadership was proud of its employees and trusted them. Management was confident that by identifying and developing good people, Blizzard would continue the legacy of success. I recall one meeting with the claims management team where we provided an assessment of our internal control processes. The report identified a number of weaknesses that could be exploited by our employees, if not addressed. The senior vice president of claims dismissed the report by saying in an offended tone, "Our employees are *not* stealing from us," and then he walked out of the meeting. My team's work suggested there were clear signs of trouble, including one case involving almost $100,000. However, many in the organization believed that these were isolated instances rather than a pattern of behavior, and did nothing to address the situation.

A Single Suspicious Check

We had just concluded our weekly staff meeting, and it was almost lunchtime. The cafeteria got crowded at noon so I usually tried to get down by 11:45, right before the rush. I was just about to leave my desk when the phone rang. The call came from Ron, our newest employee. As the person responsible for monitoring one of our fastest-growing markets, Ron had strong knowledge of the claim-handling process but was often surprised by stories told by other analysts who had identified questionable behavior. Ron asked me if we could use our payment database to identify check disbursements containing certain names.

One of Blizzard's claims representatives in his local office had noticed a payment made on a file he was handling, but he had not issued it. The check was made out to Henry or Artie Olson — Artie was our customer, but Henry was not listed on the policy. I hadn't seen payment information like that before, as most of our checks containing two names used the word "and" rather than "or." Ron told me that Hank Olson was an employee at his office and asked if I could identify all the payments made to him because he was curious to see if this was an isolated instance. I would typically create an ad hoc query, perform a cursory review of the results to ensure that the data I provided were consistent with the request and then send it for a more thorough review. I created a query based on Ron's request but was completely surprised by what I found.

The query identified 40 payments containing the name Henry Olson as a copayee. The other name changed often; there didn't appear to be a pattern to the copayees, but Henry appeared on all 40 checks. There also was no a pattern regarding who issued the checks; I saw at least ten different claims employees issuing them. I noticed something else interesting: The payments were issued for 18 consecutive months and then suddenly stopped. The amount of the disbursed checks exceeded $265,000.

I went to lunch with Rudy, one of the analysts who worked out of the office with me. Rudy had joined our department four years ago. He had a great understanding of technology and was enthusiastic about our work and in making a difference in a very large company. I told him about the case over lunch. We discussed possible explanations for the payments but discounted all but one — that Blizzard Insurance was the victim of an embezzlement scheme. We agreed that the checks to Henry Olson were a concern and felt additional work was needed.

Suspecting there was more to this story, I approached my leadership team. Our vice president, Mike, had joined the company about two years ago, while my immediate boss, Earl, had been with the company much longer. It seemed that everyone at Blizzard knew Earl. While Mike was relatively new to the company, by Blizzard standards, he quickly established an excellent reputation for his objective, firm-but-fair management style. As for Earl's style, he had one rule: Don't do anything to embarrass the department. To me, this meant I had to have facts to support my suspicions before bringing them up. Being almost right was not an option. Both Mike and Earl would provide any support we needed with senior management, but in return we had to ensure that we fully understood the information we analyzed. Based on the information known at the time, both Mike and Earl agreed that additional work was warranted. We had found what we believed to be a significant loss of funds, but we wanted to ensure that the loss wasn't even larger before confronting Hank.

Ron, Rudy and I had a conference call to discuss what we had identified and to develop our plan of action. We took a closer look at the payments made out to Henry Olson and noticed that the "other" payees came from all across the state. We could not identify a pattern in these customers; some had been insured by Blizzard for a long time, while others were not. However, one commonality was that all of the checks containing Henry's name were supplemental payments — that is, an initial disbursement was made to the insured only. The payment made out to "Henry or XXXX" was always made *after* the claim had seemingly been resolved. Also, none of the claim files mentioned Henry Olson until the payment was made. Next, we analyzed the endorsements and found that all of the checks were endorsed by Henry, never by the other payee. These facts led us to believe that the other person listed on the check most likely had no idea that another check had been issued on the claim. All of the checks were deposited into the same bank account.

It seemed that Henry had identified a significant opportunity and took full advantage of it. But we also wondered why the payments suddenly stopped. Did Henry become concerned that his scheme would be detected? We created a timeline to help us identify key events based on the facts. The payments to Henry had stopped right around the time that Hank was no longer a temp and had become employed by Blizzard. Could there be a connection? Maybe Hank didn't want to risk losing his new job? Or was there another explanation for the change in his strategy?

Climbing the Fraud Ladder

The team went back over the results of our initial investigation and discovered that the scheme was connected to customers who shared Henry's last name. We ran a query to identify the customers in Hank's state with the last name Olson. Every Olson who reported a claim in the 18 months before Hank was hired had a subsequent payment on which Henry was listed as a copayee. Faced with these facts, none of us believed that the embezzlement had simply stopped. Hank's scheme appeared to have resulted in a loss of $265,000 without detection; what would have made him cut off an undetected flow of easy money?

We theorized that, because Hank could only issue checks to himself based on the number of Olson customers who filed claims with Blizzard, perhaps he had grown frustrated with the limitations of his scheme. What if his frustration led him to find another way to embezzle funds? We didn't know what that scheme could be, but we were concerned that the Olson checks were the proverbial tip of the iceberg.

We went back to our timeline and saw that when Hank was hired by Blizzard, he was granted the authority to issue checks for up to $10,000 without needing management approval or a second signature. We created a query to identify all the checks Hank issued after he was hired. The number was significant — he had issued more than 6,000 payments worth more than $12 million since coming on board with Blizzard. Rudy, Ron and I dug into the details to see if there were any red flags lurking in the data.

We also obtained historic organizational charts for the office and noticed that Hank had been asked to serve as a liaison for vendors who provided repair services to our customers. Vendors would forward bills to him for review and payment, as warranted. Therefore, it made sense that he would issue a large number of checks to vendors. I referenced Blizzard's list of approved vendors and saw that Hank had made payments to all of them. In particular, he made a large number of payments to Stars Cleaning, a company that was well respected in the office — it received accolades from our customers for prompt and courteous service. However, in addition to the payments to Stars Cleaning, Hank issued more than 500 payments to Starz Cleaning — with a z, not an s. These might have been typographical errors; after all, the s and z are close to each other on the keyboard.

Rudy and Ron reviewed public records to see if we could find a company named Starz in the area. We checked with state agents, but they did not have a record for incorporation using that name. We checked the Internet for a website but did not find anything. There were no online reviews by customers. Starz appeared to be an anomalous company — there were dozens of firms that provided similar services, and Starz didn't advertise, have a website or register with the state. Despite this, Starz had received more than 500 payments from Blizzard Insurance.

We selected a few of the electronic claim files and dug into them to see if there was an explanation, and again we found a pattern. A customer would report a loss, and a Blizzard claims adjuster would inspect the claim. The customer then received a payment, and the file notes did not indicate that another firm had assisted in the cleanup. The files did not contain references to concerns about the quality of work or customer complaints. Nevertheless, a second payment was then issued to Starz, without an explanation.

In some files, the adjuster handling the claim questioned the Starz payment issued by Hank. The notes indicated that Hank said he had made an error, and the Starz payment belonged to another claim but had been mistakenly applied to the wrong claim. Hank thanked the adjuster for helping him find the payment and promised to move it to the correct file immediately. The adjusters were satisfied with this explanation; after all, mistakes can happen to anyone, and Hank had promised to correct it.

This is where our company's culture of trust worked against us. The staff members thought of each other as family, so the fact that Hank acknowledged his error and said he would fix it was sufficient for most people. However, Hank never moved the payments or offered further explanation. I had a sinking feeling as the pattern repeated itself with each file reviewed.

We discussed the possibility that the other adjusters could be involved in Hank's scheme, but the claims in question involved a wide array of other Blizzard staff members. Our theory was that Hank did not involve others in this scheme but took advantage of his positive reputation in the office to convince his coworkers that he would rectify the problems. The other claim representatives simply trusted Hank to do what he said he was going to do. The customer had been paid and any potential issue was an internal one.

The 500 payments to Starz issued by Hank exceeded $2.4 million, and they were all within a range of $3,000 to $9,900, which is highly unusual. Hank didn't seem interested in wasting his time with checks worth less than $3,000, but he didn't want to issue checks for $10,000 or more because they would require approval from his supervisor.

Next we obtained copies of the checks to Starz and Stars. The payments to Stars were deposited in a local bank account. The payments to Starz went into a different bank — the same account used to deposit the checks made payable to XXXX or Henry Olson. I also noticed that the endorsements on the Stars and Starz checks were different. A stamp with a restrictive endorsement was used by Stars, but Starz had handwritten endorsements. The evidence seemed overwhelming.

Surprise Interview

Our team arrived at Hank's local office to interview him on a Tuesday. Given the magnitude of the suspected embezzlement, Blizzard's leader of corporate security, Scott Walton, was going to conduct the interview. Gina Lon, the regional human resource manager, also attended. Scott and Gina were well versed in our findings and had copies of the checks and file documentation, along with a copy of Hank's personnel file, including his job application and most recent reviews. I accompanied them on the trip to take notes and provide additional insights based on Hank's explanation. We arrived at the office at 7:00 a.m., knowing that most of the staff started at 7:30, and set up in the conference room. Hank arrived at his usual time of 7:45, and his manager asked him to join us in the conference room.

This was the first time Scott, Gina and I had met Hank. He was taller and a bit older than I had imagined. He greeted us in a friendly manner and asked how he could help us. After exchanging the typical pleasantries, Scott told Hank that we were investigating some payments and that we hoped he could help us understand the reason that some checks had been issued. We started by asking Hank to state his full name. Interestingly, he gave us a different middle name from the one on his employment application. When Scott asked Hank to clarify the discrepancy, I noticed Hank's demeanor began to change. He started fidgeting and repeated the question as if he were buying time to formulate a response. Finally, he said he didn't know why his application had a different name.

Scott and Gina confirmed Hank's background and that he had been assigned to work at Blizzard by another company to provide extra help but was hired by Blizzard 18 months later. Gina showed Hank a copy of the code of conduct that each employee signs on an annual basis, and Hank confirmed that he had signed it.

Scott then laid out our concerns about several checks written to Henry Olson, and Hank denied knowledge of them. I was shocked when he continued to feign confusion, even after Scott showed him that all of the checks had ended up in the same bank account. He disputed that the endorsement was his but acknowledged that it was similar to his signature on the code of conduct. The mood in the room had gone from cordial to hostile as Scott referenced claim number after claim number where Henry Olson's name appeared on a check but had no connection to the claim.

Hank asked to take a break. We were somewhat surprised when he returned, given the contentious nature that the interview had taken on. We asked if he was familiar with Starz Cleaning Services, spelled with a z. Hank said he knew of Stars with an s and that it was a well-respected vendor. Scott showed him a check and asked why it was made out to Starz instead of Stars. Hank shrugged dismissively and said he must have made a typo. When Scott pointed out that there was no invoice from Stars in the file, Hank said it must have been misfiled. He stubbornly repeated the same explanation for the next ten checks that Scott showed him.

Finally when Scott showed him evidence that both the Henry Olson and the Starz checks had ended up in the same bank account he used for his paychecks, Hank stared down at the documents in silence. He stopped the charade and did not try to explain or offer excuses. He simply stood up, announced his resignation from the company and left the room. He walked over to his desk to get his car keys and left without saying a word to anyone.

Where Did It Go?

We then contacted the state's Department of Insurance, the Internal Revenue Service Criminal Investigation team, the Federal Bureau of Investigations and the U.S. Postal Inspection Service to discuss the case. Because the computers that processed Hank's illegal disbursements were located in another state, his actions led to federal charges.

During our investigation, we learned that Hank had never been married and did not have any children. The pictures on his desk were not his family; they were just part of his larger plan to earn his coworkers' trust so he could get away with embezzlement. We later learned that Hank used most of the funds he stole to open a nightclub. Rudy and I were curious enough to visit the club (before it was closed) and saw that Blizzard's money had gone to a number of high-end finishes, including a very large mahogany bar.

Faced with the overwhelming evidence, Hank pleaded guilty to one count of conducting a monetary transaction with criminally derived funds. He was sentenced to more than 80 months in prison and was ordered to pay $2.8 million in restitution.

Lessons Learned

For Blizzard Insurance, this case was a wake-up call regarding the need to improve our internal controls. The reality that one employee had stolen more than $2 million before anyone noticed was a significant problem. With thousands of employees authorized to issue checks, if even 1 percent of the staff engaged in similar behavior, the company's exposure was dramatic. Management believed that if we hired the best people and treated them fairly, we would minimize our risk. However, we should not have relied solely on those practices.

We also learned that our background check failed to identify a previous, unrelated conviction for Hank, which would have immediately made him ineligible for hire. We learned the importance of prevention, as the money that was stolen was spent and there is almost no chance that we will ever recover the full amount. To date, we've collected approximately $50,000.

Recommendations to Prevent Future Occurrences

Unfortunately, manual processes were used to analyze large amounts of data instead of leveraging technological advances. The world had changed, but parts of our oversight process had not been updated to take advantage of technology advancements, and Hank exploited this for his personal benefit.

Having the proper tools is essential to do our jobs, and after this case, Blizzard invested in technology to alert us to unusual payment patterns. The output is reviewed by a team of trained individuals who understand data analysis and the claims process. We built models to warn us of suspicious payment patterns. Being proactive in seeking out tools and training that can make us better examiners is invaluable to preventing and detecting fraud.

About the Author

Joe Bonk, CFE, is a Certified Public Accountant and has worked on external and internal fraud risk management in various capacities for over 20 years. His work has been used to develop tools that help identify high-risk transactions that warrant further attention.

The Twin-Cities Machine

BOB WEIR

Medical clinic fraud is a complex business. A typical clinic employs owners, doctors, office managers, clerical staff, marketers and transportation staff. Machine Medical Clinic (MMC) had all of these employees and then some. MMC seemingly came out of nowhere and grew to a high-volume, high-dollar clinic in the Twin Cities of Minneapolis and St. Paul in a very short period of time.

Jim Johnson, M.D., was a licensed medical doctor who worked at reputable medical clinics for most of his long career. Johnson was a small man who was very soft spoken and always seemed to be nervous and looking over his shoulder. But late in his career Johnson decided to leave his employer and start his own medical clinic.

Igor Dimitrov was a Florida resident, originally from Moscow, and a partner in a clinic management company, TP Management, with another individual. He moved from Miami to Minnesota to start a joint venture and expand his operations with chiropractors and medical doctors in the area. Igor had a very direct and intimidating personality, which he used to coerce individuals into doing what he wanted, when he wanted it.

Running a Machine

Johnson established Machine Medical Clinic and was the registered owner, according secretary of state records. Medical clinics in Minnesota are required to be owned and operated by licensed medical professionals. MMC marketed itself as a one-stop shop for all the medical needs of residents in central Minneapolis. The clinic employed multiple chiropractors, physical therapists and massage therapists along with Johnson, who worked as a general practitioner.

After a few successful years in Minneapolis, Johnson decided to expand and opened a second clinic in St. Paul. However, this new location was not central as the Minneapolis clinic, and most run-of-mill patients would have difficulty accessing it. It nevertheless employed as many therapists, doctors and staff.

Igor had formed TC Management in Florida a few years before he moved to Minnesota. At the time, medical clinic management companies were focusing heavily on Minnesota due to the ease of medical coverage from the personal injury protection (PIP) portion of an automobile policy. This coverage was very lucrative for medical carriers; the legislature in Minnesota required a minimum of $20,000 in PIP coverage per person in the vehicle. The ease of accepting medical claims and payments made fraudulent schemes very popular, challenging to catch and essentially had few repercussions for the perpetrators.

The Team Versus the Machine

Jasmine Collins and I were coworkers in the Special Investigative Unit (SIU) at Holm Insurance Company. We frequently collaborated on investigations and discussed what cases should be pursued. We were a very good team. Jasmine had top-notch analytical skills and the patience necessary to complete medical clinic investigations. She and I complimented each other very well, as my skills were stronger in the interviewing and confrontational aspects of investigations.

One winter day Jasmine asked me for my opinion on a medical clinic she was looking into. She said some of our internal claims representatives told her that a new clinic called MMC had opened and was billing at a very high rate. She did some background screenings on the clinic and found it was recently incorporated. She then ran an internal report to see how many times MMC showed up in records and was alarmed at what she saw. This is when she came to me. We both had an extensive history of dealing with medical clinics, and we were astounded by the number of our policyholders who were using MMC.

Our next step was to begin reviewing some of the medical claims. I started with one patient, then two and then three. A pattern was already beginning to emerge and continued as we kept looking at claims. We saw a lot of low-impact car accidents involving minorities. The treatment for each person was very similar, according to the medical records. The accident victims went to see Dr. Johnson, who then ordered chiropractic, physical and massage therapy for each patient. One initial treatment, called *spirometry*, stood out to me. It is a test of lung functioning conducted by having the patient, in simple terms, blow into a tube — a highly unusual test for a low-impact motor vehicle accident. Finally, we noted some of the "same old lawyers" representing these policyholders.

Jasmine and I discussed the case with our supervisor and decided to open an investigation and pull all of MMC's claims into the investigation unit to handle.

Ambulance Chasers, Runners and the Mob

All of MMC's claims were transferred to me to handle through the conclusion of the investigation, and Jasmine was going to be co-leading the case. The first order of business was to protect our rights and obtain legal representation, so I sent the files to our best external legal counsel, Shana James. Shana was a petite woman but she had a lot of spunk and fire. She was relentless, and I had never seen her lose an argument. She was a born attorney who loved a good battle of wits. I informed Shana of the issues Jasmine and I had identified, and together we determined that the best investigative method for this case was to request examinations under oath (EUO) from our policyholders. An EUO is similar to a deposition but does not occur during litigation; it is a requirement under an automobile policy, and the person being interviewed is sworn in under oath and a court reporter records the interview.

Shana immediately began requesting the EUOs and setting up dates for the policyholders to come in and give their statements. She sent requests to the policyholders who visited MMC and received mixed responses. The individuals who had traditional — dare I say reputable — lawyers who were unaffiliated with the clinic industry were gracious about providing information and documentation. Conversely, we also had to deal with some ambulance chasers who knew us. When Shana sent them letters requesting the EUOs, they filed for arbitration. At least we knew to expect it; it was all part of the game. And they knew we would ask for the arbitration to be denied because the claims exceeded the allowable arbitration value. In our industry, it was the regular song and dance.

A common technique used by certain attorneys was to waive thousands of dollars in claims to keep the case in arbitration. This technique only supported our theory they were not valid claims. If a patient's treatment was necessary, why would he or she waive so much money? One potential reason could be the cost to litigate — arbitration was much more affordable. The second and more common reason was that plaintiffs' attorneys in insurance disputes are much more successful in arbitration than in district court. In arbitration, the odds of getting another plaintiff attorney as the arbiter are well above 50 percent. We continued our background screening on Johnson's clinics and employees, patiently preparing the case without alerting Johnson or TP Management to the investigation. Management and staff at the clinics had no idea who we were, making it easier to drive or walk by.

Jasmine and I discussed with legal counsel if we had the ability to gather information understate statutes that allow an insurance carrier to ask for specific information from other insurance companies if there is reason to believe fraud is occurring. Shana agreed, and we began gathering data from other carriers. In addition, agents with the National Insurance Crime Bureau (NICB) contacted me and began asking questions about MMC. Involvement of NICB agents was typically an indicator a clinic was an industry-wide problem. It also usually meant that law enforcement was being engaged.

Jasmine was contact by Joe Hancock, a law enforcement agent, a few months after NICB contacted me, and he asked for information about the MMC case. Although the authorities did not provide us with many details, we learned it was beneficial that MMC management was unaware of our identities. Not only did it provide Jasmine and me with autonomy to be near the clinic, but Joe told us it was also a safety issue. He warned us to be careful with the leaders of the clinic, particularly those working for TP Management, because the funding was coming from "questionable" sources. Law enforcement was interested in MMC as a money-laundering operation. At this point, my supervisor instructed Jasmine and I not to step foot in the clinic without his approval. He told us we were potentially dealing with . . . the mob.

As Jasmine and I continued reviewing documents from a safe distance, we noticed many of MMC's managers (nonmedical professionals) maintained active addresses in other states. This seemed odd in itself, but then I noticed one particular local address appeared on a number of employees' personnel documents and motor vehicle records. Jasmine and I decided to visit this address. We drove by in morning, around 9 A.M. The house was completely dark, the garage door was shut and a couple cars were in the driveway. We made another pass to get the license plate numbers and then left. All in all, we were in the neighborhood under five minutes. As we put the pieces together, we realized the house was a staging ground for the alleged perpetrators and a place for them to stay when they were in town.

Another pattern we found was that the vast majority of MMC's patients were minorities from low-income neighborhoods, as were the drivers employed by MMC to transport drive patients to and from the clinics. One aspect that did not make sense was the distance that patients traveled to visit the clinics. In any part of the Twin Cities, someone looking for treatment could find all of MMC's services within five to ten miles of his or her home. However, these patients traveled 20 to 30 miles to go to MMC. This was our initial indication that MMC's drivers were actually *runners* — individuals who purchase police reports, contact people involved in accidents and offer to drive them to a clinic for free. Doctors and clinic managers pay the runners based on the number of people they bring into the clinic; they are willing to pay up to $1,000 per person as long as they treat them a specific number of times.

Interviews

For each policyholder, Jasmine and I completed a medical record and treatment review. We found that the exams and follow-up visits were very extensive, which was important for us to note because we like to explain the tests to patients and see if they were actually completed. If a doctor does not complete a thorough initial exam, it brings the entire treatment plan into question.

While Jasmine and I worked our way through reams of documents, Shana was able to schedule some EUOs. Typically we start EUOs by asking general questions about an insured individual's medical treatment, and then we follow the tangents that arise from their answers. Several patterns emerged during the EUOs. The first was the patients could not describe their exams and follow-up treatments to the extent that the medical record reported. Second, not all treatments claimed on the bills were actually administered. As we continued our interviews, patients kept contradicting the treatments on the bills. At this time we learned that MMC's employees were starting to leave the clinic. Jasmine went into tracking mode to locate them so we could interview them.

Only two former employees agreed to speak with us, but they provided a lot of information. The first was a man named John who worked as a physical therapist at MMC. The second was a very confident woman named Kathy who clearly did not take guff from anybody. She was massage therapist. They both said they started working at MMC assuming it was a legitimate business but quickly learned there were unethical practices occurring. They each commented on a man named Igor — they said that after they put in their notice, Igor threatened that they would be hurt if they spoke to anyone about how MMC was run. Jasmine and I suspected that all the employees who left were similarly threatened. Kathy and John also confirmed our suspicions that Johnson was not the actual owner of MMC; he was being told what to do, and "the Russians" were running the place. They explained that Igor's team of managers did not live in the Twin Cities but visited often to check on the clinic. Kathy also confirmed that the transportation company was in fact a runner organization.

Medical Mill

In each case submitted to arbitration, we requested a EUO of the policyholders and Johnson. In most arbitration cases, we end up with a plaintiff attorney who ultimately says no to all of our requests, but we needed only one arbitrator to grant us the deposition of Johnson, and eventually we were successful. Johnson still had no idea who we were, but now he had to answer questions about his background, the treatments he was giving, what symptoms would lead to the treatment and the ownership structure of his clinics.

During the deposition, Shana questioned Johnson about how medical records were developed and treatment plans were determined. Johnson said he administered all of the initial exams and treatments, including the lung testing; however, he did not do a good job of explaining *why* the patients required lung testing. Our lawyer asked Johnson if the policyholders sustained any chest injuries or had breathing difficulties that required the use of spirometry, and Johnson admitted that they did not.

Johnson told us that he had purchased a medical records system that provided him with standard formatting of medical records. The e system allowed him and his associates to cut and paste standard medical record comments and formats. What this meant was each patient was treated the same and had no originality or differentiation. It was the definition of a *medical mill* — where all treatment and records are the same.

Next Shana asked Johnson to verify that all the treatments he billed for had actually been administered to the patients, and he confirmed that they had. We showed him transcripts of patients stating that they did not receive some of the treatments and tests on their bills. Johnson said the patients were wrong and must not have understood their treatments. We told him that we had explained every treatment to the patients we interviewed and they had denied receiving such treatment. We told Johnson that his clinic appeared to be a machine through which patients were processed with the exact same treatment simply to make money off the insurance companies. Johnson of course denied this.

Out of Sight, Not Out of Mind

It was a normal, cold day in January, and I really didn't want to go in the field. When I got to the office I heard rumors that Johnson's St. Paul clinic had closed overnight. Policyholders called me with questions about what to do now that the clinic was closed. Jasmine and I bundled up and headed out to the St. Paul clinic to see what was happening. Sure enough, on the door was a sign saying the clinic had closed, with no forwarding address or instructions for patients.

A few weeks later, the Minneapolis clinic closed as well. This time we didn't even bother to go and look. Instead, we validated the date it closed and made sure we did not receive any medical bills after this date. Holm Insurance denied all the claims from the two branches of MMC, and we placed Johnson on a list of doctors to track going forward. The case was closed, and Jasmine and I moved on to other assignments.

Holm Insurance maintains a list of medical providers that we track on a quarterly basis using internal and external systems and share with other insurance agencies. We receive reports showing new and old medical clinics that we received claims from. With these reports, we could look at the medical bills and records to identify doctors. If we had previously investigated a doctor who reappeared later on a tracking report, the investigator who completed the initial investigation was notified. In addition, we tracked people using background search engines. We would run queries by name and Social Security number to see if a new address showed up to see where they moved. Perpetrators who evaded justice once almost always pop up later if we're patient and steady about tracking them.

That summer I received a call from an investigator at Interstate Insurance Company in Minneapolis who was investigating a clinic. He said, "What was the name of the guy you looked at last winter with the two clinics?" I told him it was Johnson, and he said, "I found his new clinic; I am staring the door."

I quickly asked for his location, grabbed Jasmine and we headed straight over. We found an unmarked door, so we walked around to the back of the office building and saw some guys walking in with computer equipment. About ten minutes later we saw Johnson walk out of the office. He looked at us, threw his arms in the air and we were able to lip-read his exclamation — "You have to be kidding me!" His new clinic never opened.

The Big Picture

From our investigation, we were able to piece together the story behind MMC. Igor and his cohorts had moved to Minnesota and recruited Johnson to run a medical mill and pose as the owner. The Russians funded the lease of the building, the medical equipment and even the payroll, presumably with dirty money that they needed to launder. Together with Johnson they hired the employees, found the ambulance chasers and runners and determined how much to pay runners for bringing in patients.

Johnson was responsible for treating patients but was given a directive from Igor that each patient had to receive a predetermined treatment plan. Their formulaic treatments ensured that MMC would receive the full $20,000 in patient benefits in four to six months.

MMC's unwritten mission statement was to churn through as many patients as possible, doing the least amount of work and billing the insurance companies excessively. Igor and TP Management handled the paperwork, and they unbundled medical charges to bill for higher rates, billed for treatments the patients did not receive and billed for patients the clinic did not see.

In total, Holm Insurance Company had about 100 claims from Johnson's two clinics with a combined exposure of $2.8 million. The company had paid less than $100,000 in claims before the investigation began, and management chose not to pursue a recovery. In addition, each of the claimants was entitled to lost wages and other benefits, which totaled $5.6 million; we paid less than $50,000 toward these claims and again chose not to pursue recovery.

A few months after the closures of MMC, I ran into Joe Hancock, the law enforcement officer who worked on the case with us. He indicated we had "run them out town," and at this point the police investigation into Igor and TP Management was closed. He said that that no one had been charged at the time and would not comment further on the money laundering or ties to the mob. He did, however, mention that he found "business papers" that Igor kept. One page had the license plate and a description of the car Jasmine and I were in when we made our very short trip to the staging house. The house had looked empty when we drove by, but someone had been watching us.

Lessons Learned

I learned many lessons from this investigation about methods to identify and prevent insurance fraud. The first was to conduct a proper review of suspicious medical clinics. MMC was the first clinic I ever investigated that was not genuinely owned by a medical professional. The classic red flags were there: an external management company and a one-stop shop for everything, with excessively high volumes of patients. If we had not completed the proper review of the ownership and TPP Management, we would have quietly moved on and put all the blame on Johnson.

Keeping your identity unknown can be an advantage during an investigation. Typically fraud examiners, including myself, want to visit the clinic and see what is happening inside. In this case, not going to the clinics worked in our favor. It allowed us to observe the clinic without being noticed. Most important, we had several months' worth of investigative time on the case before MMC leaders knew the claims were being questioned. If they had known who we were or been tipped off that Holm Insurance was investigating them, they might have employed methods to inhibit our ability to investigate.

Johnson was unaware of who we were until his deposition, and he commented, "I'm surprised you have not come to clinic before." He tried to make small talk by saying "Everyone was interested in meeting you at MMC." This reaffirmed our position that keeping our identities concealed was the right move, particularly in light of what Joe Hancock told me later.

Money is king when it comes to prosecution of insurance fraud cases. Law enforcement and NICB declined to prosecute this case based on the amount of the fraud. We caught onto the scheme quickly enough that Holm Insurance had not paid much out of pocket; the damages were not as large as in most prosecuted white-collar crimes.

Recommendations to Prevent Future Occurrences

I highly recommend that insurance companies track individuals after they shut down a clinic. This worked for us when Johnson was about to open a new clinic. In addition, track people to other states and notify investigative partners there about the subject and your previous investigation.

The most important method to preventing future occurrences is knowledge. The front-line staff at insurance companies has to understand billing codes so they can spot suspicious claims and know what questions to ask the policyholders. The investigators at Holm Insurance provide constant training about new trends that we see in fraudulent billing, and this helps everyone in the company play a proactive role in preventing and detecting fraud.

About the Author

Bob Weir, CFE, is a 1998 graduate of the University of Wisconsin-Stout. Following college, he began his professional career with a national insurance company where he handled injury claims and later was placed in the Special Investigative Unit. During his time in this role he investigated injury claims, property damage, homeowners' claims and medical clinic fraud. He transitioned to a new company and role in 2007, where he completed internal audits and financial investigations. His current role, which began in 2012, is in sourcing operations where he negotiates logistics contracts. Mr. Weir became a CFE in 2010 and continues to maintain his active status.

With Friends Like These...

JOHN FIFAREK

James Anthony was in his early 20s, and, like so many other people living in Detroit, he had no job and no prospects. In fact, he had never held down any kind of work for very long at all. He made his money the same way everyone else he knew did — by taking what the streets had to offer. That's where he was born and raised, and it was a place where petty crime and drug dealing are career choices. Friends and family came and went. Some escaped by finding long-term work, while others ended up in prison or dead. James had been to jail a few times for possession of narcotics and drug trafficking, but now that he was free he set his sights on a different goal.

Martin Davidson had been friends with James since childhood, and they grew up together. However, Martin tried to find a more respectable path in life than the one James chose, and eventually the two men drifted apart. Martin lived with his mom in Detroit and was saving money for college tuition. He liked to tell his mom about his plans to get a good job after school and move her out of their dangerous neighborhood.

The American National Insurance Company was a national leader in the industry. It was often described with the words *prestigious, strong, stable* and *conservative*. The company reputation was sterling and well deserved. It was also one of the company's greatest assets, and executives were mindful to maintain and preserve it. "Doing the right thing by our policyholders" was engraved on the wall inside the lobby at company headquarters. Every business practice and decision was driven by the client, sometimes to the detriment of the bottom line. When a claim was made, customer service was king. Professional skepticism had to take a backseat.

I was a fraud investigator with American National, one of six in the Special Investigations Unit (SIU). We were there to protect the company and its reputation, customers and assets. We worked investigations for people across the company with diverse needs. One day we might be investigating a case for a claims examiner and the next for an attorney in the legal department. Being a fraud examiner at American National wasn't without intrigue, but, like any other job, it had its fair share of the routine and mundane as well.

We received cases from a variety of sources, and one way for people to contact us was through our anti-fraud tip line. It was set up so that any employee, customer or a Good Samaritan in the general public who saw something suspicious could call in and alert our group. The incoming calls bounced around from phone to phone in the SIU until they were answered or went to a dedicated voice mail if the office was closed. The nature of the calls ran the gamut from benign to outlandish, but we looked into each one regardless. That being said, it was natural to let out a little groan when a call bounced to you. That's what I did when I picked up the phone on a Tuesday afternoon in late summer. The call was from Steve Kennedy, the branch manager at a bank in downtown Detroit. "We have someone here trying to cash one of your checks, and we have some questions," Steve said.

"Okay, what can I do for you?"

"Well, it's for $25,000, and something just doesn't seem right about this. Can I fax you a copy of it? This guy does not look like he should be cashing a $25,000 check."

False Alarm?

Steve was able to buy time with the customer and place a hold on the check for further review. I received the copy he faxed and knew what kind of check it was right away — an access check. When life insurance proceeds are paid to a beneficiary, they typically do not go out as one check for the lump sum of the policy. Instead, the funds are put into an access account, and the beneficiary is issued a book of checks to use to draw funds from the account. I studied the check. The handwriting looked like it was made out by the beneficiary to himself — but who was he, this James Anthony? From the number on the check, I surmised that it wasn't the first one written he had written on the access account. I needed to review the claim file to gather more information.

I called our records department and asked to be sent full documentation for the policy number. After I reviewed the claim file, a few things were evident. First, the policy had been taken out by the deceased, Martin Davidson, fewer than two years ago and was therefore still within its two-year contestable period. Claims filed in the first two years of a policy require a more stringent review because of the increased risk of fraud, but Martin's case avoided the enhanced scrutiny because it was a relatively low payout and because of the cause of death — multiple gunshot wounds. The policy was for $250,000, which is not significant compared to most that American National Insurance Company agents issued. Claims for life insurance policies typically required only one piece of evidence for payment, a death certificate. As for the claim on Martin's policy, the death appeared tragic for certain, but suspicious? Certainly no one would purchase insurance planning to be killed in the street. According to the file, the claim was made by the beneficiary on record, the insured's uncle. He called in the notice, provided a copy of the death certificate and was promptly paid. Claim closed.

As far as my review was concerned, everything appeared relatively straightforward. However, before closing the case I took a quick look at the policy papers since it was so new. Everything looked in order there as well, but one thing caught my eye. The policy had been in force only a few months, yet there had been three beneficiary changes. When Martin took out the policy, he designated his mother, Jolene Davidson, as the beneficiary. A couple of months later, he changed it to his stepfather. Then, only a couple of weeks before his death, he changed the beneficiary yet again to an uncle, the James Anthony who had been trying to cash an access check at Steve Kennedy's bank branch. It was odd, for sure, but was it anything more than that? It is a policyholder's prerogative to make beneficiary changes as he sees fit. It seemed strange, but I didn't think it was overtly fraudulent.

Investigations can be expensive, and a $250,000 policy with no clear red flags of fraud is unlikely to warrant the time or money required to review something as seemingly trivial as a few beneficiary changes. Fraud investigations are designed to protect the customer and the company, and in this situation it didn't look like either party needed protection. In addition, I had a full caseload of work and couldn't afford to spend time chasing vaguely odd behaviors. I put the matter aside and went back to work on more important things. The suspicious check was paid.

Nagging Suspicions

There's an old saying, "Out of sight, out of mind," that might ring true most of the time, but it certainly did not apply to this situation. Sure, I went about my other business just fine, but that one detail in Martin's policy just kept thee claim in the back of my mind. It just kept bothering me, and I would find myself harking back to it in my head, asking myself the same questions: Why so many beneficiary changes in such a short amount of time? And what about the timing of that very last change? It was only weeks before Martin was murdered. Does it mean anything? Does it matter? A policyholder was killed and we paid out the benefit. Isn't that what is supposed to happen? Nobody was being cheated here.

After a few days I decided I just couldn't let it go. I revisited the claim file and decided to start with the beneficiaries named through the life of the policy. I had no idea what sort of information I was looking for but figured I needed something to put the matter to rest.

The policy documentation provided contact information for the three beneficiaries, but my efforts to reach them with the phone numbers provided failed; the numbers were all disconnected. I did, however, also have addresses to work with. I performed some online research with the information I had and found it curious that none of the beneficiaries seemed to be related or even know each other, despite being Martin's mother, stepfather and uncle. How does that work? There were no shared addresses, no shared family members and no shared last names among the beneficiaries. In fact, the only person I could positively connect to the deceased was his mother, Jolene Davidson, who was the original beneficiary on the policy.

I decided to visit the address on file for Jolene. She was easy to locate and was friendly and cooperative. She told me that her son had lived with her his whole life and was found dead only a few streets away from the house. Obviously grieving, she initially thought that I was there to talk about the search for Martin's killer. She said that the police had already come to talk to her and she hoped I had new information for her. When told that the purpose of my visit was to talk about her son's life insurance policy, she was surprised, confused and skeptical. She was unaware that Martin had an insurance policy; after all, he was only 22 and unemployed. "Why on earth would he have insurance?" she asked. "He had no money to pay for something like that."

She told me about the time leading up to her son's death, how he spoke of going back to school and getting away from the neighborhood that he felt was holding him down. When I asked if anything different or unusual had happened prior to his death, she thought for a minute. She told me that for a couple of months, she was having a lot of problems with her mail. After going for weeks without receiving any mail, she contacted the post office and was told that someone had changed her address on file, and not once but twice. She remembered the trouble she went through to get it straightened out and then, after it was finally fixed, happened to see someone stealing mail from her mailbox. She said the man ran off when she opened her front door to see what was happening, but it was too fast for her to see what he looked like. For the life of her, she just couldn't understand why she was having so many problems with her mail.

This information was useful, but she didn't stop there. What she shared next would transform an oddity into to a full-blown insurance fraud case, and more. She told me that Martin had no other family besides her. When I told her that the final insurance benefit was paid to Martin's uncle, she protested.

"How on earth would my boy have an uncle without me knowing about it?" she asked.

"James Anthony is not your son's uncle?"

"I know James, but he is no relation!"

She knew James Anthony all right. She said he was Martin's childhood best friend. They had known each other since kindergarten and all the way into high school. They were inseparable when they were kids, she said, but then they started to drift apart in their teens. James, she said, had begun to get himself into trouble and started running with the wrong crowd. It was only recently that she began to see him around the neighborhood again, and he and Martin had rekindled their friendship over the last couple of months before he died. She said she thought Martin was a good influence on James. Nevertheless, she couldn't believe that Martin would leave his insurance money to James, and definitely not over his own mother.

Mounting Dread

The interview with Jolene answered some of my questions but left others glaringly unanswered. Just who was James Anthony? Why was he the beneficiary on Martin's policy? Had he and Martin really become that good of friends again in the few months before Martin's tragic demise? Worst of all, I dreaded the possibility that American National's insurance policy played a role in a murder. A dark premise was beginning to form in my mind.

My attempts to locate the second beneficiary — supposedly Martin's stepfather — were fruitless. The phone number listed on the policy was disconnected, and my visit to the address revealed a different resident with no knowledge of Martin or the others involved in my case. With nothing else to go on, I decided to ask around Martin's neighborhood to see if anyone could provide any new information. A few people who lived in the neighborhood and were willing to talk about Martin's death said they knew that he was shot but nothing more than that.

I approached the case from every angle but had little to go on. I searched the Internet and various databases for information about everyone involved. I was searching for something — anything — that would get me out of the dead end and give me another avenue to investigate. The online searches revealed that the individuals associated with the phone numbers and addresses on Martin's policy had changed, and then changed again, and then yet again. Overall, there were dozens of names associated with various phone numbers and addresses. While I was sifting through my search results, I noticed a theme. Often once, twice and three times removed, one name reappeared: James Anthony. Some databases even showed him sharing an address with Martin and Jolene Davidson. I also noticed shared addresses between James Anthony and Martin's second beneficiary, the phantom stepfather.

Next I decided to reach out to the agent who sold Martin's life insurance policy, Woody Klein. His office was in the affluent Detroit suburb of

Bloomfield, Michigan, miles away from the inner city where the insured lived. During our interview, Woody said he hardly ever remembered the details of any given policy he sold, but one thing made his exchange with Martin Davidson more memorable than most. He said Martin had just walked into his office one day, without an appointment, and asked to buy a life insurance policy. Woody said that had never happened to him before and that most of his sales came from cold calls and referrals. He pulled out Martin's file and read from his notes that Martin said that he wanted the insurance for his mother and baby sister if something were ever to happen to him. Woody gave me a copy of Martin's driver's license that was filed with the application. After the interview my leads were exhausted and I was left with was a grainy copy of a driver's license and chilling hunch. The photo in the license looked nothing like the photos that Jolene Davidson showed me of her beloved son.

Now What?

At this point I had a tough question to answer, and I knew I couldn't do it myself. I took it to my supervisor and the five other fraud examiners in American National's SIU. I filled them in on my findings thus far and then asked, "What should we do?"

Almost instantly we split into two camps. The first camp could not believe what we thought we were seeing. It seemed far-fetched, sensational and potentially damaging to American National's good name and reputation. Then there was my camp. We advocated that the case had turned out to have little with insurance fraud and money and much more to do with justice. Could it be that James Anthony had something to do with Martin Davidson's death? To me it was clear, and I had a responsibility to do something. We held meetings to discuss the case — emotional meetings — and finally my camp was able to convince the others of our moral obligation. We had enough information and I was going to contact Detroit's homicide police.

Before the series of events that my call set into motion, Detective Shirley Mathis only knew one thing for sure, that 22-year-old Martin Davidson was dead. His body had been found on the edge of a street, gunned down during the night in what appeared to be a random act of violence with no clues or leads. His death was another unsolvable crime that would see little to no police resources, which were already stretched so thin in Detroit. My phone call changed all of that.

Justice

In my line of work, interaction with law enforcement was common, but this situation was different. Typically I was the one contacted by police officers or government agents who needed information and leads for cases. However, in the case of Martin Davidson, the onus was on me to find a way to convince a police detective that my case was relevant to a recent homicide. Somehow I had to find a way to pique Detective Shirley Mathis' interest. It ended up being easier than expected.

Detective Mathis told me the Martin Davidson investigation was at a standstill because the few leads they had went nowhere. I could almost hear her attitude change from near resignation to renewed interest as she listened to my story, chronicling the series of events that had led me to contact her. During our conversation, she shared some information with me that validated our decision to reach out to her. One thing she said was that the police didn't know an insurance policy for Martin existed; however, they were familiar with James Anthony, having interviewed him as part of the preliminary investigation. We discussed my case and the possible new motive. She thanked me for calling her and said she would be renewing the investigation.

From there it was out of my hands and into Detroit homicide's, but I continued to follow the case as best as I could. The information I shared provided vital missing pieces to the puzzle and allowed the police to complete the picture of an innocent victim done in by a friend turned identity thief and murderer. James Anthony, a trusted boyhood friend of Martin Davidson, betrayed his trust by posing as him to fraudulently obtain a life insurance policy, only to kill him in cold blood for the insurance payout. With our new evidence, Detective Mathis built a solid case against James Anthony, and the district attorney agreed to prosecute.

Six months after I received that fateful call from Steve Kennedy about a suspicious check, a jury convicted James Anthony of first-degree premeditated murder, illegal possession of a firearm by a felon and false application for state identification. The police investigation revealed that James Anthony exploited his friendship with Martin Davidson for financial gain. James devised a scheme to rekindle his broken friendship, but the whole time he planned to assume Martin's identity and insure his life. He named Jolene Davidson as the beneficiary to avoid suspicion when he took out the policy, but then he intercepted the insurance mailings by unlawfully changing her address and, finally, by stealing her mail.

James then orchestrated a series of beneficiary changes that involved an accomplice who played the role of Martin's phantom stepfather. However, this accomplice backed out of the agreement for fear of his life after learning details of James' plan. After the accomplice dropped out, James had no choice but to name himself as Martin's final beneficiary and pose as Martin's uncle. When all the pieces were in place, he committed the final act in his grand scheme. He asked Martin, his childhood best friend, to meet him late one night. Then James shot Martin multiple times and left him to die in the street. Today he is serving a life sentence for his crimes.

Lessons Learned

Looking back, this was one of my most memorable cases. Most investigators might describe their most memorable cases as the ones that required a lot of work, or the ones that saved a lot of money, or even the ones that garnered some recognition for their part. This case will stay with me for one simple reason — it was a key to serving justice. As anti-fraud professionals, our focus is generally on the dollars. It is the white-collar criminal whom we typically pursue, after all, and we tend to assume these criminals are nonviolent. This case taught me how dangerous that perception can be; as anti-fraud experts, we should never underestimate the lengths that some people will go to for money.

This case was also a reminder of the personal side of insurance fraud. The victim was American National, which lost about $100,000 (the amount James Anthony had already taken from the access account before the investigation), but the real victims were Martin and Jolene Davidson.

Recommendations to Prevent Future Occurrences

The case highlighted various strengths and weaknesses in American National's business processes and red flag recognition. As a result, my team and I made the following recommendations to our controls department.

1. James Anthony might have never been brought to justice had it not been for a phone call to a fraud hotline. We now hold frequent training for our staff and vendors to spread awareness of our hotline and the red flags of insurance fraud they should be watch for. Third-party awareness worked in the case of James Anthony, and we want to make sure it continues to work in the future.
2. This case emphasized the importance of knowing your customer. James Anthony found it too easy to impersonate the victim with a false state ID. All of our agents are now required to conduct background checks on new clients and verify their identities.
3. American National's practice of streamlining the payment process for low-dollar claims was also called into question. We recognize the importance of good customer service, but it should never be to the detriment of effective review practices.

About the Author

John Fifarek is a Certified Fraud Examiner who currently resides in Denver, Colorado. He is an experienced investigative professional who has performed investigations for the insurance, credit card and banking industries.

CHAPTER

All the Buzz

DALENE BARTHOLOMEW

Georgia Getty was a 58-year-old wife and mother who enjoyed music and spending time with her family, and she was especially close with her youngest daughter. Some of her family members were in a band, and Georgia liked to attend their concerts and listen to them play. Georgia was known for her exceptionally long hair and her long, perfectly manicured and brightly colored fingernails. She had worked for Buzz Agency in the neighboring city for more than 15 years, providing data entry and basic accounting support.

Buzz Agency was the parent company of *Buzz Magazine*, a weekly publication that started more than 100 years ago. It had a great reputation for providing local and world news coverage as well as fun, smart and interesting stories. The company was also known as an excellent employer and provided staff with generous wages and benefits, including disability insurance coverage. Unfortunately, the challenges of the economy had taken their toll, as had competition with online news sources. The magazine suffered a decline in advertising and readership. Although the agency was able to remain current and competitive by creating an online forum and other innovative ideas, management had to reduce overhead, which included making some very tough decisions for the best interests of the company overall. As a result, it was common knowledge that the Buzz Agency was going to face a reduction in workforce, which set many staff members, including Georgia, on the defensive.

Partnerships in Action

One afternoon I received a call from Jamie Hill, a claims adjuster working at Fyne Claim Services, a company that provided professional claims administration for self-insured corporations and government entities. My employer, Probe Information Services, had a partnership with Fyne Claims Services to investigate their suspicious and fraudulent claims, and as the vice president of the special investigations unit (SIU), I had worked with Jamie many times during the last five years. Our efforts together had resulted in 17 prosecutions for insurance fraud plus dozens of claims where early intervention prevented fraud from occurring by stopping the payment of unwarranted benefits.

Jamie was a senior examiner at Fyne in the workers' compensation (WC) unit, and her primary client was a large self-insured employer, Buzz Agency. Jamie coordinated a meeting for us with Paula Lane, the risk manager of Buzz Agency, to discuss a claim she felt was suspicious. During my conversation with Jamie, I could detect the concern and sense of urgency in her voice; therefore, I cleared my calendar, and we scheduled to meet the following day. A workers' compensation defense attorney from Fyne, Lavern Lynn, also attended the meeting.

During this initial meeting, Jamie and Paula explained that Georgia Getty, a longtime employee at Buzz, had filed a WC claim based on a carpal-tunnel injury to her hands and arms. The claim had been accepted and benefits had been administered immediately. Buzz's management was eager to provide medical treatment and help Georgia return to work.

Buzz Agency provided a robust return-to-work program for employees who were injured or faced other physical challenges, so management was prepared to provide Georgia with a modified position to accommodate her condition. Georgia received medical treatment inclusive of physical therapy, medication and a minor surgical procedure for a carpal-tunnel release on one wrist. Despite the medical treatment that her doctors noted as "successful," Georgia said she had not regained use of her hands and was unable to return to work. As a result, she continued to receive temporary disability payments while not working. In fact, she had told her doctor that her hands had become completely useless and were folded over in a shape like claws. Jamie, Paula and Lavern were all concerned that this condition, which they believed initially was a compensable injury, had veered toward a potential fraudulent situation.

Confirmed Suspicions

My 15 years of experience investigating suspicious insurance claims had provided me with the knowledge and expertise to fairly and objectively evaluate claim evidence and provide specific recommendations. I had been specializing in WC claims for eight years, including claimant, provider and premium fraud cases. The scenario presented in Georgia's claim was unfortunately very familiar to me, as I had seen an increase in abuse and theft of WC benefits with the downturn in the economy.

I reviewed the evidence in Georgia's case, including her medical records with complaints about not being able to use her hands. She told her doctor that her fingers and thumb permanently touched "like a claw" and she couldn't open her hands. However, based on her medical treatment, she should have been mostly, if not completely, recovered from her injury. Medical records indicated that she could return to work in at least a modified capacity. Her doctors observed no medical reason why Georgia had not improved, and they were confused by her worsening complaints. During this time Georgia remained off work, and she was continuing to be deemed temporarily disabled as a result of her subjective complaints. Jaime was understandably suspicious and had already been authorized to order surveillance, which had been conducted and filmed for one day.

My review of the evidence included watching the surveillance video, and I saw Georgia using her hands normally for a few hours. The video was inconsistent with her complaints, but one day of surveillance video is typically not enough to make a determination pertaining to fraud. My recommendation was that Jamie continue surveillance to determine if Georgia was able to use her hands without restrictions consistently, or if she was perhaps videotaped on a "good day" or on a day when she had taken additional pain medicine or had other treatment that allowed greater mobility. Jamie agreed with my recommendation and received authorization to continue the surveillance.

The surveillance effort resulted in hours of footage showing Georgia using her hands without any signs of restriction or limitation, over multiple days and doing various tasks. We saw her driving, texting on her mobile phone and holding her phone in her hand while she conversed for long periods of time. The footage also depicted Georgia opening and closing doors, running her fingers through her long hair and eating with utensils. She attended a concert performed by family members and danced and clapped along to the music. Georgia set up a tripod and a camera and recorded the concert.

Lying Under Oath

After the surveillance was completed, I met with the team again. We strategized the case and specifically discussed Georgia's upcoming deposition, which Lavern had arranged. I stressed the importance of asking specific and detailed questions and ensuring that Georgia provided direct responses. On the day of the deposition, Georgia entered the room with both of her hands folded over in the shape of claws, with her thumb touching her four fingers; she kept them in that position throughout deposition, which lasted several hours.

She was sworn in and testified under oath about her injury, including that her hands were always in a clawlike position, that she was unable to open them normally and that she had no use of them. When Lavern asked how much weight she could pick up, Georgia said that she could not pick up anything, not even a coffee cup. When Lavern asked if she could hold anything in her hands, she testified that she could not even hold a pencil.

Georgia said that the limitations on her hands were the sole result of her carpal-tunnel injury sustained at Buzz. She said pain medication did not help her symptoms and she never had good days because her hands were always useless. She testified that she was not able to return to work, even in a modified capacity, because she could do absolutely nothing with her hands. Georgia also explained that her youngest daughter had to help her with household chores and daily grooming activities, including bathing and brushing her hair.

Her deposition testimony was in stark contrast to the surveillance video and the medical reports. After a full analysis of all of the evidence, I concluded that Georgia had made numerous misrepresentations during her deposition and to her medical providers with regard to her physical limitations and restrictions. I further concluded that this case currently had three of the four elements of fraud.

Understanding the Elements

The four elements of fraud are: (1) misrepresentation, (2) intent, (3) knowledge and (4) materiality. The case had several egregious misrepresentations that Georgia made with full knowledge that benefits were being determined based on her statements. Further, there was a clear intent to commit fraud based on the misrepresentations she made both under oath in her deposition and to her doctors. Georgia had knowledge that she was making misrepresentations and that to do so would prolong her disability benefits. However, the case was lacking the forth element — materiality. Consequently, I determined that the next step was to present the evidence to the medical providers to determine if Georgia's misrepresentations were material to the claim and if she received benefits that she was not entitled to as a result of her lies.

I gave Georgia's medical providers the surveillance evidence and deposition transcript, and they reported that she had indeed made misrepresentations about her physical restrictions and limitations. She had been deemed disabled as a result of her subjective complaints; based on the evidence, they thought that she could have returned to work following her initial treatment. The doctors concluded that Georgia was not entitled to the disability payments she had received as a result of her material misrepresentations, thereby confirming the theft of benefits.

Georgia had filed not only for WC, but also for long-term disability benefits, and she was receiving payments from both of those claims. It appeared that Georgia was attempting to obtain a medical finding of 100 percent disabled to receive both WC benefits and permanent long-term disability benefits. The amount of theft I had computed in the WC claim was only a part of the overall benefits that she stole.

Preparing for Legal Action

As a Certified Fraud Examiner with years of focused dedication to fighting insurance fraud, I am experienced at investigating suspicious cases and determining if a case has sufficient evidence to package and present to law enforcement. My professional analysis of the evidence determined that there was enough to prove that Georgia's material misrepresentations resulted in her theft of WC and disability benefits. I packaged the case per the guidelines of the District Attorney's Insurance Fraud Division. The package included: (1) a summary of the fact pattern, (2) a timeline of events, (3) recommended criminal charges with documented corresponding evidence, (4) exhibit list and all evidence, (5) current status of the case, (6) date of discovery of the fraud and (7) a full witness list. Providing the date of the discovery of the suspected fraud was essential so the deputy district attorney (DDA) could determine if the case fell within the statute of limitations.

I delivered the fraud referral personally and discussed the case with local DDA Armando Martinez in the District Attorney's Insurance Fraud Division. We watched the surveillance video together, reviewed the deposition transcript and went over the elements of fraud. DDA Martinez accepted the case, and I called Jamie to give her the status update. Soon thereafter DDA Martinez filed criminal charges, and Georgia was arrested.

Armando charged Georgia with 12 criminal counts; two were misdemeanors and ten were felony charges. The charges included:

- Seven counts of insurance fraud
- Three counts of presenting false statement concerning payment from an insurance policy
- Two counts of attempted perjury

Georgia pleaded not guilty at the arraignment and was provided a court-appointed criminal defense attorney. DDA Martinez provided a full and complete copy of all of the evidence (including the surveillance video) to Georgia and her attorney. The date was set for the preliminary hearing, and I coordinated with Martinez to prepare my witness testimony. At the preliminary hearing a portion of the evidence was presented in court, including some of the surveillance video, excerpts from the deposition, testimony by the investigators and a portion of the medical records. The judge ruled there was sufficient evidence for the case to move forward. The case was then calendared for trial, and I expected Georgia would hope for a plea deal. Martinez did offer her reduction from the 12 counts to two counts with no jail time if Georgia would plead guilty and make restitution payments. She declined the offer, did not make a counteroffer and the case was calendared for trial.

Realities of the Courtroom

The date of the trial arrived, and the attorneys appeared at the court to learn that a courtroom was not available and that the trial date would be calendared again. We were not surprised because the criminal courts are very full and, in my experience, it is rare for an insurance fraud case to be assigned a courtroom on the first try. While I was prepared for the trial date to be bumped, I was unprepared for what happened next.

Georgia's attorney advised the judge that his client was "not fit to stand trial." He offered various reasons, including stress, anxiety and a dependence on pain medication. This situation put the burden on the prosecution to prove Georgia could stand trial, and I was not confident that the county would pay the cost for the two independent psychologists who were required to analyze Georgia, as that is an expense that the county must cover. However, I was relieved when DDA Martinez ordered the two independent evaluations. In the meantime, the case was taken off of the trial calendar and we anxiously awaited the results.

The evaluations were conducted, and both psychiatrists independently found Georgia fit to stand trial. Consequently the judge ordered that the case be put back on the calendar for criminal jury trial. After the case was bumped two more times due to overbooked courtrooms, and as the third date approached, DDA Martinez made a similar plea deal. Again Georgia declined the offer. It appeared that she wanted her day in court.

I was in disbelief the day that the jury was selected because I had always believed Georgia would eventually plead guilty. Twelve jurors and two alternates were seated, and for the next two weeks they heard evidence of a crime. Perhaps they were expecting a driving under the influence case, or a drug-related crime or maybe even a murder. I imagine they were rather surprised and maybe disappointed when they learned that the suspect had been charged with insurance fraud.

During the trial, the jury heard how workers' compensation benefits are administered, learned the details of Georgia's claim and viewed the evidence. Opening remarks by DDA Martinez explained that Georgia sustained a legitimate industrial injury and was entitled to WC benefits including medical treatment and temporary disability while she was unable to work. Martinez advised the jury that evidence would prove that Georgia abused the system and lied to medical professionals to steal temporary disability benefits from her self-insured employer. After opening remarks, the first to take the stand for the prosecution was the claims administrator, Jamie. She laid the foundation for the claim and had the task of explaining to the jury how WC claims are handled and how the benefits are administered. The next to take the stand was Paula, the risk manager from Buzz Agency. Paula explained to the jury the return-to-work program that Buzz offered and the availability of Georgia's job throughout the course of her claim. All of Georgia's medical providers involved in the claim testified that Georgia had an injury but then misrepresented her physical abilities and remained off work, receiving disability benefits to which she was not entitled. The surveillance investigators testified after the video was shown to the jury. I took the stand to provide information regarding the investigation, including the gathering of evidence, chain of custody and discovery of fraud.

During my testimony, I was questioned about the surveillance and if it was possible that the investigators might have turned off the video camera when Georgia was showing signs of pain or limitation, and only filmed her doing activities that made her appear to move normally. I testified that it was not possible because our investigators always videotape all activity and they never make determinations about what should or should not be captured on film. Doing otherwise would destroy the admissibility of evidence and our credibility.

Then the defense provided their witnesses. Georgia took the stand and testified that she had no use of her hands. She told the jury and the judge that her hands caused her severe pain constantly and that she was not able to use them to perform normal daily functions. Georgia's youngest daughter testified on behalf of her mother. The defense subpoenaed medical providers who were not involved with Georgia's claim, but who testified that she had an industrial injury that resulted in pain, loss of strength and diminished ability. These medical providers also testified that Georgia might need future medical care, including medication and therapy as a result of her injury.

DDA Martinez provided closing arguments that the evidence proved Georgia misrepresented her ability to work in order to obtain WC disability benefits to which she was not entitled, thereby stealing from Buzz Agency.

The jury deliberated for three full days and watched all of the surveillance video again in chambers. I worried that we might have a hung-jury situation, given the amount of time they were deliberating. It's not unheard of for juries to be overwhelmed by the technicalities of fraud cases and be unable to come to a conclusion. I felt nervous when the announcement finally arrived that the jury had reached a verdict, and I held my breath as the verdict was read.

The foreman of the jury announced that the jury found the defendant, Georgia Getty, guilty on all 12 counts.

The Verdict Is Only the First Step

The judge thanked the jury for their service and set a date for the sentencing hearing five weeks later. I gathered the data and provided DDA Martinez with the restitution figures and supporting evidence of the amount of theft. In addition to the benefits stolen, we were seeking the money that Buzz Agency paid for the surveillance costs and my fees since those expenses would not have been incurred in the normal course of a claim and were incurred only as a result of the fraud. The total restitution DDA Martinez wanted exceeded $60,000.

I returned to court for the sentencing and heard the defense recommend that Georgia not serve any jail time because she had no prior criminal record. He asked instead that she be sentenced to community service, probation and an order for restitution. The judge said he was unable to order community service considering that Georgia's entire defense was that she could not do anything with her hands. The judge said that because community service was inappropriate, Georgia would serve 90 days in jail. She was also ordered formal probation upon release and payment of restitution.

Georgia's attorney attempted to negotiate the terms of the sentencing, saying that the terms were predicated on Georgia's conviction of 12 counts, ten of which were felonies. Georgia's attorney made a formal request that the ten felony counts be reduced to misdemeanors, but the judge immediately denied the request on the grounds that Georgia had been given ample opportunity to negotiate a plea bargain but chose not to accept any of the offers made by the DDA. The amount of her restitution payment was the final issue to be decided.

DDA Martinez asked the judge to grant a forensic audit of Georgia's finances to determine her ability to pay restitution. He argued that Georgia could not simply be asked what she could afford based on the fact that she had just been convicted of 12 criminal counts that involved lying. The court scheduled a follow-up restitution hearing two weeks later for further discussion and consideration of restitution. The judge advised that he would take into consideration the terms of the probation and restitution amount then.

At the hearing two weeks later, the judge acknowledged that Georgia did not manufacture her entire claim because her carpal-tunnel surgery was necessary, but said she had exaggerated her symptoms after the surgery. Although Georgia did not have a prior criminal record, the judge said probation was warranted and imposed the maximum term of five years. Additionally, mandatory fines were imposed, and the judge ordered Georgia to repay the full amount of restitution that DDA Martinez asked for. To conclude the case, Georgia was ordered to surrender into custody to serve her 90-day sentence.

Lessons Learned

Jamie and Paula were able to successfully identify Georgia's suspicious behavior and report their concerns quickly to me, their fraud consultant. Specialists in the insurance industry should be able to contact a fraud specialist as soon as they have suspicions; this is critical to halting unwarranted payments quickly, securing evidence and obtaining a positive outcome, including prosecution when a crime has been committed.

Successfully fighting fraud is a team effort. In this case, a claims adjuster, risk manager, defense attorney and fraud specialist played essential roles in the effective fraud-fighting team. We learned the importance of communicating effectively and regularly to discuss and strategize the case to ensure we maintained a cohesive plan of action. I have observed many times in my career as an anti-fraud professional that emotions can sometimes dictate decisions instead of a carefully considered plan. In cases similar to this one, I have seen employers become angry when they see evidence of an employee stealing from them, and they react to that emotion, sometimes by immediately terminating the employee. I have also had many experiences wherein insurance industry professionals who do not specialize in fraud believed that surveillance footage was sufficient evidence to prove fraud. Those cases were not developed to prove fraud beyond a reasonable doubt, and insurers were later disappointed that law enforcement could not file criminal charges. Many industry experts who are experienced in insurance or risk management might not understand the elements of fraud and how to gather evidence sufficiently for law enforcement. To prove the crime of insurance fraud, four elements are needed:

1. **M**ateriality
2. **I**ntent
3. **L**ie (misrepresentation)
4. **K**nowledge

These four elements are easy to remember if you think of the acronym MILK. Each element is required for a district attorney to prove insurance fraud beyond a reasonable doubt. An experienced fraud investigator who specializes in insurance fraud can direct the investigation, ensure evidence is gathered legally and ethically and then determine if the case warrants law enforcement involvement.

Recommendations to Prevent Future Occurrences

To successfully combat insurance fraud, a knowledgeable fraud-fighting team is needed. Risk managers, executives at self-insured companies, insurance defense attorneys and other members of the insurance industry should partner with a fraud specialist or SIU that is proactive, understands the fraud laws and regulations and has positive relationships with law enforcement in order to successfully prosecute insurance fraud. This partnership should provide resources, experience and cost-effective solutions to identify problematic claims early and help prevent insurance abuse, stop unwarranted benefits and coordinate the prosecution of insurance fraud when a crime occurs.

Regular anti-fraud training for members of an insurance claims team is a critical tool in preventing future fraud. My employer's SIU provides customized training to its strategic partners to educate the claims teams and managers

(Continued)

about red flags to look for, innovative tools to stop abuse, pitfalls to avoid and updates on fraud trends. We are a resource for our clients, providing consultation, discussion about cases and strategizing when needed.

Insurance fraud costs all of us through increased insurance premiums and higher costs charged by employers for goods and services. The National Insurance Crime Bureau (NICB) reports that insurance fraud is the second costliest white-collar crime after tax evasion. The NICB also estimates that one-third of injuries are exaggerated. We should focus on building strong fraud-fighting teams and creating strategies to proactively combat this fraud that affects us all.

About the Author

Dalene Bartholomew is a Certified Fraud Examiner, Certified Insurance Fraud Investigator and vice president of the SIU at Probe Information Services, Inc. (www.probeinfo.com). She began directing Probe's highly successful, compliant, innovative and award-winning insurance fraud team in 2004. Ms. Bartholomew is a recognized speaker, anti-fraud trainer, author and insurance fraud consultant.

Getting Rich from the Elderly

JOHN R. HOLLEY

Betty Lincoln (maiden name Thomas) was born in and raised in a small town in Montana. She was the only child of parents who were deeply conservative and moderately religious. Betty's parents were successful business owners, and Betty was accustomed to having everything she wanted. She took several minimum-wage jobs while in high school for spending money.

After high school, Betty attended a local college and majored in marketing. Just prior to her graduation, she attended a sorority party and met a boy named Bob Lincoln. Bob was a recent college dropout whose only dream was to be a long-haul truck driver, and he was about to begin with a big oil company's truck driver training program.

Bob and Betty started dating and a courtship soon developed. They married six months later. After having completed his training, Bob learned that there were plenty of jobs for a truck driver in Alaska. Moving north, he and Betty settled in Wasilla. Bob got a job hauling freight for the oil companies. His pay was good, but Betty soon realized she could not have the lifestyle she craved on his income alone.

Betty took a job as an insurance agent in a local agency where she specialized in handling annuities. The commission was adequate, but she saw the owner of the agency making large amounts of money from her work. Betty longed to keep that additional money and dreamed of what she would do with it. She was looking for different ways to get rich quickly, and Betty decided her best option was to open her own agency. She did research to discover which insurance products paid the highest commissions.

During this time, both of Betty's parents became ill and had to be placed in long-term-care facilities. Betty took over their finances, paying their expenses. Her parents had their money conservatively invested in the stock market and in savings. While talking to several of her parents' friends, Betty learned they had similar financial portfolios. Betty saw her opportunity.

In her research, Betty saw variable indexed annuities as her ticket to wealth. She used her marketing knowledge to develop a plan directed at the elderly. Betty held seminars at the various senior centers on financial planning, promising free food and drinks for those who attended. She bought the names of potential clients from a company on the Internet. She mailed invitations to those on her list and paid local kids to distribute flyers on cars parked at local senior centers.

Betty's seminars were packed. She began by telling those in attendance about the dangers of investing with untrustworthy stockbrokers and highlighted the recent negative media coverage of the stock markets' fiascos. Betty explained her discovery of a surefire way to make money. It had a rate of return of more than 40 percent, and the money would always be available. She was careful not to mention the word *insurance* or any penalties incurred for early withdrawal.

In the weeks after a seminar, Betty would meet individually with those interested in her financial plan. Prior to a meeting, Betty would find out personal information on the potential client. She would ensure that the person's favorite foods or flowers were in the conference room. On one occasion Betty noticed an individual's volunteer service with a pet shelter, so she went so far as to place a box of puppies in the corner of the room and she told the woman she was trying to find them good homes. That client signed on with Betty immediately.

Betty was successful in persuading people to liquidate their portfolios and transfer the funds to an annuity through her underwriter, Continental Annuity. She was careful not to let her clients read the paperwork they were signing and told them that they could trust her help and judgment.

Betty started by holding one or two seminars a month. Her client base grew so quickly that she needed to conduct only one seminar every three months to attract new clients. In nine months her client list went from zero to more than 300. Her newfound wealth gave her the means to obtain the things she wanted.

Betty was now able to hire an employee as well as the services of a private investigator to perform background checks on her prospective clients. She was able to better screen them and go after the ones with the highest net worth.

The Promises of the Plan

Linda Jones had just retired from a lifelong career as a teacher. Linda had the natural authority and outspokenness common to teachers, and she lived a modest lifestyle since the accidental death of her husband and daughter some years earlier. She had her retirement money in a 401k that was making modest gains. She was looking forward to retirement and was trying to stretch her dollars.

One day Linda received an invitation to a seminar on that very subject. The invitation stated that the event was free, that food and drinks would be provided and that there was no commitment required. The only requirement was an RSVP; Linda immediately signed up.

At the jam-packed seminar, Linda was mesmerized by the speaker, Betty Lincoln. Betty reminded Linda of her own late daughter. Betty seemed to be speaking directly to her when she spoke of the dangers of dealing with stockbrokers and the normal types of investing. Betty spoke of a method, which she referred to as "the plan," that promised a return of 40 percent. This caught Lisa's attention immediately, and she wanted to learn more.

Linda contacted Betty after the seminar and arranged to meet with her privately a few days later. Before their meeting, Betty had Linda thoroughly researched and learned, in addition to Linda's favorite flowers and foods, that Linda's late daughter was of the same age and build as Betty. She was able to locate a picture of the daughter and had her hair styled to match, along with getting some identical glasses. Betty was able to tell from the private investigator's report that Linda had a rather sizable portfolio. Betty was ready for her meeting with Linda.

Linda met with Betty in Betty's office. Linda was impressed with the antique furniture in the room and the fact that some of her favorite flowers, tulips, were present in the room along with blueberry muffins. The smell of the tulips along with fragrance of the warm muffins was exquisite. Linda was astounded at the resemblance between Betty and her late daughter. Linda felt at ease and sensed that she could trust Betty's advice.

After reviewing Linda's present financial portfolio, Betty told Linda that she would be in broke in five years if she did not do something to change her future. Betty said if she changed over to "the plan," she would be set for life financially. When Linda asked Betty about whether she would have access to the money if needed, Betty told her that she would have complete and total access at any time. Linda was sold. Betty produced a stack of documents and told Linda that if she really trusted and believed in the plan, there was no need for her to read them. Linda signed immediately.

Things went well for several months. With Betty's help, Linda was able to work out an adequate budget that met all of her day-to-day needs. Betty had arranged for a monthly withdrawal from the plan to cover those needs. Betty would call Linda weekly just to chat about things and occasionally sent her little cards. Linda was happy with her decision to go with the plan.

Then one day Linda started feeling ill so she went to her doctor. The doctor was concerned and, after some additional tests, he confirmed the worst — Linda had developed abdominal cancer. The disease had been caught early, and Linda's prognosis was good but the treatment would be expensive. Linda, though upset about the disease, knew that she could rest assured that she had the money in "the plan" to fall back on.

A Different Side of Betty Comes Out

After getting home from the doctor's office, Linda pulled out the sealed envelope containing the paperwork she had gotten from Betty. She was surprised to learn that what she thought of as "the plan" was actually an indexed variable annuity and that there was mention of a 30 percent penalty for early or additional withdrawals. Linda was able to determine that Continental Annuity was the company identified as holding her money.

Linda immediately phoned Betty about what she learned. Betty told Linda that it was a misunderstanding and hung up. Linda tried to call back but was told by the receptionist that Betty was busy. Linda even went by Betty's office several times but was unable to meet with her. Linda contacted Continental Annuity and, after finally reaching a sympathetic ear, filed a complaint about Betty. The agent at Continental assured her that they would look into it.

About this same time Bob Davis, who was a mild-mannered, recently retired carpenter, attended a seminar at his local senior center because of the promise of free food and the chance to get out of the house. He had been a recluse since the death of his wife several months before and needed the company of other people. The speaker, a young woman named Betty Lincoln, spoke of the untrustworthy practices of stock brokers, and he was very alarmed when she mentioned the name of the stock brokerage that he used.

After the seminar he arranged for a one-on-one meeting with Betty. He was surprised by the clothes she was wearing; Betty looked just like his late wife looked when she was younger. There was a box of his favorite cigars, and Betty even offered him one of his favorite beers. Betty reviewed Bob's portfolio and advised him of the lifestyle he could have after he had changed over to "the plan." Bob was tempted but told Betty he had to think on it first. Betty tried repeatedly to persuade him to change his mind, but Bob refused to be pressured.

After the meeting, Bob went to see his stockbroker and longtime friend Bill Harris to tell him what Betty had said. Bill had never seen Bob so irate before. Bill was able to put Bob's mind at ease about the safety of his money, but over the next several days, he was contacted by no fewer than eight other clients who told him the same thing about Betty; three of them withdrew all their funds from Bill's brokerage.

Bill decided to do some investigating of his own. He managed to get an invitation to one of Betty's seminars and was appalled by what he heard. He realized that what Betty was saying was not true and that something needed to be done about her. He filed a complaint with the State Division of Securities about Betty.

The Complaints Keep Coming

I was born and raised in the Bible Belt of the deep South. Due to my strict upbringing, I developed a black-and-white view of things that has helped me during my 20-plus years in law enforcement. After a messy divorce, I moved to Alaska, where, with a new family, I have settled. I went to work as an investigator with the State Division of Insurance and have handled various types of complaints.

After intensive studying, I was able to obtain the credentials of a Certified Fraud Examiner. I have been able to apply the knowledge I learned in the successful solving of my investigations.

A complaint was filed with the division by Continental Annuity concerning their insurance agent Betty Lincoln. In the complaint, Continental alleged that Betty had been less than truthful with her clients during the presentation and sale of the product involved, variable indexed securities, and had used unauthorized sales materials. Continental advised that it had refunded the insured, Linda Jones, the funds in her entire annuity, had not paid Betty any additional commission on the sale of the product to Linda and had warned Betty that she would be dismissed if such behavior continued.

The next day I got a phone call from a friend a who was an investigator with the State Division of Securities asking if I had heard about an insurance agent named Betty Lincoln. After I told him yes, he told me about the facts concerning the complaint filed by Bill Harris concerning Betty's seminar presentation. It seemed that the date of that seminar was after the date that Betty had been warned by Continental. I told him to forward me a copy of the complaint, and I, with my director's blessing, launched an investigation into the matter.

I was able to determine that Betty Lincoln was indeed licensed to sell insurance in the state. She was not, however, licensed to sell securities or offer financial advice.

My research into variable indexed annuities revealed that they can produce a high rate of return, but they may not be suitable for everyone. This type of annuity has an average term of about 20 years, often has high penalties for unscheduled withdrawals and is based on the performance of various stock markets. According to state insurance regulations, an agent has to tell clients that they are in fact buying an insurance product. Based on this information, I set off to find out what Betty was really up to.

I interviewed Linda Jones about her dealings with Betty. It was easy for me tell that her health was failing fast. It was also easy to tell that she had become distrustful of everyone, including those who wanted to help her. Linda told me how she had received Betty's invitation in the mail and about attending the seminar. She told me how the meeting with Betty had been, about the antiques, flowers, muffins and how Betty had reminded her of her daughter. Linda told me that Betty never mentioned the word *insurance* or that any withdrawal penalties were involved. Linda told me that she would never trust anyone again. I felt sorry for Linda and realized how devastating Betty's actions were; they caused far more than financial damage.

I interviewed Bill Harris next, and he told me about his conversation with Bob Davis after he had attended one of Betty's seminars. Bill gave me a copy of the invitation he had received along with a copy of the materials that had been distributed at the seminar. I reviewed the materials; there was no mention of insurance or penalties associated with "the plan." The seminar materials did describe all stockbrokers as being untrustworthy and listed the rate of return for "the plan" as 40 percent.

I interviewed Bob Davis, who told me of his dealings with Betty Lincoln and what she told him about "the plan." Bob confessed to me that he had secretly, without Bill's knowledge, cashed in one of his stock portfolios and given the money to Betty to invest in "the plan." When asked why, he said he trusted her because she reminded him so much of his late wife. Bob said that Betty never described "the plan" as being insurance nor did she inform him of any penalties for early withdrawal.

I requested and reviewed documentation from Continental for all policies sold by Betty Lincoln. Of those 300-plus policies, I discovered that there were only two in which the policyholders were below the age of 55. I discovered that in one instance an 85-year-old gentleman was sold a $500,000, 20-year annuity that technically locked up his money for that time period.

While I reviewed the policies, I was able to determine that the vast majority of the policyholders — 85 percent — were either widows or widowers at the time their policies were issued. I also noticed that, other than the signatures, each of the policy applications bore the same handwriting. I did a comparison to the known handwriting of Betty Lincoln, and each of the 300 applications appeared to have been completed by her. I randomly selected 15 other policyholders to interview.

I conducted those interviews and heard similar stories about how they had attended Betty's seminars and then set up private meetings with her. They all told me about how surprised they were that Betty shared their tastes in foods, flowers and hobbies. Each interviewee told me how he or she only signed on the dotted line and left the other stuff for Betty to complete. Her clients said they trusted Betty and were shocked when I told them that they had purchased an insurance product; they each told me that was not their intention and that they would not have done so if they had known. They told me they felt as if they had been violated by Betty.

I interviewed Betty Lincoln about the complaints filed against her. Betty, who was 30 minutes late for the interview, acted shocked that anyone would file a complaint. She denied any wrongdoing and of ever being warned about her behavior by Continental. Betty also denied having completed policy applications on behalf of her customers after the fact and said that she had never heard of "the plan." I had the strong suspicion that Betty was trying to manipulate me during the interview: She cried in disbelief about the "hurtful" allegations made by people she was genuinely trying to help.

When that did not work, she stopped on a dime and tried to befriend me by talking about sports. At one point she offered to get me hockey tickets. I realized she had had her private detective investigate me. When I refused her ploys, she became defensive and ceased to answer my questions.

Unwelcome Visitors

The next afternoon I received a phone call from Lindsay Mason, who claimed that she was a current employee of Betty's. Lindsay told me how she had been hired by Betty to perform the background checks and even surveillance of prospective clients. Lindsay told me that Betty would use the information to gain the clients' trust. She told me that after Betty had returned to her office from the interview with me the previous day, Betty was mad and had ordered her to destroy all the background and surveillance reports. Betty also shredded all the seminar materials in the office. Lindsay told me that she did not feel right doing so at the time. After thinking about it all night, she decided to contact me. Lindsay supplied me with copies of some of the background and surveillance reports that she had managed to keep. One of those files was that of Linda Jones.

I reviewed the findings of my investigation with Brenda Thompson, the director of the Division of Insurance. She decided to have a business audit conducted by division employees Frank McDonald and Leroy Spiegel to look into the actions of Betty and her agency. She told me to take them to Betty's office to meet her.

A few days later Frank, Leroy and I went to Betty's office, where I introduced them to her. Frank and Leroy told Betty that their exam would include random interviews of clients, employees and a review of the client files. Betty said she would cooperate, and I left Frank and Leroy to perform their duties.

During their interviews of two clients, Frank and Leroy were verbally assaulted and accused of messing up their investments. One of them threatened to kill Frank and Leroy. The Division of Insurance employees told Betty what had happened and asked her to help calm the clients down, but she refused and said she did not blame her clients for being upset. Betty told Frank and Leroy to get out of her office and not come back.

Frank and Leroy were shocked by Betty's response. Instead of reporting her actions immediately, they decided to wait to see if she calmed down. Betty did not and refused to let them continue their exam.

The Plan Fails

From my investigation, I was able to determine that Betty Lincoln had indeed violated several sections of the state insurance code. The following events happened as result of my investigation.

1. No criminal charges were filed against Betty Lincoln.
2. The Division of Insurance filed administrative charges against Betty for her behavior. Betty agreed to a voluntary permanent surrender of her insurance license.
3. Continental Annuity reimbursed all the policyholders whom Betty had taken advantage of. Continental also forced Betty to repay all the commissions she had made on those polices.
4. The Division of Securities filed an administrative action against Betty for unlicensed activity, which resulted in her being levied with a large fine. Betty did not fight the action.
5. Betty closed her business and left the state. She and her husband got a divorce.
6. Frank and Leroy suffered internal disciplinary actions for their failure to immediately report Betty's change in behavior.
7. Frank later left his employment with the division because of the way he was treated by Betty and her clients.

Lessons Learned

I always try to take away new lessons from every case I investigate. Betty's fraud was an eye-opener for me because I had never had a case involving annuity products. I learned how these products work with the markets and the wide range of annuities that are available. I also gained a new appreciation for the importance of proper and thorough record keeping; Betty had hundreds of clients, and keeping track of all the records was essential to the investigation.

On a more personal level, I learned the importance of immediately reporting any significant change in behavior by a suspect or witness to my supervisor — I didn't want to undergo the same disciplinary actions that Frank and Leroy endured. And as a consumer, I have a new appreciation for the need to conduct due diligence before making any investment. One day I'll be a retiree, and I would hate to fall victim to the predatory actions of someone like Betty.

Recommendations to Prevent Further Occurrences

Betty's fraudulent practices are all too common. She recognized a weakness in elderly investors and had no qualms about exploiting it for personal gain. Her behavior was despicable, but there are plenty of people who lack the basic moral compass that directs most of us. To avoid falling prey to these "advisors," I recommend that everyone conduct thorough research into all investments before committing to them. Talk to friends and family about your plans, and carefully read any paperwork before signing it. It is also a good idea to diversify your portfolio to reduce risk.

About the Author

John R. Holley is an investigator with the State of Alaska, Division of Insurance. In addition to being a Certified Fraud Examiner, he has more than 20 years of law enforcement experience, having successfully conducted investigations involving insurance fraud, financial elder abuse, forgery, embezzlement, theft, robbery and homicide.

CHAPTER 18

Transparent Greed

JOSEPH LICANDRO

Behind every company contaminated with fraud usually lies a group of perpetrators willing to risk jail and the company's long-term sustainability for personal greed. Glass Star, the most popular glass replacement store in the northwest region of the state, with more than 20 branches, was no different. What made Glass Star's fraud unique was not that contamination occurred but that two independent actors committing the same type of fraud prospered simultaneously while upper-level management looked the other way the entire time.

Sure, greed was a strong motivation for Casey Thomas and Chet Sterling, but that was not their only motivation. For Casey, who came from one of the two families that founded Glass Star's nearly three-quarters of a century ago, fraud was about exerting control and implementing his vision — remaking the company from a local brand to a state powerhouse. For lone-wolf Chet Sterling, who married into the company almost 15 years before and was handed the job as manager of the Broad Street store, fraud was more personal. Chet was a taciturn, socially awkward individual with few friends, and he never bothered to make any at Broad Street. Sure, Chet enjoyed the bonuses he earned from his inflated insurance bills. But to him, fraud was also about demonstrating to all of his doubters and detractors that he could run the most profitable store in the company.

Casey Thomas steadily rose through the ranks of his family's glass company during his nearly two decades of employment. Although he knew from a very young age that he would always have a job waiting for him at Glass Star, it was not a foregone conclusion that he would attain the title of vice president and become one of the most powerful men in the company. Casey had to earn that role. He was not a terribly imposing figure, standing a head shorter than most of the other men in the company. But for whatever Casey lacked in stature, he made up for in charisma, hard work and self-confidence.

After a five-minute encounter, a stranger could tell that Casey suffered from a Napoleonic complex, and although this probably sparked his inner drive, it also fueled an arrogance that attracted him to fraud. A results-oriented number cruncher to his core, Casey strived for a way to cut corners and maximize profits.

Beginning at the company as an entry-level customer service representative (CSR), Casey steadily ascended the corporate ladder, working in all three divisions of Glass Star — branch stores, corporate management and warehouse and inventory. Glass Star's president, Jack Gulley, called upon Casey to turn around the 19th Street store by naming him head of the store, but it was not the ideal place for a first-time manager. It used to be one of Glass Star's most profitable locations, but it had fallen on hard times when its customer base plummeted due to a deteriorating surrounding neighborhood.

Business as Usual

Casey did not introduce fraud to Glass Star. Fraudulent billing of one kind or another against customers and insurance companies had occurred sporadically at a few other branches. For years, other store managers had suspected Chet in particular of fraudulent billing because his profits consistently surpassed every other branch's, yet his sales were in the middle of the pack. There was no other way to explain it. No one knew precisely how Chet was making so much money, and no one from corporate management cared to ask.

After only a few months as manager, Casey realized that the 19th Street store did not have the client base to compete against Chet's Broad Street location. However, Glass Star used an electronic billing system to submit insurance claims through a third-party vendor. The insurance companies had no oversight in the process, and the opportunity to fudge the numbers was ever present. Casey suspected that Chet was taking advantage of this opportunity by submitting invoices to the third-party billers indicating that his technicians installed dealership glass in cars when in fact less expensive, aftermarket glass was installed. Casey decided to test his theory a few times over the course of two months.

He was careful to use the login number of his assistant manager, Frank Washington, when submitting improperly coded bills. As he predicted, nobody from the insurance company noticed or asked about it. After all, Glass Star was not required to submit supporting documentation showing the type of glass that was actually installed in the automobile. Casey had figured out how Chet was making so much money without ever having to ask him.

Imitation Is the Highest Form of Flattery

Casey decided that Chet was on to something good, and he wanted to exploit it as well. Casey instructed his store employees to bill this way going forward, knowing that they would not refuse. Frank Washington was perpetually late for work and battled personal demons, which kept his employment in perpetual jeopardy, and Casey took full advantage of it. Most of the CSRs were impressionable young women who were not going risk their jobs by standing up to Casey, a member of the founding family.

Not surprisingly, Casey turned around the profitability of 19th Street in only few months, falling behind only Chet and his incomparable Broad Street store. This dramatic turnaround helped Casey earn the promotion to Glass Star's vice president. With Jack Gulley essentially acting as a detached figurehead, Casey had attained unrivaled control of the daily operations. With this newfound power, he wanted to expand Glass Star, and that meant recruiting outsiders and conspiring with others whom he trusted to carry out his dirty work.

Glass Star's Evolution

Glass Star had been one of the most recognizable independent companies in the river city for more than 80 years. Portraying itself as the consummate workingman's company rooted in the traditional family values of hard work and integrity, Glass Star had grown from a single neighborhood store into the most successful glass replacement company in the northeast region of the state. With more than 20 locations and new stores cropping up outside of its geographic base, Glass Star had strategically positioned itself for sustained economic growth and success. It was a full-service glass company providing auto, residential and commercial glass, but auto glass was the company's proverbial bread and butter. Regarding this aspect of its business, management prided itself on being able to offer customers a choice between aftermarket glass and dealership glass.

To know why fraud pervaded Glass Star, it is important to understand this particular time in the company's history. Glass Star was in transition from the old guard who built the company into a city-wide chain to the new guard beholden to loftier sales goals set by corporate management. Some members of the old guard had worked at Glass Star for more than 30 years. Beginning their long careers as entry-level technicians straight out of high school, many moved up to store managers and enjoyed considerable autonomy.

With the increased use of credit cards, computers and the Internet and with the growth of the insurance and automobile industries, the old guard witnessed dramatic changes in the way the company conducted business. Long gone were the days when billing a customer's car insurance company for replacement glass was conducted with a phone call and a handwritten invoice in the mail. Now virtually all glass replacement bills were submitted by a click of a mouse. The bills were not sent directly to the insurance company because Glass Star's management had begun employing third-party billing companies to save costs . . . or so they thought.

With members of the old guard starting to retire, the new guard started to take over management positions. As my investigation would reveal, there seemed to be unspoken tension between the old and new guard. While members of the old guard had put in their time to earn their leadership roles, some of the younger employees were thrust into lucrative management positions with sometimes less than a year on the job. Casey handpicked many of the new managers, not necessarily for their acumen or talent but because he believed they would be loyal to his cutthroat, profit-maximizing vision for the company. In exchange for their lucrative compensation, Casey demanded that they meet his profit expectations.

Although he was aware of the laws in place prohibiting insurance fraud and the severe penalties for breaking them, Casey regarded the law not as a roadblock but as a mere stop sign to roll through. When he was managing the 19th Street store, corporate leadership took a "hear no evil, see no evil" approach and turned a blind eye to the billing practices of both Chet and Casey. Now Casey was part of corporate management whose primary responsibility was to supervise the store managers. There was no one else in the company to stop him.

The New Guard in Full Swing

Tyler Burns and Kyle Lawson were two store managers whom Casey held to high expectations. Tyler and Casey had been known each other since high school, and when Glass Star needed to hire more glass technicians, Casey recruited Tyler from a rival store by offering him a significant pay increase. A few weeks after Casey became vice president, the midtown store's manager retired and Tyler was promoted to fill the opening — after less than two years as a glass technician. Unlike most members of the old guard who climbed the company ladder, Tyler did not have to put in any time as a CSR or as an assistant manager. Casey explained to Tyler that the midtown store made average profits and attributed the mediocre performance to the previous manager's antiquated ways and unfamiliarity with computers. With Tyler at the helm, Casey expected the store to become a profit powerhouse like Chet's store.

During Tyler's first few months in charge of the midtown store, its profits dipped below those his predecessor achieved during his last few months — a fact that that Casey pointed out to Tyler on multiple occasions. For the life of him, Tyler could not understand how Chet had been so successful. Initially, Tyler thought he and his CSRs were simply bad salespeople who could not convince customers to buy dealership glass. Despite his best efforts, Tyler had not been able to turn his numbers around after six months on the job.

Late one Friday afternoon, Casey visited the midtown store to deliver Tyler's quarterly status report, and he took Tyler to the office and closed the door. He explained to Tyler that if his numbers did not turn around, Tyler would not be a store manager much longer. When Casey again explained that Tyler needed to be more like Chet, Tyler asked, "What does Chet do? I can't figure it out." Casey had hoped to insulate himself by letting Tyler figure out the billing scheme on his own, but clearly that hadn't happened.

Casey then used Tyler's computer password to log into the billing system and showed Tyler how easy it was submit bills for dealership glass when aftermarket glass had been installed. The next Monday, Tyler showed his CSRs this "new way to bill." A few months later, Tyler had turned around the store's profits, exceeding company expectations and earning a nice quarterly bonus.

Casey met Kyle Lawson at a bar when the two struck up a conversation about golf and fishing, and they quickly became regular drinking buddies. Kyle was almost 20 years younger than Casey and had been working odd construction jobs since failing out of college. One day Casey offered Kyle the opportunity to manage a new store that Glass Star was opening in Magnolia Park. Before the store opened, Casey arranged for Kyle to visit Chet's store and learn how to bill. Chet was a subtle trainer, but Kyle was observant. When Magnolia Park opened, it did not take long for him to implement Chet and Casey's preferred billing procedures.

A Holdout from the Old Guard

Jimmy Hopkins prided himself on running his Princeton Street stores the right way. After serving ten years in the Navy, Jimmy started his own glass repair store in the Crestwood area of town. A few years later, Glass Star's former president Buck Thomas (Casey's uncle) offered to buy out Jimmy's store, pay him a healthy salary and make him the manager of the company's new Crestwood location. Although Jimmy enjoyed being his own boss, the financial opportunity was too great; plus, Glass Star had an outstanding reputation at that time.

Jimmy's nearly 30 years at Glass Star were successful and enjoyable. The Crestview location performed well financially, and his customer satisfaction rating was always near the top. However, the last few years had been tough on him. Ever since Casey took the reins as vice president, he had been after Jimmy to improve his store's statistics. Jimmy also did not care for the way Casey pitted the store managers against one another. Casey created an incentive mechanism, dubbed the "Profit Game," in which managers had to compete with each other for best store profits. Casey sent a company-wide email with the results of each manager's periodic profits to shame low-performing stores and reward the high performers.

Casey also set profit goals for each manager. While Jimmy did not find anything inherently wrong with the concept of profit goals, he thought Casey's goals were unrealistic. Moreover, Casey was not shy about letting a manager know if he failed to meet his expectations. Worst of all, Casey had no qualms about embarrassing low performers in front of all the other managers at their quarterly meetings.

Hanging on the wall inside Jimmy's office was a poster with bold letters detailing the criminal penalties for committing fraud. One day when Jimmy was out to lunch, Casey visited his store and showed a CSR named Tammy how the store could make more money by "altering" third-party bills. Casey told her that billing this way would improve the store's standing in the Profit Game. When Tammy told Jimmy about the plan, he pointed to the sign in his office and reminded her that insurance fraud was a crime. He warned her that if he caught her committing billing fraud, he would fire her on the spot.

Although Jimmy was not privy to Casey's conversation with Tammy, he had no reason to disbelieve her, especially when another CSR corroborated her account, so Jimmy decided to conduct an investigation. Two years earlier, Glass Star had switched to a company-wide network system, and it was now possible to pull a warehouse order and the matching invoice submitted to the third-party biller for any particular installation. Jimmy had long heard the rumors about Chet, Tyler, and Kyle, so he decided to start with them. Over the next few weeks, Jimmy meticulously reviewed the billing records from the three managers' stores. While Jimmy was not surprised that they were committing fraud, he was shocked by its volume. Jimmy also suspected that the scheme stretched beyond the previous two years, but those were the only numbers he could access on the network. Earlier records were kept at corporate headquarters.

Jimmy called the state insurance fraud hotline to report his findings and received a call back from Detective Patrick. They set up a meeting, and Jimmy laid out his findings. His motivations were clear and pure: Jimmy respected the hell out of Buck Thomas and the rest of the old guard who built the company into a trusted brand, but most of these people had retired. Jimmy did not like the direction Glass Star had been moving in since Buck had passed the torch. It was one thing for Casey to needle him about profit numbers, but it was another for Casey to instruct Jimmy's direct employees to commit billing fraud.

After Detective Patrick met with Jimmy, he tipped off the victim insurance companies. He also subpoenaed relevant records from the third-party billing company going back a decade. These records corroborated the information Jimmy had provided covering the previous two years.

To support his analytical research, Detective Patrick visited some random Glass Star customers from the previous two years whose warehouse records did not match their billing records to see what windshields they had installed. Dealership windshields can easily be spotted by the manufacturer's insignia printed on the windshield; aftermarket windshields do not contain an insignia. As Patrick expected, all of the windshields he examined were aftermarket. He photographed the windshields to preserve them as evidence and then drafted his case report and brought it to my desk.

Brand New to the Job

I was a young prosecutor who had been promoted to the economic crimes unit from the burglary unit less than a week before, so when Detective Patrick presented me with his report, I was a little nervous. I had never prosecuted a case where the defendants committed a crime in a corporate setting for the direct benefit of their employer — not that these defendants did not have their own selfish motives. The voluminous amounts of bills and computer records did not make the task seem any easier.

My two primary tasks became readily apparent to me when Detective Patrick placed his initial case report on my desk: I needed to build a successful prosecution against Casey and ascertain accurate restitution figures. Regarding the first challenge, Casey had successfully distanced himself from the fraud, and not one single fraudulent bill was issued using his unique computer login. While all of the Glass Star employees who submitted fraudulent bills deserved to answer for their crimes, the ultimate success of the prosecution hinged on whether we could hold Casey accountable for his actions. To do that would require Tyler, Chet, Kyle, Frank and lower-level CSRs to cooperate with the investigation and point the finger at Casey. Of course, I had no guarantee anyone would cooperate. When the president learned his company was under investigation, he initially suspended the employees identified as fraudulent billers. It was doubtful that they would roll on Casey with their jobs hanging in the balance.

To ascertain the restitution figures, I needed to review Glass Star's inventory warehouse order forms and match them to each bill the company submitted to the insurer. Subpoenas to Glass Star were not going to suffice because I doubted the leadership team would cooperate, and I could not know if they provided the complete set of records. When Detective Patrick reached out to Glass Star's attorneys requesting additional records, he was met with stiff resistance. The attorneys assured him that Glass Star's internal investigation had uncovered the full amount of the fraud, which allegedly dated back only two years. Detective Patrick also had very little luck setting up interviews with employees.

Meanwhile, as Detective Patrick and I launched our investigation, several of the victim insurance companies began seeking compensation from Glass Star for the overbillings. Jack Gulley and his attorneys tried to placate them by insisting the fraud was isolated and unknown to the corporate management. Gulley then cut a check to each company covering the fraud and contractual penalties.

Jack Gulley's claim that the fraud went back two years — whether he believed it or not — was inaccurate. Jimmy sent Patrick and me a company-wide email that Casey sent from over three years before, describing an investigation into a similar fraud at a different local business. The email did not instruct employees to refrain from such practices but warned them that "we do not want to bring a similar situation onto Glass Star." Essentially, Casey was telling employees that they could engage in fraud provided they did not get caught.

Detective Patrick arranged an interview with Glass Star's former marketing director, Bill Jones, and it proved to be quite revealing. Jones had left the company about a year before Jimmy blew the whistle. When Patrick advised Bill that fraudulent billing had been occurring at Glass Star over the past two years, Bill said that he was surprised because he thought Gulley and Casey had stopped the problem three years ago when Casey sent out the email. At a minimum, Jones' statement revealed that some members of corporate management had knowledge of fraudulent billing occurring prior than the past two years.

Patrick then procured a search warrant for Glass Star's email and billing records. As we hoped, Glass Star's management was caught off guard when the search warrant took place, and they had no time to destroy records. The records yielded from the search confirmed our suspicions that the fraudulent billing had been occurring at the company for almost a decade. The warrant also generated negative media attention. Although we will never know for certain, the negative publicity seemed to force Gulley's hand. Within a few weeks of our search, Glass Works officially cut ties with all the employees linked to the fraudulent billing, with one glaring exception — Casey Thomas.

Gathering Witnesses

The records had identified Frank Washington as a prolific fraudulent biller — clear proof that someone working directly under Casey's was involved in the scheme. Frank had been dismissed a year before for consistent tardiness and other problems. While Patrick and I eagerly anticipated interviewing Frank, we also needed more witnesses to come forward against Casey. Favorable testimony from Frank alone would not be enough to build a strong case. Casey could portray Frank as a vengeful former employee whom defense attorneys would accuse of operating out of pure spite. Frank's testimony combined with that of other codefendants would be more credible.

Initially, I issued arrest warrants for Chet, Tyler, Kyle, and the CSRs whose computer identification numbers appeared on the fraudulent bills but held off on issuing a warrant for Casey; I wanted to lock down the cooperation of my witnesses first. One by one, each former employee agreed to cooperate and testify against Casey because the threat of significant jail sentences weighed heavily on their minds. All of these defendants, particularly Tyler and Kyle, provided credible and damning testimony against Casey. To one degree or another, they testified that Casey either directed them to fraudulently bill or made statements showing his approval of the fraudulent billing Chet initiated. Interestingly, Chet told us that he originally learned his billing "technique" at a professional seminar for auto-glass repair companies.

None of our witnesses had evidence that Gulley or other members of corporate management actively encouraged the fraud. Although Detective Patrick and I strongly believed that Gulley knew, neither his willful blindness nor negligent supervision could serve as grounds for fraud charges under state law. The fact that we did not file charges against Gulley might have actually strengthened our case against Casey, as he could not claim the prosecution was overreaching or vindictive.

After Casey's attorneys exhausted all of their legal maneuvers, Casey pleaded guilty to fraud charges and is now a convicted felon. The judge sentenced Casey to house arrest, probation, community service, repaying costs of investigation and heavy fines to the state. Casey's prosecution also spurred Glass Star to repay nearly $1 million in restitution to the victims dating back almost a decade when Chet first brought fraud into the company. Jack Gulley later suspended Casey's employment. The other defendants received lesser sentences based on their cooperation.

Lessons Learned

Given my limited experience prosecuting white-collar crimes, I was initially apprehensive about pursuing this case, but my fears quickly subsided. Detective Patrick's professionalism and the depth of his investigation put me at ease. During the course of the prosecution, we developed a strong working relationship; we interviewed several witnesses together and held joint strategy sessions. Our open line of communication was vital to the prosecution's success.

I also learned to never underestimate the lengths that fraudsters go to in order to prevent the truth from being discovered. Maybe it was naiveté, but I genuinely thought that Glass Star's attorneys would encourage the company to cooperate fully in an effort to avoid negative publicity and the fallout sure to come with its customers. Then again, the media's coverage of investigators cordoning off the company's headquarters with yellow police tape as the search warrant was executed did not ingratiate us with Glass Star's upper management or its attorneys. I believe, though, that the real reason for the lack of cooperation was a coordinated effort to protect Casey.

Only a small percentage of Glass Star's employees engaged in fraud, and it is wholly unfair to think that the entire company was corrupt or dishonest. Although it was depressing to discover how easily some employees succumbed to greed and corporate pressure, it was uplifting to observe the courage Jimmy displayed. If he had not tipped off the state insurance fraud division, I doubt the fraud would have ever been discovered. As the prosecution of Casey unfolded, Jimmy retired. Sadly, when it came out that Jimmy was the whistleblower, many of his friends at Glass Star ostracized him. This case underscores the necessity for fraud hotlines and for companies to create internal mechanisms for employees to report fraud without fear of repercussions.

Recommendations to Prevent Future Occurrences

From an outsider's perspective, Glass Star appeared to be a close-knit, family-owned company. In reality, it was a loose affiliation of stores in which managers enjoyed autonomy over billing practices. As Casey learned before becoming vice president, there were no controls in place, and the leadership had not implemented any anti-fraud measures. This coupled with Glass Star's heavy emphasis on internal competition encouraged fraudulent behavior. While competition can be healthy, if left unchecked it can push employees too far. There was also nowhere for whistleblowers to turn within the company itself. In the end, this case demonstrated the need for companies to implement anti-fraud strategies and to educate employees about the dangers of fraud. Above all, management must emphasize to employees that fraud causes irreparable damage to an entire company's reputation.

The victim insurance companies also bear some of the blame. While the move toward third-party online billing systems reduces expenses, it also leaves insurance companies susceptible to fraud. Insurers can protect themselves by performing vendor audits. In this case, the insurance companies might have avoided the fraud by requiring Glass Star employees to submit proof, such as a photograph or an inventory receipt, that the glass on the bill matched the glass installed in the vehicle. As a deterrent, insurance companies might also consider providing anti-fraud training workshops to major claim generators, such as repair shops and medical providers.

About the Author

Joseph Licandro, J.D., is a prosecutor for the Fourth Judicial Circuit in Duval County, Florida. He is a member of the Special Prosecution Division, which focuses on white-collar and organized crime. His primary area of focus is insurance fraud. Mr. Licandro graduated from the University of Notre Dame and the University of Florida, Levin College of Law. He is married to his beautiful wife, Catherine, who is also a prosecutor for the Fourth Judicial Circuit. They are the proud parents of two young children.

19

Fault of Fortune

JYOTI KHETARPAL

Most economies around the world were facing problems at the time of this case. Big corporations were suffering steep declines in revenue, and the service industry was hit hard on the bottom line as turnovers dropped. Management started pressuring their sales teams to meet unbelievably high targets, insurance companies included. Organizational leaders had started resetting their budgets for the next couple of years based on this downtrend, and layoffs were commonplace.

Sean was born and raised in a small town. He had been a below-average student since childhood. He was brought up in a large family and received little individual attention. His family was so preoccupied with meeting their daily needs that his below-average school performance was hardly noticed. He had a chance to get a basic education, and that was enough for him and his family. Neither his academic performance nor his family encouraged him to attain a professional degree.

After he finished high school, he could not find a job anywhere in his hometown, but he had to support his two youngest siblings and his elderly parents. Even the most basic, entry-level positions he applied for had steep competition due to the economy, and Sean's poor grades in school knocked him out of the running quickly. He searched for almost a year before deciding to start looking in towns and cities nearby. Finally his father asked one of his brothers to help his son in the job hunt. Sean's uncle, Oscar, was an insurance policy advisor with the county regulator, and he had a great network of connections in corporate insurance. With his uncle's help, Sean finally landed a job at Credentials, a well-respected insurance company, as an insurance agent for medical policies.

The Ethical Dilemma

Sean was also a below-average performer at work. He was always low on the bell curve and didn't earn performance bonuses. Although he managed his workload somehow, everyone expected him to be the first one asked to leave if Credentials had to lay off employees. So when, as the global economic downtrend worsened, management at Credentials was ordered to reduce its workforce by 100 employees, no one was surprised that Sean's name was on the list. However, his manager, Derrick, knew about Sean's personal situation and felt uneasy about laying him off. Sean had a large family to look after. By that time he had a wife, three kids and two elderly parents depending on him.

Derrick was unsure of what to do. Sean had been hired on the request of Oscar, a senior figure in the industry. Derrick thought of a way out by giving Sean three months to improve his performance as a special case. Derrick set certain monthly goals for Sean to achieve in order to save his job, and he categorically told Sean the implications of not achieving these goals.

After hearing that he had three months to save his job, Sean desperately started chasing clients, but with little success. At the end of first month, when Sean could not meet his first month's target, he got panicky and started to think of unconventional ways to improve his performance. He took a day off to brainstorm. He left his house early in the morning and went to a secluded park to clear his mind and focus on his job, which was not possible at home with so many family members around. When he returned that evening, his wife noticed his expression, which had been troubled when he left that morning, had become calm. He smiled and told her not to worry because he had thought of a way to fix the problem.

The next morning Sean was completely recharged and ready for a day at work. After reaching the office, he piled all of Credentials' policy and procedure manuals on his desk and started reading them in detail while making notes in his personal diary. He also prepared a list of doctors who could refer him to their clients and a list of potential clients from Credentials' database. Then he started visiting doctors.

Sean made a unique proposal to doctors, and they found it hard to refuse. He said that if the doctors would advise their clients to switch their medical insurance to Credentials through Sean, he would ensure their medical claims were approved. The doctors had to make small changes in their diagnoses to make the medical claims fall under Credentials' approved list. He lured doctors with more clientele and promised to share a part of his commission with them.

When he started visiting potential clients, Sean promised them complete health insurance coverage, even if they had certain diseases that Credentials would not cover. The clients not only liked his idea and signed with him but also referred him to many other clients.

Sean's clientele base increased quickly. Many customers moved from other insurance companies to Credentials due to Sean's new approach. He assured clients that, come what may, he would make sure their claims were approved.

The Consortium and Its Needs

To fulfill his commitment to clients, Sean had to create a consortium of doctors. To cover all types of medical claims, he connected with doctors from specialty hospitals to small nursing homes and everything in between.

Sean gained knowledge of approved diseases and treatments through Credentials' policy manuals and then shared the information with his network of doctors to ensure a mutual understanding of what could be billed on their medical claims. He not only advised doctors to manipulate their diagnoses, but he also made his clients get treatment from a few select doctors who were part of his consortium.

Sean had become smart enough to maintain a database of all his clients, doctors and their claims, and he also maintained a timeline of when medical providers could submit claims for smooth sailing.

Sean created a situation that he thought was favorable to Credentials, definitely to its clients and clearly for the doctors. Credentials' clientele grew as Sean recruited more individuals with his incentives. His clients were happy to receive treatment and have their claims approved. Doctors were getting clients through Sean just by manipulating their diagnoses a little bit. As promised, Sean was also sharing a part of his commission with doctors. In few instances, he was even sharing a small percentage of his commission with clients who promised not to present any claims in near future. It seemed like a win-win situation for all the parties involved, but it was impacting Credentials' revenue terribly.

The Reservations

Sean, with the success of his scheme, kept promising his clients unconventional offerings. His performance records were showing drastic improvement. Derrick was surprised by Sean's sudden and extraordinary performance. He not only retained Sean but gave him tougher targets to achieve. Sean was able to meet Derrick's higher expectations, and within one year he earned a high-performance award.

Nevertheless, Derrick had doubts. He reviewed Sean's client lists and number of claims versus policies ratios. Everything seemed in order, but he had reservations. Derrick could not understand how a below-average performer started beating the top performers at Credentials. He noticed that Sean began checking Credentials policy manuals more often, while other employees rarely looked at them.

The Investigation

Derrick had the responsibility of heading his department with integrity. Though apparently Sean's achievement was beneficial for the company, Derrick wanted to be completely satisfied with the process Sean had adopted to achieve targets.

Derrick called me to get my opinion on the situation. I owned and operated an independent consulting and investigation firm and had handled insurance fraud cases in the past. Derrick explained what was going on and his apprehensions about Sean's performance. After few queries, I suggested two steps. First, give Sean the benefit of the doubt because at times people under certain pressure can turn around after performing poorly. Second, make Derrick's most trustworthy employee, Chris, receive training from Sean to better understand his way of soliciting clients. Derrick liked the idea and told me that he would call me later, if needed.

One week later, I got a call back. Derrick explained that Sean treated his colleague Chris well and explained to her importance of visiting clients personally. However, he did not take Chris into his client meetings but made her wait outside. According to Chris, Sean also visited doctors regularly and made her wait outside during these meetings too.

When Derrick asked Sean's reason for leaving Chris out of his client meetings, Sean said he did not like to share his way of interaction. He said Chris was smart enough to overtake Sean in getting new clients if she knew his communication strategies and, if that happened, how could he know his job was secure in the future? Moreover, Sean said he was not mentored and guided by any senior sales associates when he learned how to solicit new clients. Why should Chris enjoy a benefit he didn't get?

Derrick also asked Sean about visiting doctors regularly, but Sean explained it logically. He said out of his targets, he achieved a 60 percent success rate with those who were present at a doctor's clinic or at some hospital for treatment without a policy. He said when someone falls sick and has to pay hefty bills, they realize the importance of purchasing a medical policy. Although Sean's logic was acceptable, it raised further doubts. I asked Derrick to send me Sean's resume and his appraisal documents from the past few years. I also requested a list of his clients and details of his approved claims. Derrick provided all the documents and also dug up a list of clients and doctors who were involved in Sean's insurance claims.

My team reviewed the documents and prepared an analysis of Sean's performance over the years. I asked them to support the analysis with his clients and claims data as well. The analysis revealed the expected, sudden spurt in Sean's performance after the threat to his job. The number of claims under him had also increased manifold, while he maintained permissible limits set by Credentials.

We short-listed a few doctors and claimants from the compiled list. After preliminary inquiries, I figured these people would not reveal anything about their relations with Sean. But there was no harm in trying, so I told two of my investigators to speak with a few randomly selected doctors and clients. And as expected, none said anything except "Yes, Sean is a medical insurance agent from Credentials." The symmetry of responses made us believe that they were scripted.

Veracity Test

My team had prepared a list of the options we had to reach to a conclusion in this investigation, and we organized a brainstorming session to ascertain the best suitable alternative available. We commonly sat down for sessions like this to hash out different plans and collectively decide on the best approach.

While we were running through the options, one of my junior employees, Nancy, peeked in through the conference room door. We generally advise other staff members not to disturb these intense discussions, but she seemed to be in hurry, so I went out to talk to her. She asked me for early leave, and I joked that she should put on some makeup because she was probably going to meet her fiancé. Nancy said that she had to visit her insurance agent to purchase a family medical policy, and the agent just moved up her appointment time. I gave her permission to leave early and suddenly realized what a great opportunity Nancy had just given us.

I asked her not to buy the policy that day as I had better options for her. I dismissed the brainstorming session to explain Nancy's new role in the investigation.

I described our investigation into Sean to Nancy and asked her to contact him for a quote on a similar medical policy. I instructed her to ask for as many benefits as she could get from him while maintaining the confidentiality of the case. I told her if he was convincing, she could even purchase a policy through him and I would reimburse her.

Nancy understood her role. She knew that with her help we could reach a conclusion in the case, and my company was ready to bear complete medical insurance cost for her family because of her contribution. Nancy prepared a spreadsheet of all the options she received from agents from Credentials and other insurance companies. Whereas other agents openly offered benefits to her over the phone, as if they knew the benefits by heart, Sean was more reserved. Nancy was surprised that he did not explain the benefits over the phone but insisted on a personal meeting.

I advised Nancy to be on alert and try to remember verbatim what Sean suggested, because she had to submit a written report on the meeting. Nancy met Sean in the lobby of a hotel to discuss the options. She was blown away by the benefits he offered her.

Too Good to Be True

Nancy said that Sean not only offered discounts from his commission but promised to get her medical claims approved if necessary. He had a list of approved diseases and a strong network of doctors to manipulate diagnoses. While doctors were treating one disease, they were writing claims for another close disease on the approved list to have it cleared smoothly for medical claims. In order to maintain his claims ratio, Sean also manipulated the timing of claims. This way he was able to pass along no-claim benefits to his clients and then have their claims reimbursed by Credentials at a later date, with the help of the doctors.

Nancy said that Sean had the air of a simple, kind man from a small town. She said you would never think he would try to do anything deceptive by the way he carried himself. Sean first presented the various benefits offered by Credentials' policies and then explained the extra benefits of signing a policy with him. Nancy feigned ignorance to the plan, so Sean had to explain the complete process to her.

Sean told Nancy that he had a panel of doctors who worked closely with him, which allowed him to get all his claims approved whenever necessary. Nancy told him that she preferred to be treated by her family doctor. Sean, eager to accommodate, asked Nancy to give him the contact details of her doctor so that Sean could add him to his panel.

I asked Nancy what her family doctor was like, and she assured me that he would never agree to Sean's unscrupulous ideas. I told Nancy not to pursue the case any further with Sean and to take the medical policy from the best suitable agent she liked.

I set up a meeting with Derrick so I could fill him in on the developments. We talked about Sean's unethical approach to signing clients, and Derrick confirmed that it was completely unacceptable under Credentials' codes of ethics and conduct. Unfortunately, we knew that none of Sean's doctors or even clients would divulge anything about the process to us.

On my suggestion, Derrick asked everyone on his team, including Sean, to submit a schedule of their meetings and locations at the beginning of each day for a week as an audit exercise. Derrick then asked a few of his trustworthy agents to relocate some of their client meetings to places where Sean was scheduled to meet his clients, but for the other agents to arrive shortly before Sean would. Sean was aghast at the presence of his colleagues and their potential clients at his designated meeting places. In that week, his performance dropped radically.

After analyzing the data of that week, we decided to conclude the investigation quickly. By that point we understood how Sean had improved his performance, and we had analyzed Sean's personality traits. He had one of those manipulator personalities, and the fear of losing his job did not make him a better or more honest worker; it made him a worse person.

The Interview

Derrick and I decided to speak with Sean directly. We took him to a conference room with closed-circuit cameras. He seemed very reserved at first, until we asked him to tell us how he had improved his job performance. Sean proudly dedicated his turnaround to his hard work and spoke in glowing terms about how his confidence and diligence made him successful.

When we told Sean that we thought there was another angle to the story, he was quiet. He did not expect us to know anything about his scheme. We explained precisely what he offered to his clients and then asked him if such a sales pitch complied with Credentials' ethics and value statements. Sean did not utter a single word.

We asked Sean to accept his guilt, but initially he denied the allegations. He said his jealous colleagues had been spreading lies about him. When we asked why his performance fell drastically the previous week, he could not offer a reason. We told Sean that we knew about the consortium of doctors helping him and had spoken with some of them. When cornered with a few clients' names as well, Sean confessed to the fraud.

Sean told us in detail the method he had adopted and gave us a list of the doctors on his panel. He agreed to help the investigation against the doctors; he knew his career was finished, and it would be better to support the investigation than try to hide his fraud. While the doctors argued that Sean's scheme did not benefit them, Sean provided proof of how he provided new clients for the doctors and evidence of how they tweaked their diagnoses to submit false claims. At the conclusion of the investigation, Sean was jailed for one year. The doctors on his consortiums were suspended for two years each with heavy penalties for breaching their professional code of conduct.

All the pending claims brought up by Sean's clients were put on hold and investigated individually to segregate false claims from genuine ones. Not to our surprise, more than 90 percent of the pending claims were false. Sean's clients who submitted false claims were also charged with fines.

In light of Sean's situation at home, Credentials' management hired his wife to support the family after Sean was let go. Nina was unaware of Sean's fraud and was shocked when she learned about it. Credentials wanted to set an example for their employees, so after Nina passed the test to qualify as an insurance agent, she was promoted from an administrative position to an insurance agent.

Credentials also started a severance fund for future layoffs. Management knew that layoffs were unavoidable, but they also realized the importance of supporting employees in their hours of need.

Lessons Learned

This investigation was complicated, but the method of fraud adopted by Sean was pretty simple. Those involved in the scheme helped Sean because they all benefited from it — except for Credentials, of course. Derrick stood for integrity, and he understood the importance of upholding the company's code of ethics.

This case gave us a new stream of lessons learned. Sean was at fault, but management at Credentials also realized the harm they had caused by setting unachievable goals for the insurance agents. Lessons we learned include:

- Sean, under pressure, turned to crime. A regular, honest employee can turn into a fraudster based on circumstances and opportunities. To avoid the situation in the future, Credentials employed Sean's wife to set an example that management was ready to take care of their employees in need. They stressed to employees the importance of being honest.
- Economic downturn affects everyone, and we should all be better prepared for such ups and downs in life.
- There are no shortcuts to prosperity; success in a short span of time through wrong means leads nowhere.

Recommendations to Prevent Future Occurrences

I met with Derrick a few months after this case ended, and he told me about some changes that were made at Credentials to prevent such frauds from occurring in the future. He works closely with management and his staff to ensure that the goals set are realistic and can be measured ethically. He has an open-door policy so employees can come to him with problems and they can work on a positive solution together. He also monitors the sales practices of insurance agents more closely and conducts surprise audits of their records. Another change he implemented requires employees to bring a colleague to their meetings with clients if Derrick requests it, so everyone knows they can be monitored at any time. Derrick also told me with a smile that Nina is doing very well as an agent and has become a model employee for Credentials' ethics policy.

About the Author

Jyoti Khetarpal is an India-qualified Chartered Accountant (CA) with over 15 years of corporate experience with such reputed organizations as Dun & Bradstreet and American Express. Ms. Khetarpal has been instrumental in outlining risk management methodology, analytics and assessment. As the managing partner of bRiskCheck, she is a risk mitigation and management advisor to PEs, venture capitalists, banks, other investors and corporate. She is a regular writer in international publications and a speaker with international organizations.

Going Blind to Fraud

KAREN WRIGHT

Optometrist Charles Cooper owned and operated All Eyes Optometry Clinic in a small, rural farming town. Dr. Cooper, tall and very personable, was liked and trusted by his patients. Dr. Cooper's wife, Marilyn, a take-charge country woman, was the office manager. The Coopers' adult children also worked at the clinic.

All Eyes had been in business for more than 20 years when the state tax commission received an anonymous tip that Dr. Cooper had avoided paying income taxes. In December of that year, the commission notified Dr. Cooper that his tax returns from the prior three years would be audited. While the audit was ongoing, Dr. Cooper refused to meet with auditors and failed to provide the requested records. Steve Barton, the audit supervisor, filed affidavits for search warrants of Dr. Cooper's home and business. The search warrants were executed simultaneously, and three police officers were present at each location. Steve Barton read the warrant while local police officers entered and secured the scene. Steve and his team from the tax commission conducted the search.

Deputy Attorney General Joseph Gaston presented evidence seized during the search to the grand jury, which returned an indictment of three counts of felony income tax evasion. Dr. Cooper's defense attorney moved to have the evidence suppressed, stating that the search had been conducted improperly. The defense attorney argued that state law required search warrants to be served by peace officers. The search conducted on Dr. Cooper's home and business had been performed by state investigators who were not peace officers. The police officers had little or no knowledge about the case and performed no meaningful role during the search of the residence or business; they were the token police, which was a relatively common practice at the time. The court agreed and granted the defense's motion to suppress the evidence and quashed the indictment.

Three years later, the case reached the state supreme court, where, ultimately, the trial court's decision was upheld. The case was dead in the water.

Several justices dissented with the majority opinion. They reasoned that tax commission investigators, and even the judge who issued the search warrant, made an honest mistake. This was not an intentional violation of constitutional rights by corrupt government workers. Dissenting justices felt suppression of the otherwise valid evidence was too harsh.

Word of the court's decision spread through state agencies, where numerous civilian investigators were working similar cases. I was an investigator working for the state department of insurance at the time. This decision would have adversely affected one of my cases, if it weren't for the fact we had obtained consent and did not need a search warrant.

The court's decision materially altered the activities of civilian state investigators. No longer could we act as primary case agents when serving search warrants; police officers had to be brought into complex fraud investigations and thoroughly briefed so they understood exactly which documents needed to be seized during searches. Because police officers often carry heavy caseloads involving easily recognizable victims, they needed to be convinced of the criminal aspects of the complex and voluminous fraud cases and of the value of their own involvement. Subsequently, civilian state investigators were not always successful in sparking the interest of police officers.

In the years following the court's decision, the state legislature passed a bill approving the establishment of a Medicaid Fraud Control Unit (MFCU) under the attorney general's Criminal Law Division. Receiving 75 percent federal funding and 25 percent state funding, the MFCU was set up to investigate medical provider fraud. Agents did not investigate welfare beneficiaries but focused entirely on doctors, dentists, home-health workers and other healthcare providers. The attorney general took the state supreme court's decision into account when creating the new MFCU and mandated that some of the investigators hold peace officer status so they could serve their own search warrants.

Popular with the Auditors

Tax issues were not Dr. Cooper's only encounter with auditors or with the criminal justice system. Prior to the tax case, he had come to the attention of a Medicare auditor named Linda Stothers. This stylish petite lady was also a knowledgeable and aggressive auditor. In analyzing the claims data, Linda later told me, "I saw that Dr. Cooper was an outlier, billing services that significantly exceeded the frequency with which they were rendered by all other optometrists in the state. I found that nearly all of his patients had costly optometry tests done without clinical justification. He also unbundled services and billed unnecessary, extended services. Medicare required

Dr. Cooper to refund $14,000 and told him that continuation of billing for services not medically indicated and other inappropriate practices could result in his being excluded from participation from the Medicare program." Provider education of inappropriate billing practices is good evidence in future cases of knowledge and intent. This should have been a warning to Dr. Cooper.

Fifteen years after auditing Dr. Cooper and recovering funds for Medicare, Linda Stothers was working for the state Medicaid program when, unbelievably, "Dr. Cooper again stood out as an outlier for the exact same issues for which he had been sanctioned before," Linda said. Upon making this discovery, Linda contacted a few local health insurance plans to compare notes. By this time I had left the department of insurance and was working as an investigator for Mountain Health Benefits, Inc., a private insurance company. Mindful of Linda's reputation as a credible auditor, when she contacted me about the optometrist, I was eager to dig into claims data to see what I could find. I searched Dr. Cooper's claim history and found a low number of claims; evidence of fraud just wasn't there. Dr. Cooper had not been billing private insurance in the same manner as he had billed Medicaid and Medicare, so I moved on to other cases.

Having previously educated Dr. Cooper about his inappropriate billing practices with Medicare, which apparently had no effect, Linda did not just publish audit findings and demand a refund from Dr. Cooper this time around. She referred the case to the new MFCU as a suspected fraud. The MFCU investigator assigned to the case, Brian Grant had recently graduated from the peace officers standards and training academy. As luck would have it, he would turn out to be instrumental in the investigation against Dr. Cooper, whose previous state supreme court case contributed to the creation of Grant's own job. Though still quite young compared to his colleagues, Brian Grant was not only a peace officer; he was a Certified Public Accountant (CPA) and a Certified Fraud Examiner (CFE).

Mountain Health Benefits was a nonprofit health insurance company offering a full line of products, including major medical, vision, dental and pharmacy benefits to employer groups and individuals. It also offered a Medicare replacement plan.

The fact that Mountain Health did not initially have much in claims exposure in response to Linda's inquiry was significant because most private insurance carriers offer separate coverage for vision services. Typically, vision coverage allows for a yearly eye exam and glasses or contacts. If the patient has a medical diagnosis, such as glaucoma, the claims can be processed through major medical coverage, which pays at a higher rate and has higher limits. Usually a private insurance carrier would not see a large number of high-dollar claims submitted to major medical coverage by an optometrist.

A year or so after Linda's Medicaid audit, Mountain Health suddenly began to see a significant increase in claims submitted to major medical by Dr. Cooper. Whether because of the Medicaid audit or because Mountain Health offered him a contract as an in-network provider for the Medicare replacement plan, I'll never know. (Patients with Medicare replacement plan coverage are covered only if they use an in-network provider. The Medicare replacement plan contract allowed Dr. Cooper access to this expanded patient population.)

This sudden increase in claims first came to my attention through a provider contract specialist, Lisa Rogers, who had been with Mountain Health for some time and had a lot of expertise in Medicare. Her job was to contract with medical providers for the Medicare replacement plan. Lisa was also an asset to this case because she had previously worked in an optometrist's office.

Second Opinion

Lisa selected a sample of claims for six of Dr. Cooper's patients and requested supporting medical records. After receiving the records, Lisa sent them to an external expert, Dr. Dawson. The review was double blind, meaning the expert did not know Dr. Cooper's name and none of us knew the expert's name until after he conducted his review. Dr. Dawson's report was scathing, with comments like these:

- "There are no findings consistent with glaucoma, nor reason to do so many tests and to have repeated them."
- "There is overutilization of services. There is clearly an unnecessary and unfounded diagnosis of glaucoma."
- "There have been no records convincing of glaucoma nor is there seen any treatment started."
- "There is an outrageous abuse of medical necessity in this case, with overutilization of tests performed."
- "Clearly there is an overdiagnosing of a glaucoma condition that does not seem to exist."

Mountain Health's special investigations unit had purchased a fraud detection software product that used predictive analytics to review claims histories and detect outliers. It filtered claims data through various questions to compare providers to their medical specialty peers, producing a detailed report for each provider. Lisa asked me to take a look at Dr. Cooper with the fraud software. Rachel Shipley, our fraud software "superuser," who was also an experienced nurse and computer techie, created a model to look at optometrists submitting claims to our major medical plan. The results showed that Dr. Cooper was off the charts for optometry testing and for diagnosing patients with glaucoma, the second leading cause of blindness. In his entire state, this small-town optometrist had the most patients with glaucoma-related diagnoses, he billed for more glaucoma-related tests than any other optometrist and he ranked number one in the entire state for total dollars paid.

Lisa and Dr. Dawson met with Dr. Cooper and his wife and confronted them with the independent medical review report. In relating the meeting to me, Lisa said, "We waited for Dr. Cooper to provide a reasonable explanation. Dr. Cooper suggested he had been billing glaucoma because he was trying to rule it out (which has not been a practice in the healthcare field for decades and would not explain the repeated tests). Mrs. Cooper attempted to blame the problem on a former employee who did the billing." This also would not explain the repeated tests. Blaming a former employee is the single most common explanation for questionable billing practices I hear from providers. Other than those comments, Lisa said, "Dr. Cooper and his wife offered very little during the meeting."

We concluded that our original sample was insufficient because it had focused only on claims for the Medicare replacement plan. We needed to look at Dr. Cooper's claims for our commercial products. My supervisor asked me to officially take over the case and conduct an onsite audit of All Eyes Optometry.

The First Visit

I conducted a thorough background report on All Eyes Optometry Clinic and Dr. Cooper. I extracted data from our claims processing system and imported it into a spreadsheet. I sent a list of Dr. Cooper's patients to our internal audit department to pull a statistically valid random sample using our sampling software, which selected 30 names. I then sent a certified letter to Dr. Cooper notifying him of the upcoming audit, providing some possible dates and asking him to respond within two weeks. Thinking back on my days as an investigator for the department of insurance, I cringed at the thought of giving a provider the opportunity to alter records by announcing our visit beforehand, but this was required by our provider contract. In accordance with our policy, I did not provide him with a list of names in advance, and Dr. Cooper had a very large patient population.

Once the letter was in the mail, I began researching optometry, glaucoma, optometry tests, the type of equipment that optometrists use and vision insurance coverage. Dr. Cooper's deadline was fast approaching when I received a call with a familiar voice from the past. It was Carter Phillips, a well-known local defense attorney who had handled some very high-profile cases, including one of my cases with the department of insurance. Carter explained, "I represent All Eyes, and they sent me a copy of your audit letter." Carter and I then scheduled the audit. He didn't question the fact that I would not provide patient names other than to say "Well, if you want to let us know in advance, great, but if you don't, we will be happy to do it however you want to do it that day." He was, however, going to be present during our visit.

We scheduled my site visit first thing in the morning on a cold winter's day. Concerned about being punctual, I stored our scanner in the trunk of the car the night before. It was critical to be professional and polite during the clinic visit and for everything to run like clockwork. A site visit like this typically takes three investigators. In addition to Rachel, I brought Carmen Sadler, a highly reliable investigator and a cheerful woman willing to do whatever was needed to get the job done. When we arrived at All Eyes, we introduced ourselves to Carter and presented our list of patient names.

While staff located the files we requested, we set up our scanner but when we turned it on, the screen was black . . . not good. After rebooting it several times, the scanner finally started working. I made a note to myself — never leave a delicate piece of electronic equipment in the trunk of a car on a cold winter's night. I took a tour of the clinic with Carter and Marilyn Cooper. Dr. Cooper was conspicuously absent. I snapped pictures of the equipment and exam rooms to demonstrate whether Dr. Cooper had the equipment needed to perform the services for which he billed. While Rachel and Carmen scanned patient files, I interviewed Marilyn and Carter. We did not finish in one day and returned a few days later. Once we finished scanning all the patient files, we conducted a quality check to ensure we scanned every page correctly.

Audits and Reports

Upon returning to the office, I made a CD of the scanned records and sent it to Carter. I then began performing a desk audit by organizing records in chronological order and reviewing each patient file to get an understanding of what was in the files. On the second pass, I compared each date of service to the corresponding insurance claim. During one of these passes I noticed the intraocular pressure (IOP) test, which is the primary indicator of glaucoma, had been altered in numerous patient files. I also found many test results were missing and several other services billed for had not been documented. The records consistently mentioned eye drops used to treat glaucoma, but the files contained no copies of written prescriptions. I reviewed patient claim histories and found no claims for glaucoma drops and no other doctors treating the patients for glaucoma. This couldn't be. From my research, I knew glaucoma had to be treated with drops to prevent progression of the disease. Not to treat glaucoma would be malpractice.

In the following months, we ended up returning to All Eyes two more times to scan more patient files. I found more altered IOP measurements, but I also found something else — tests we had not seen in previous files.

After several reviews of files and comparing them to claims, the additional tests started to look familiar. I took a couple of the graph tests, put one on top of the other and held them up to the light. They were exact clones, except for the patient names and dates of service. I had seen this in insurance broker fraud cases but never before in a healthcare case. I went back through all of the records looking for documents that appeared to be photocopied and found two types of tests. One was a handwritten Farnsworth colorblind test, and the other was a computer-generated visual-field test. No two of these tests should look exactly the same for different patients.

At the end of several months, I produced two audit reports, the first addressing events leading up to the investigation and the results of my audit for our commercial lines of business and the second addressing my audit findings for our Medicare replacement plan, including the cloned tests. I supported the audit reports with source documents, each referenced as a specific exhibit. The audit reports with exhibits consisted of seven large binders and were available in electronic format.

The total loss identified thus far for 55 patient files was around $15,000. Since my background was in investigations, not healthcare, I based my findings entirely on whether a service was documented or whether a claim was supported with a cloned test result. Even when the IOP had been altered, I could not conclude that a glaucoma diagnosis was inappropriate. I suspected, however, that almost all of the files contained false diagnoses, and as such, almost all of the testing billed would have been unnecessary. That amount was in excess of $100,000.

Fraud Referral

Because of the cloned tests, altered records and lack of glaucoma treatment, I suspected fraud. In the wake of healthcare reform, the terms *fraud, waste* and *abuse* have been thrown around as a single concept — FWA — but they are not the same. *Waste* can be explained by a simple example. Imagine using a small amount of an expensive drug from a large vial, throwing away the rest of the drug and then billing the entire vial to insurance. An example of *abuse* would be giving every patient the same panel of lab tests, regardless of whether the patient needed them. *Fraud* is intentionally submitting a material lie in support of a claim for money or benefit to which the provider is not entitled.

In cases of waste or abuse, we typically tried to recover overpayments and educate providers. In cases of suspected fraud, we had certain obligations, including reporting suspected fraudulent claims to the state department of insurance. If the suspected fraud involved our Medicare replacement plan, we were required to report it to the MEDIC, the Centers for Medicare and Medicaid Services (CMS) contractor responsible for overseeing all Medicare replacement plan anti-fraud activities. We were audited regularly by the department of insurance and CMS to ensure we were in compliance. I held a meeting with my audit team and concluded that we were obligated to report Dr. Cooper for suspected fraud.

One of the drawbacks of leaving the public sector to work for a private company was Rule 6(e) of the Federal Rules of Criminal Procedure, which established rules for grand jury secrecy. Basically, now that I was no longer a government investigator, I could not be privy to grand jury investigations. Let me tell you, it was quite a shock to be left standing out in the cold. Because of Rule 6(e), I was unaware of how deeply involved agents from Health and Human Services, Office of Inspector General (HHS OIG) and the Federal Bureau of Investigation (FBI) were in their investigation of Dr. Cooper.

I was to learn later that about the time we were making site visits and auditing records, federal agents were interviewing Dr. Cooper's Medicare and Medicaid patients. They also interviewed some of his employees. In addition to Brian Grant, the MFCU investigator, Joni Sweeny, special agent with the HHS OIG, and Robin Miller, a special agent with the FBI, were investigating. Joni, who I had worked with before, was tall and slim with a fresh, midwestern look. Robin, who I had met but not worked with, was petite and looked like she could have been anywhere from her teens to her early 30s. They were both bright, professional and exactly what one would hope for in two federal agents. After the conclusion of the case, I learned more about what these agents had been up to.

According to Agent Sweeny, when she interviewed one of Dr. Cooper's former employees in October that year, she asked her to keep the interview confidential and not tell the Coopers, but tell them she did. Agent Sweeny said, "This tip-off coincided with a major switch in billing practices by Dr. Cooper." He virtually stopped submitting claims with glaucoma or a glaucoma-related diagnosis. Dr. Cooper's billing for glaucoma never returned to previous levels, but he significantly increased billing for tension headaches, pain in and around the eye, optic atrophy, punctate keratitis and nonexudative macular degeneration.

Similarly, I had been pulling updated claim histories in response to a subpoena I received after referring the case to law enforcement, and I noticed an abrupt change in Dr. Cooper's billing pattern. He virtually stopped billing Mountain Health for glaucoma on September 24, just one day after Dr. Dawson and Lisa Rogers confronted him with the independent medical review report.

Armed with additional information from private payers with subpoenas, the agents continued with their investigation and interviewed numerous Medicare, Medicaid and private-pay patients. Only one in ten Medicare patients interviewed was appropriately diagnosed with glaucoma and was being treated for it, which falls in line with the national average of less than 10 percent for Medicare-age clients. We found parents who told us that Dr. Cooper diagnosed their children with glaucoma but said he wanted to monitor it, not treat it. Glaucoma occurrence among juveniles is extremely rare at less than 1 percent of the population.

Federal agents hired an expert who examined the children and found no glaucoma or related conditions in any of the cases. Agent Sweeny told me, "One particular Medicaid patient, a ten-year-old girl, was so distraught after being diagnosed with glaucoma, she cried with her mother about the diagnosis. Even after being examined by our expert and told she did not have glaucoma, she still believed she would go blind."

Agents compared Dr. Cooper to all other providers in the state, not just optometrists, and found that Dr. Cooper saw 4 percent of the Medicaid population but billed for 92 percent of the total Medicaid population with glaucoma. However, glaucoma-related conditions were not the only diagnoses Dr. Cooper apparently falsified: His patients with acquired color deficiency accounted for 99 percent of the state's Medicaid population with that diagnosis. Just as I had found, agents identified copied or cloned tests. They found 141 Farnsworth colorblind tests in 109 files consisting of 14 distinct photocopied tests. Agents also identified falsified diagnoses of primary open-angle glaucoma, chronic angle closure glaucoma, optic cupping, acquired color deficiency, photokeratitis, trichiasis, superficial injury of cornea, recurrent erosion of cornea and pre-glaucoma.

Tallying the Losses

Brian Grant, the MFCU investigator, was instrumental in coming up with a unique way to identify the loss amount by focusing on Dr. Cooper's change in billing practices. At the conclusion of the case, Brian explained, "We knew that Dr. Cooper's scheme was to diagnose patients with something they didn't have and then bill for tests they either didn't need or he didn't do. The problem was that he was also providing some legitimate services." To separate the legitimate services from the fraud scheme, Brian created a spreadsheet. Focusing on the primary diagnoses, Brian listed the patients Dr. Cooper saw with a particular diagnosis and what he was paid for that patient's visits each month. Brian explained, "I had about 12 diagnoses I was looking at. Once I had all the data entered, I graphed it out and noticed that he would use a certain diagnosis for a while and then switch to something else. It was especially blatant when his employee told him he was being investigated. He dropped all the diagnoses he had been using and started with new ones." The total loss amount Brian identified after weeding out the legitimate claims exceeded $1 million.

Olivia Walsh and Michael Kelson were the Assistant U.S. Attorneys handling our case. AUSAs Walsh and Kelson were two of the best prosecutors I have ever had the pleasure to work with, and they easily comprehended complicated and voluminous fraud cases. They presented the case to the grand jury, and Dr. Cooper was indicted on 105 counts of executing a scheme to defraud a healthcare benefit program under Title 18 United States Code § 1347. The indictment alleged that Dr. Cooper "defrauded Medicaid, Medicare, Mountain Health and two other payers of more than $1 million in healthcare benefits program reimbursements, by making material false statements, and by submitting material false, fraudulent and fictitious claims for reimbursement to these healthcare benefits programs."

After several trial postponements and months of negotiations, Dr. Cooper pleaded guilty and was ordered to pay $1 million in restitution. According to the sentencing memorandum, "Each fraudulent billing required the creation of false medical records." False records not only existed in Dr. Cooper's office but also in the files of several insurance companies. The sentencing memorandum pointed out that those records "may follow the patients into the future, affecting their future medical care or their future ability to obtain affordable insurance."

At his sentencing hearing, Dr. Cooper took sole responsibility and said, "It was definitely greed that prompted my actions. I just got caught up in it, and couldn't get out." In sentencing Dr. Cooper to three years in federal prison, the judge said, "It would appear what happened here is out of character for you, but when you think about it, it's your perceived character that made it possible for you to do what you did."

Mountain Health received more than $30,000 restitution, which was substantially less than the company's actual losses but fair considering losses to Medicaid and Medicare.

Lessons Learned

Fraudsters rarely stop until they are caught. Dr. Cooper's first escape from prosecution brought about a sequence of events that led to his ultimate imprisonment. Simply recovering overpayments, which is the primary focus of health insurance companies, is sometimes not enough to deter criminals. Teamwork, both internal and external, is key to successful outcomes. It is crucial to forge strong relationships with local, state and federal law enforcement agencies and be willing to cooperate and assist as allowed by the law and privacy regulations.

Recommendations to Prevent Future Occurrences

Had Mountain Health been more proactive in using anti-fraud software, Dr. Cooper's scheme would have been detected earlier and losses would have been less. We have since implemented a procedure to proactively review and audit different specialty groups each year.

The external medical reviewer helped us prove that Dr. Cooper was falsely diagnosing glaucoma and conducting unnecessary tests on his patients. In future cases I will recommend that a larger sample of medical records be sent for external review. It is costly, but the return on investment in this case would have been worthwhile to demonstrate the extent of Dr. Cooper's false billing and receive more restitution.

Prepayment review is a process of examining claims, requesting records and talking to patients before payment is made. It is time consuming and requires resources, but if we had implemented it early in this case, we could have stopped fraudulent claims from being paid in the first place, which is better than trying to recover payments later. Although we could not go back and implement stronger controls with Dr. Cooper, we are taking all the lessons we learned from his case to prevent frauds like this from occurring in the future.

About the Author

Karen Wright works for a health insurance company investigating fraud, waste and abuse. Ms. Wright's experience includes serving in the U.S. Army Military Police, as a Medicaid Fraud Control Unit investigator, as a trial assistant in the prosecution of complex crimes and as an investigator with a state insurance department. She became a Certified Fraud Examiner in 2002.

CHAPTER

21

Going Against the Cartel

LOFTIN C. WOODIEL

"He knows who I am. He knows my schedule, where I am at any time during the day, as well as the names and ages of my family members. He knows the schools my children attend and the market where my wife shops on Thursday afternoons. He is all too close to me yet I know nothing about him — not even his name. I am afraid for the lives of my family and my own."

Believe it or not, I heard this terrifying account from an insurance claims adjuster, as he was relating an encounter he had during a routine visit to the scene of a car crash — and I was about to discover it was not an isolated incident. Why would someone threaten insurance claims adjusters and their families?

The Mexican drug cartels were ruthless, killing anyone who interfered with their operations accidentally or intentionally. Armed conflicts between the cartels and the Mexican government, and among the rival cartels, permeated the fabric of our work and social structure. At the time of this case, three cartels competed for jurisdiction over our city: the Gulf Cartel, Los Zetas and Los Negros. The Gulf Cartel had dominated the drug trade for years. It hired corrupt, elite, former military soldiers to serve as its private army, eliminating anyone who stood between the cartel and its mission. However, these brutal military elite soon realized they could logistically run drug trafficking operations on their own and spun off as a separate cartel, Los Zetas. It quickly became the most feared cartel and a rival of their former employers in the Gulf Cartel. Los Negros formed to counter Los Zetas and Mexican security, law enforcement and military forces.

Finding dead bodies in our neighborhood streets was no longer unusual, as the three cartels and the government fought. To be killed by a stray bullet or marked as an unfortunate witness was a tragic but common side effect of being in the wrong place at the wrong time. The cartel members acted like organized crime families and sought to fill their coffers with drug money and profits from any illicit activity that presented itself as worthy.

The Cartel Climate

My employer, Poco Coche Rojo, was one of the largest private organizations in Mexico. It was a wealthy and profitable insurance company owned by a foreign car manufacturer as part of its financial services corporation. Poco Coche Rojo (which translates to "little red car") was a full-service operation offering auto, home, business and other forms of insurance to thousands of customers in hundreds of locations throughout Mexico. Five years ago, our headquarters city, Aguas Profunamente, was considered the safest major city in Mexico. In fact, our metropolitan area was publicized as the second safest city in all of Latin America. There was a saying that the cartel leaders lived in Aguas Profunamente but never worked where they lived. However, that changed rapidly, and the following years brought turf battles among competing drug cartels. It became evident that our city was in the midst of a fierce battleground and that our police forces had become corrupt and could not be relied on to protect and serve the shell-shocked citizens. The Mexican military commonly closed roadways and conducted car-by-car searches of the passengers and their belongings. Army personnel surrounded major hotels and businesses and searched every floor. Heavily armed patrols were all around the metropolitan area, but average residents were no safer because of it.

The security environment in Aguas Profunamente presented a persistent and serious challenge for Poco Coche Rojo, and special safety measures for our field agents were no longer an option; they were a necessity. Insurgents were engaged in a sustained campaign against businesses. Kidnapping posed a severe and persistent threat to ranking nationals and foreign staff. It was clear that the government did not have control of the cartels and their threats. Failure throughout all levels of government and in private institutions became evident, as violent crime rates rose and scams targeting businesses and foreigners were common. There was a high level of incidental risk to our staff and especially our travelers and expatriates as a result of the random cartel violence. In the midst of all this chaos, we struggled to continue "business as usual."

Acceptable Expenditures

Last spring an auditor at Poco Coche Rojo named José Garza had identified a loss column in the financials labeled "acceptable expenditures" and examined it in depth. After a lengthy review, José found the expenditures were quietly attributed to organized crime payments. The audit trail revealed that the cartels had expanded their enterprises beyond the drug trade to include taking insurance company profits via car thefts and staged accident claims. Organized criminals intimidated and coerced employees at Poco Coche Rojo to certify claims that were obviously staged and fictitious. Year-on-year figures demonstrated that false claims cost the company in excess of $7.6 million with an additional $500,000 a year in extortion expenditures.

In Mexican cities like Aguas Profunamente, insurance companies dispatched field claims adjusters to the scene of auto thefts and accidents. Police were not sent to such incidents as a general rule unless there was a death or extreme road blockage. After José's audit revealed the troubling payments to drug cartels, my supervisor tasked me with interviewing claims adjusters to understand their experiences in the field. I had been hired by Poco Coche Rojo six years earlier as a security and compliance consultant, and I had conducted staff interviews countless times at the company. Over the years, I gained the trust and respect of the employees, and they were usually forthcoming in my interviews with them. After meeting with all the claims adjusters at my local office, I learned that at least a handful of them had been assaulted and threatened with future harm if they did not approve and pay the cartel members' fraudulent claims in full.

Based on the results from my local interviews, corporate investigators, myself included, interviewed all of Poco Coche Rojo's field adjusters throughout the region to determine the extent of the extortion and fraudulent claims. After meeting with more than 100 staff members, it was evident that these occurrences were not isolated. A majority of the adjusters told stories of being greeted by "bad people" when they arrived at the scene of reported thefts and accidents. An individual would present identification information and, in the case of alleged accidents, photos of the damaged cars with recommended repair costs. The cars were never at the scene. Although the situations were obviously suspicious or fraudulent, the cartel member at the scene typically asked the field adjuster questions like these, which a field adjuster related to me during an interview:

"You are Rodrigo Jimenez, yes?"

"Yes," the adjuster replied.

"You are the husband of Lucinda and the father of Matteo who attends university, Louisa who goes to the neighborhood school for girls and little Clara who attends Gato Nursery School?" the cartel member asked.

"Yes, but what does that have to do with your claim?" demanded Rodrigo.

"Your wife sure enjoys driving her 2009 red convertible to the Pueblo Market on Thursday afternoons, doesn't she? It would be a shame if something were to happen to her on the way to the market one afternoon," the cartel member stated ominously.

With a conversation of this nature, the deal was sealed. On the rare occasions that field adjusters did not cooperate, assaults and kidnappings were realities. When the adjusters did cooperate, I learned through my interviews that they did not report the incidents to company management for fear of losing their jobs or, worse, the lives of loved ones. It takes very few of these violent repercussions to ensure complete compliance by the field adjusters. Too many headless bodies were found alongside the roadway for anyone to pretend the threats were empty.

Coercion of Poco Coche Rojo's employees did not end with the field adjusters but also affected our regional claims agents, as I soon found out. After interviewing all the field adjusters, I decided to move up and question agents at our regional centers.

Poco Coche Rojo operated six regional centers in Mexico. If an agent thought a claim was suspicious, he or she would have the claimant come to the nearest regional claim center to meet and explain it in person. The regional claims centers had many points of entry and exit, and none of them had surveillance or physical security measures in place; cartel members could come and go as they pleased. The interviews I held with 75 regional claims agents revealed that it was extremely common for them to be threatened and coerced while on company property in a similar fashion as the field adjusters. The claims agents were consistent in the facts they related. A cartel member would approach the agent in a manner clearly intended to gain the element of surprise, either while the agent was doing paperwork in the office or in a casual environment, but almost always while he or she was alone. One agent explained to me, "One minute I was in my office by myself and the next minute a man was there. The message was clear and direct: Pay or suffer the consequences. More than once I had a knife pressed against my skin where no one else could see." Another agent evaluated the threats he experienced in these words: "There are far too many bullet-riddled automobiles in our adjacent salvage lot with bloodstained interiors for us not to take these situations seriously." The combination of so many building exits, the private offices of adjusters and sufficient time for cartel members to state their case made it conceivable that threats were delivered, received and a claims check was written without anyone else in the building knowing it happened. Indeed, this occurred many times.

No arrests were made in these cases. Staff at Poco Coche Rojo, like most Mexican citizens at the time, did not trust law enforcement personnel because the level of corruption eliminated any hope that the police were not on the cartel's payroll. The federal officers were considered to be somewhat reliable, but they had more pressing matters to attend to. The military, while invested with arrest authority, were more concerned with the violent crimes that frequently occurred in mass numbers. For federal agents to become involved, the needs of our staff members were going to have to multiply drastically. In light of all these factors, the corporate objective was simply to mitigate the financial loss while protecting our employees.

Strange Bedfellows

We at Poco Coche Rojo realized that we could not be the only company facing this problem with the cartels. Our security director, Vicente Zamora, initiated a collaborative meeting with his peers from the three other leading insurance companies — Escudo Claro, Seguridad Social and Protección Verde. His "security summit," as we nicknamed it, revealed that staff members at the three other companies were experiencing similar issues, confirming our suspicions. However, the security director from one company, Protección Verde, was content with the extortion and considered the cartel expenses and harassment simply the price of doing business in Mexico. Verde's security officer left the meeting with concerns that even speaking in the collaborative meeting would cost his employer collateral damages. The directors from the three remaining agencies, the largest in their number of policies and revenue, banded together to establish a common strategy to fight back against the cartel. After they agreed on a plan, Vicente reached out to trusted federal police officers and army commanders. He briefed them on the ideas generated during the security summit, and they offered their support for the plan.

Collectively, Vicente and his two counterparts drafted policies and procedures to meet the overall needs of the three companies. The plan was to present a standardized and consolidated front in dealing with the threats from cartel members. Each security officer would then go back and refine the tactics as necessary within his company's corporate structure. From these policies and procedures, we at Poco Coche Rojo developed training programs for field adjusters and claim agents that focused on detecting, investigating and documenting fraudulent claims related to the cartel. I helped develop the training initiatives and drafted how to communicate the new approach to staff members. The fact that our efforts supported the employees' duties and that the project was a team effort requiring common action drove home the message that both management and each employee were in this change together — we had a point of mutual, pledged support. We placed special emphasis on the potential for workplace violence and defusing hostile situations.

The Plan in Action

Cartel members began to see changes when the three major insurance companies started issuing informational warnings during every field adjuster's first contact with the "victim" of a car theft or accident at the scene. Cartel members onsite were given written notices stating that the insurer was now placing increased due diligence on investigating all automobile claims. The notice clearly stated that, while the field agent would take any and all information that witnesses provided at the scene and include it in the report, the decision to release funds would not be made until a thorough, third-person investigation was completed. The notice explicitly said that the field agent had no sway in the outcome of the investigation and identified the legal options of the insurance companies should fraud be detected or should harm come to their employees. Although a mere written notice does not typically deter fervent criminals, they often move like water flowing through the points of least resistance — in this case, to Protección Verde. Poco Coche Rojo, Escudo Claro and Seguridad Social enjoyed a significant decline in threats to our field adjusters after we began issuing notices. We could only assume that Protección Verde saw an inverse spike in run-ins with the cartels.

For the next phase of Vicente's strategy, our regional claims centers underwent security enhancements. Because the final determination to pay or reject claims happened at the centers and checks were issued there, they represented the last point of illegitimate influence for the cartels. We needed to tighten controls so that cartel members could not walk in and out as they pleased. After the security enhancements, monitored cameras first detected visitors to a regional center as they approached the compound perimeter. Armed guards — whom we had thoroughly vetted from a pool of trusted contacts in police and military organizations — then identified all who entered the compound. If the visitors passed this first step of clearance, they were allowed to park in our secured lot. At this point cars were inspected for explosive devices and other weapons. Visitors entered the claims center through one consolidated entrance, where they were greeted by another security guard in a separate area that had no access to the claims agents or the financial resources held within.

The security guard in the entry area was positioned in an adjoining office and communicated with the guest using an intercom; the guard's office was made of bulletproof glass. The guard notified the claims agent that an identified guest had arrived. While seated in the quarantined area, awaiting the arrival of the claims agent, guests' actions were monitored by surrounding cameras and one or more plainclothes security agents who were in charge of our day-to-day security operations. These agents were also vetted former police managers or army officers. After the claims agent greeted the visitor in the quarantined area, if the agent determined the visitor was legitimate, the guest was escorted through locked doors into a group claims area where digital monitoring continued.

When the meeting was over, the visitor was escorted out. In addition to wall-to-wall monitoring and control, we installed duress buttons throughout the building in appropriate locations, and security forces would respond immediately to calls from these buttons. At any time, a guest could be removed by request or force, if necessary. The bottom line was that absolute identification and control over visitor movement reduced the number of surprise visits from cartel members operating with anonymity, in secluded spaces, with freedom to coerce our staff members into furthering their fraudulent purpose. As a result of these security measures, we saw a sharp decline in criminals attempting to access our regional claims centers.

David Beats Goliath

While the collaborative actions of the three major insurance companies and the individual actions of Poco Coche Rojo were not totally foolproof, they provided solid evidence that one can fight the cartel and win not because we were stronger in force, but because we were smarter in planning and executing our strategies. All the policy and procedural changes we implemented, plus the cost of training and security reconstruction, were completed for less than Poco Coche Rojo's projected six-month loss to cartels. The ongoing salaries and benefits of security personnel to manage and maintain operations represented only a fraction of what the cartel members were taking from us every month.

At the time of my departure from Poco Coche Rojo, cartel activity had been removed from the expenditure column; no doubt, the cartels are now enjoying a feast from another point of least resistance. The big win in this endeavor was our ability to alleviate the stress and fear experienced by staff members. The confidence of Poco Coche Rojo employees that they were safe and in a violence-free work zone allowed them to concentrate on their jobs and thus increased productivity.

Lessons Learned

Three lessons became clear to me as a result of my experience at Poco Coche Rojo during this time. First, building trust and confidence between management and staff must be based on honest communication. The root failure that brought this case to fruition was the inability of claims adjusters to talk about a difficult situation without perceived penalty. They worried about the security of their jobs and were afraid to tell their supervisors what they were experiencing in the field.

The second lesson I learned was that sometimes your best ally is your competitor. Vicente took a big risk when he reached out to the security directors at our competitors, but it paid off. Building a relationship with the other insurance companies in this matter of mutual significance helped us overcome insurmountable odds, and, in the end, our consolidated approach removed the cartel influence in this case. I imagine that the director from Protección Verde regretted his decision to walk out of that meeting.

Third, this case taught me the importance of reading and digesting the monthly audit reports, watching for trends and then asking questions. One diligent auditor, José Garza, was able to bring this massive fraud to light. Had the irregularly upward trending of Poco Coche Rojo's "acceptable expenditures" been questioned earlier, millions of dollars could have been preserved.

Recommendations to Prevent Future Occurrences

Based on my experience with Poco Coche Rojo, I have three recommendations to prevent similar future occurrences, not only in environments similar to cartel-ridden Mexico but also for insurance companies in general.

1. Monthly auditing of trends is essential. I highly recommend rotating different audit teams on analyses. This comparative approach provides an opportunity to get a fresh set of eyes to examine the landscape of the company's finances.
2. Monthly or quarterly peer meetings can reap dividends in staying ahead of developing trends. In this case, the meetings were among security directors at competing insurance companies, but the same principle can be applied for insurers around the world. There are opportunities to meet with competing corporations and agencies that are positioned similarly to yours. The issues to be discussed will vary widely, of course, but industry-wide communications can have positive effects regardless of the concerns in a specific region.
3. In any political environment, monthly coordination with intelligence resources provides a great opportunity to understand changes in the operational landscapes that might affect the profitability and safety of your company.

About the Author

Loftin C. Woodiel, Ph.D., CPP, is a graduate professor of criminal justice at Missouri Baptist University. He has 20 years' experience in international corporate security leadership serving the financial services and transportation industries as well as ten years' experience years in law enforcement operations. Dr. Woodiel is an avid researcher, writer and public speaker.

CHAPTER 22

Falling Prey to Online Charms

TINA HANCOCK

Rick Alley had been out of work too long. Money was running low, and he wasn't comfortable accepting help from his wife's family. One day, while at home surfing the Internet, he saw an advertisement about making a living working online. The ad described how he could learn how to sell insurance from the comfort of his home, and it sounded ideal. All he had to do was pay $39 for the e-book sold on the website and he would be able to run his own agency. Rick paid the $39 with his credit card and downloaded the insurance manual onto his computer. He flipped through the pages, excited at the prospect of getting back to work again.

After finishing the manual, though, Rick didn't feel so confident. Running his own agency sounded a lot more difficult than he imagined. About that time, Denny Morfine, the book's author, called Rick to follow up on his purchase. Denny said he was sure that Rick could pass his state licensing exam. Although Denny was in a southwestern state and Rick was living up north, Denny assured him he would be there every step of the way to help him with the insurance agency. Rick thought, "What do I have to lose?" He eked through the licensing exam and started his insurance business online, right out of his home.

Denny built a website for Rick's agency, which he named Insurance Alley, to help market the business online. Ads were targeted to small-business owners looking for commercial liability insurance. Denny also helped Rick manage the agency's bookkeeping, taxes and bank accounts. Denny was like a business partner and assisted with day-to-day operations, so Rick didn't mind that he took a percentage of the business returns. After Rick expanded his agency to several states, Denny hired Doon Ritter to help Rick answer the phones and return emails. Denny assured Rick that Doon didn't need an insurance license because he was just performing customer service.

Denny's help with the agency was so invaluable that Rick had time to work an outside part-time job at a grocery store to support his family. Somehow that wasn't part of his plan, but the money from the agency didn't seem to go far enough after Denny paid the expenses. As Denny said, "Running an insurance agency is expensive."

Denny was an aspiring actor who promoted himself and his training business in comical videos. Denny was the wacky professor of his online agency's course, and he danced and sang about how "insurance is fun!" He also linked his talent agency's website and his acting credits to his insurance ads, blogs and incredible success stories.

Rick was a nice guy who was just looking for a way to take care of his family. He had been unemployed and knew how hard it was to make a living. He tried to keep up with the demands of Insurance Alley, but holding down an outside job made it difficult. He trusted that Denny could make the business work for everybody. He knew that Denny had lost his insurance license, but the way Denny explained it, he had been misunderstood. And it didn't matter because Rick had his license, and he was the owner of the company.

Rockwell Construction was a small company with 40 employees. Sue and John Rockwell had built it from the ground up, with a lot of hard work and their own funding. With two young children under the age of six, the couple had their hands full running the company and caring for their family. Most days there were not enough hours to do everything necessary for the business and the family.

Rockwell built small office buildings and strip malls and won several municipal government contracts for projects in the local community. The business had done well, and the company expanded from its original ten employees to several work crews supervised by experienced foremen. Rockwell Construction enjoyed a reputation for quality work and completing projects on time. The workers enjoyed regular pay at competitive rates, and the business was like a close-knit family.

A Good Deal Gone Bad

Sue Rockwell oversaw the office management for the company, while John managed project schedules and supervised the foremen. Sue took care of the paperwork, and, of course, tried to save time wherever possible. One Thursday night in the first week of November, after putting the children to bed, she decided to work on an unfinished task from earlier in the day. She had been shopping for quotes on commercial liability insurance for a project bid. She went online and saw an ad for purchasing a business policy through Insurance Alley. Sue input the required information in the Web form to obtain a quote and was pleasantly surprised when it was lower than all the others she had gathered.

The next day Sue received a call from Doon at Insurance Alley. Doon instructed Sue to return her signed application by fax, and he took her bank information over the phone for the quoted down payment of $789. Doon said the policy would be bound that day, and he would fax to her a certificate of insurance. The monthly payments of $350 were within budget, and Sue was relieved it had been so easy to obtain the required coverage online.

Sue received the insurance certificate by fax that afternoon from Doon, but she noticed that the project was not recorded with an insured interest. She called him back, and he said that to add an insured interest would cost an additional $150. Disappointed, Sue authorized the additional charge. Doon said he would have the certificate reissued, but it would take a few days.

The following Tuesday, Sue called Insurance Alley, but there was no answer. Feeling uneasy, she called her bank and learned that the withdrawal for the down payment had cleared the day she signed the application. She called the agency several times that week and left voice messages. The following Wednesday, Doon returned her call to say the certificate was not ready and it would be another week. Over the next three weeks, Sue called and followed up with emails but still did not receive the certificate. She was getting panicky — without proof of insurance, Rockwell could lose the contract. Toward the end of December, Sue's project coordinator called and requested the certificate. Sue called Doon and explained the urgency of the situation. Doon said he would have his supervisor, Rick, look into the matter.

The next week, Sue called again and asked for Rick, who apologized and said it was an oversight by the insurance company. Sue had received her December bank statement, and realized another deduction by the agency had been processed, far more than the additional $150 due for the insured interest — $489. She called Rick again, who explained that the revised certificate had caused the premium to increase, and the certificate would be provided within a week. Several weeks went by, and Sue's project coordinator issued a final deadline for receipt of the certificate. During this time John got involved, and he was not as patient with Doon or Rick as his wife had been. John told them both that if a policy did not materialize before the deadline, he would file a complaint with the state insurance commissioner. Rick hung up on John.

Call for Help

After three months, the Rockwells still had not received the certificate of coverage. Rockwell Construction could not fulfill the terms of its contract and lost the project. Sue also had not been able to obtain two other certificates for additional projects she had ordered from Insurance Alley during the first weeks, and the company lost those projects as well. With the interrupted work flow and loss of income, the company had to lay off workers, who went to work for competitors. The stress that resulted from the insurance transactions gone awry had taken a terrible toll on the young family and their business.

Sue filed a complaint with her state's insurance department that Insurance Alley had taken her company's funds and provided an invalid commercial certificate of coverage without an in-force insurance policy. Sue said the agency failed to provide documents substantiating the additional deduction from her company's bank account. She alleged that the agency's mishandling of the transactions had cost Rockwell Construction lost contracts, income of approximately $1 million and two-thirds of its permanent workforce.

As an investigator with the insurance department in Sue's state, I have investigated many consumer complaints involving misappropriation and diversion of fiduciary funds — insurance-speak for theft of premiums — both permanent and temporary. Jurisdiction over the agents and their agencies often resulted in administrative discipline consisting of probation, suspension, fines or license revocation (termination). Many of these frauds involved forgery or submission of insurance documents with altered or false information. Other times the agent collected and retained the premium but never issued a policy.

Misappropriation and insurance application misrepresentation are felony criminal violations that are often referred to the fraud division for criminal investigation. Unfortunately, in Sue's case, Rick was in a different state, and my jurisdiction was limited to an administrative case. I knew that if the Rockwells' money disappeared without a valid policy, I would need to refer the subjects to regulatory agencies in multiple states, increasing the complexity of the investigation.

Seeing the Big Picture and the Red Flags

My first investigative action always involves looking at the big picture to determine the components: who was involved, what was done, when it occurred, where it happened and why — the five Ws. In this case, Insurance Alley took Sue Rockwell's money on three separate occasions, twice in November and once in December. I discovered that Rick Alley was the only licensed individual at the agency. Doon Ritter did not have a license, but he initiated and completed Sue's transaction. In our state, an insurance agency license was required to transact commercial lines, and Doon was not authorized to conduct the transactions.

Sue's payments occurred online and by phone, fax and email, which constituted wire fraud because Doon and Rick failed to provide contracts after taking Sue's money. Premium charges were not detailed with written documentation as required by law. The "why" was a little harder to document; but when money disappears, it's usually because someone intended to take it and use it for their own benefit. Sometimes agents divert the money and try to pay it back before anyone notices, but that wasn't the case here — Sue never received valid certificates that she had paid for.

After assessing the big picture, I began to look for individual red flags — the attention grabbers, visible markers, even my gut feeling about the case. In this case, the flags were that Rick worked out of his home selling commercial insurance (which was prohibited in our state) and that Sue Rockwell never received the insurance policy and certificates she purchased. Since Rick had been unemployed prior to opening the agency, it meant he was probably using the funds just to survive and support his family. When I saw that Denny was doing a song and dance on the Internet about his acting and insurance agency success, it was apparent he wanted attention and easy money. After all, how many insurance agents were actors and made comedy videos? Having his promotional websites linked to Rick's website illuminated their business relationship, which I explored more fully.

Another flag was that Sue called Rick's phone number in one state but reached Doon in another — an indicator that their business was not operating as a typical insurance agency. It was going to be hard to track and reconcile its activities. The lack of response to Sue's calls and emails was another sign that Rick either couldn't manage the business or didn't intend to do so. The damage to Rockwell Construction and the level of frustration after repeated efforts to resolve the matter were strong indicators that the subjects mishandled the transactions.

Knowing that I was dealing with three subjects in two other states who were operating online meant it was going to take a considerable amount of documentation to prove their activities and intent. After gathering the Rockwells' statements and documents, I requested policy documentation and correspondence from the insurance company and subpoenaed bank records for the subjects and the agency. It was important to establish the timeline of payments and when documents were due to be provided, both to the insurer and to the customer.

I checked the state database for additional filings against Rick Alley and found several other customers who lodged similar complaints. I also checked the national database and enforcement action publications of other states but found no other complaints about Rick. However, Denny's license was revoked in his home state and in 30 other states where he operated for misappropriation of funds and insurance application fraud for providing false certificates to small-business owners. As I processed Rick's case as a nonresident licensee, I referred Denny's case to his home state's department of insurance; I sent information about Doon's unlicensed activity to his home state's agency as well.

As I reviewed the third-party insurers' documents and the subpoenaed bank accounts, it was evident that Rick had treated other customers the same way he had the Rockwells — taken their money without providing policies or certificates of coverage and then ignored their requests for help. I contacted a sampling of the customers and obtained statements from four in my state and two in the states where Doon and Denny lived.

Revealing Records

I discovered documents from a finance company that had Sue Rockwell's signature authorizing a finance agreement for her policy premium, although she never mentioned it. I called her and she stated she had never even seen the document. I had her come into my office and verify that the signature was not hers.

I then ordered additional documents from Rick for the other customers I had identified. As some of them had policies canceled from several third-party insurers, I ordered documents from those companies as well.

The subpoenaed bank records revealed that Rick added Denny as an authorized signor on his agency's account one month after opening it. Denny had been using a debit card drawn on the agency's account for everyday purchases. Rick withdrew $300 per week from the account and transferred it to his personal account, while Denny spent most of the agency's income on personal expenses. The account had been overdrawn every month for more than a year with insufficient funds charges totaling hundreds of dollars. There were very few withdrawals by insurance companies for premiums.

In misappropriation cases, it's advantageous to talk with the individual to obtain additional information. I called Rick and asked him some general questions in a friendly tone and then asked him to explain the customers' transactions. I knew that I might only have one opportunity to get information from him, so I asked my supervisor to be in the room while I was on the call, as a witness to the conversation. Of course I disclosed it to Rick and said she was there to help me take notes for my report. As my tone was relaxed and friendly, Rick was not intimidated and cooperated.

In most cases in our investigative bureau, it was necessary to notify the subject of the investigation if the evidence substantiated the allegations. It was at this point, at the end of the call, that I asked Rick to put his response in writing to include in my investigative report. I already had all the evidence I needed regarding the customers' transactions, but I wanted to give him the opportunity to document his false statements in his own writing, signed and dated.

After I received Rick's written response, I called him again with the goal of getting information on the other subjects. Instead, Doon answered the phone and I verified his location. On another attempt to reach Rick, Denny answered the phone. He said that Rick's line was forwarded, and he verified his and Rick's locations. Denny even provided additional contact information for Rick. I had met my goal of verifying the existence and location of these other agents and their relationship with Rick.

Satisfied Customers

As I reviewed the documents received from the different insurance companies for the customers, it became evident that Rick misappropriated the premiums on every case I reviewed. Of the four customers in my state, all gave sworn statements that they had not received policies or valid certificates of coverage. Two were unaware they had been operating their businesses with no commercial liability coverage for at least two consecutive years, as the insurers had no record of receiving payments and canceled the policy applications. The two customers in Rick's and Denny's states were also unaware they had no coverage. Rick had used his agency address on the policy applications as the customer contact information to intercept all correspondence from the third-party insurance companies.

Of the six customers I reviewed, the average loss was the down payment premiums for two years, or approximately $1,500 each. All business customers suffered lost business income, ranging from a few thousand dollars to $1 million. Each successive policy that was sold by Rick resulted in increased premium rates, due to poor payment history.

Insurance companies began terminating Rick's contracts due to substandard business retention — too many canceled policies and late premium payments. Accounting records provided by the brokers revealed convoluted transactions of numerous policy applications, lost down payments, canceled policies for nonpayment of premiums and invalid certificates with false information on customers. Departmental budget restraints did not permit me to investigate each set of suspicious transactions, but of the ones I calculated, Rick misappropriated an average of 20 percent from each customer. In the two years of the investigation, he wrote contracts with the three insurers worth a total premium amount of $300,000, of which he took about $60,000 and repaid about $10,000. But he also transacted insurance with more than 20 companies in eight states that were not part of the investigation.

Rick had already given me a statement on the phone, and he also emailed statements regarding each customer's transaction, with copies of his credit card and bank statements showing customers' down payments. Rick had an excuse for every problem on each customer's account, and said it was unfortunate he had such a bad group of customers who couldn't keep their payments current and were too hard to please. Rick denied any business affiliation with Denny, stating he had bought the agency from Denny and they were just friends. Rick said Doon was an elderly employee who had Alzheimer's, made a lot of the mistakes at the agency and couldn't remember the customers' transactions.

I sent my written report with an evidence packet to our legal processing unit. The case coordinator analyzed it against statutory law and contacted Rick in an attempt to settle his case. Rick was apologetic at first and said he did not want an agency license in our state and had no intention of

206 Falling Prey to Online Charms

conducting business here in the future. He offered to provide refunds to his victims. After the coordinator explained the possible repercussions in detail, including felony arrest, Rick changed his position. He said he knew that once an agent was disciplined in one state, all the other states can take reciprocal action, and he didn't want to lose his entire business. Rick decided to retain an attorney and proceed to an administrative hearing to dispute the facts. He also applied for an agency license in our state. Rick continued to write policy applications despite being notified in writing several times to cease and desist transacting insurance in our state.

After a year of considerable effort, we obtained refunds for all of the customers contacted in the investigation — $10,890 in premium refunds from Rick — a paltry percentage of his overall fraud. We also revoked his nonresident license in our state, and he is currently in the process of losing his license in the eight other states in which he operated.

We referred the evidence of Denny's involvement to the department of insurance in his state, and agents there opened an investigation. Updated contact information for Doon was forwarded to that division as well.

The total time spent on the investigation in our state was 18 months, from the initial customer complaint until the case was transferred to our legal department. Additional information continued to stream in from customers as they sought to obtain refunds from the subject.

Lessons Learned

It's crucial to do a case assessment at the outset to determine the necessary resources and develop an investigative plan. As the evidence builds, it's important to develop an organized tracking system for easier reference and to determine what is still needed. In these types of cases, it's especially true that it's not what you know; it's what you can prove.

The advantage for insurance agents who operate online is that they can cross state lines and sell in an almost unlimited venue. For some agents, this allure leads them down the wrong path, and they think they have a measure of anonymity. But this same level of anonymity can be enjoyed by investigators to locate subjects, track activities and perform extensive background checks online. Establishing networking relationships with other regulatory and enforcement agencies helps to successfully determine the proper jurisdiction.

If you have a good rapport with a subject, you will be able to obtain information more easily. Having a conciliatory and helpful attitude enables you to reach a commonality with your interviewee more readily. Forgetting your ego and position while retaining your professional skepticism and employing advanced interviewing skills allows others to relax and let down their guard, creating the space they need to share the information they possess and you need. Human nature dictates that people think, "What's in it for me?" Making the benefits clear to the suspect increases the likelihood of success.

Investigating insurance fraud requires careful organization of what usually amounts to volumes of evidence. Maintaining the chain of custody is critical to preserve its integrity for trial. Transactions conducted in cyberspace, on the phone and by fax can be especially difficult to document. Sophisticated computer forensic analysis might be necessary in some cases to track fraudulent transactions.

Insurance fraud tends to be difficult to understand for nonindustry people, including law enforcement, and it is necessary to collect proof of each step that occurred in the sequence of events to make the case clearer. Reconstructing a fraudulent transaction and comparing it to a legitimate transaction helps others to see the big picture.

Recommendations to Prevent Future Occurrences

The National Association of Insurance Commissioners maintains a database of all insurance licensees, including records of the states in which they are licensed, companies to which they're appointed and reported enforcement actions. Within just a few minutes, it is possible to verify licensees' residency and industry records and find contact information for the appropriate regulatory agencies. Accessing the database at the start of a case — and following up regularly — can provide critical information. Most states reciprocate enforcement actions performed as part of another state's investigation outcome.

Searching websites of individual states can produce additional data regarding licensees and enforcement actions against them. Sometimes documents or press releases are provided online, along with Web forms to file complaints.

If evidence was uncovered in an investigation that a licensee perpetrated fraud in another state, or in a state as a nonresident licensee, it's particularly important to report the activity to the agent's home state as well as to any other states in which activity occurred. Some fraudsters may think they can commit fraud in a nonresident state and, if they get caught, it won't affect their ability to conduct business overall. Make sure you coordinate your evidence and investigative report with the other states so the subject is aware that states are united in their efforts to regulate the insurance industry.

About the Author

Tina Hancock, CFE, M.A., M.B.A., is an analyst, auditor and former insurance examiner. Ms. Hancock's loss reserves analysis led to fraud litigation on her state's largest property and casualty insurer insolvency case. As an insurance investigator, her caseload of agent and agency fraud involved data analysis, interviewing, forensic accounting and risk assessment. She shares her experience in webinars and public speaking.

Big Bills in Little Cuba

MARK STARINSKY

Every year thousands of immigrants risk their lives escaping Cuba, seeking asylum and a better life in the United States. Some travel in makeshift boats or rafts while others gain access overland from Mexico. However Cubans make it to the United States, most end up in South Florida. Maria left Cuba in the early 1970s, before the mass exodus in the 1980s known as the Mariel boatlift eventually closed Cuba's borders to exiles. She lived briefly in Los Angeles, California, before making her way to South Florida. Joe had a more harrowing experience and didn't make it to the United States until the mid-1990s. He never did reveal his life story or how he was able to leave Cuba; he was just happy to be living the American dream in the bright lights of New York City. After being in the country for five years, Joe also moved to South Florida. Although Los Angeles and New York have thriving Latin American populations, nowhere is there a larger Cuban American population than in the greater Miami area. In fact, Hialeah, a city just north of Miami, ranks second on the list of Cuban and Cuban Americans residents of any U.S. city and Spanish is the most-spoken language. Missing their families and cultural familiarities, Joe and Maria both settled down in Hialeah.

The streets of Hialeah had all the comforts of Havana: the smell of *cafecitos*, a strong mixture of Cuban coffee and sugar; the sound of dominos being played by old men in the neighborhood; the taste of the *guarapo*, a sweet juice made from raw sugarcane; and the medical clinics . . . the medical clinics? Yes, the medical clinics. It turns out that pharmacies, home health agencies, durable medical equipment (DME) suppliers and clinics dominate many neighborhoods in Hialeah.

Maria owned an interior design company, but business wasn't so great and she was looking around for a better opportunity. With no formal medical training, Maria stumbled upon a company that was seeking new ownership. K&B Equipment, a DME supplier providing breathing supplies to Medicare and Medicaid patients, had gone through nine ownership changes within its ten-year existence. Maria would be the final owner and eventually turn it into the company that is the subject of this case study. Business was good — so good, in fact, that Maria opened two other branches in Hialeah. In the beginning, the sales were legitimate. Doctors sent in prescriptions, orders were filled and patients received their medications. This is where Joe stepped in.

After heading to Hialeah, Joe set up a delivery company and turned it into a thriving business. Eventually he crossed paths with Maria and started handling all of her deliveries. The two quickly became more than business acquaintances; within a few years they were living together as husband and wife.

Running three suppliers was proving to be too much for Maria, and some questionable billings had started taking place. After a solid nine-year run, her business venture was coming to a close — but that didn't mean she was finished. With the experience she'd gained and the contacts she made, Maria set up one final company — the company that would lead to her downfall.

Dusty Shelves

K&B Pharmacy spun off from K&B Equipment and opened on a corner of one the busiest intersections in Hialeah. Walking into the pharmacy, a customer wouldn't notice any differences from a small neighborhood drug store. The shelves were packed with inventory, and there was even a small section of women's clothing in one corner. A close look at the inventory, however, revealed a layer of dust covering the boxes of cough medicine and candy bars. The pharmacy had DME — devices used by ill or injured people, such as walkers, canes and wheelchairs — on display. Under the stress of her failing business, Maria established Joe as the owner and president of K&B Pharmacy. This Cuban exile and one-time deliveryman was now the owner of a multimillion-dollar company receiving payments from Medicare and Medicaid.

Although the pharmacy had canes and wheelchairs in the windows, the only items it actually billed for were levalbuterol and budesonide inhalation medications and the items necessary for their administration. These medications are commonly prescribed to patients with breathing disorders, such as asthma. For most Medicare beneficiaries, though, the diagnosis is usually more ambiguous: chronic obstructive pulmonary disease (COPD), which can mean either chronic bronchitis or emphysema. The medications for both of these diseases are liquids and require the use of a nebulizer, a small device that uses compressed air to break up the liquid into an aerosol that can then be inhaled into the lungs through a face mask or mouthpiece. Nebulizers and their accessories are all considered DME and are payable by Medicare, Medicaid, private insurers, etc. as long as the medications are covered. Payments for these items are relatively small. For example, at the time of my investigation, Medicare reimbursed DME suppliers about $16 per month for a nebulizer rental. During this same time, a supplier could make thousands of dollars for power wheelchairs, hospital beds, or other more advanced pieces of equipment. Maria and Joe were staying below the radar with these small-dollar items — or so they thought.

In the 11 months prior to my investigation, K&B earned more than $2.6 million from Medicare alone. Unless a company has a substantial patient base or is a national chain, it's pretty difficult to earn that type of revenue when you're only making $16 a month per patient. It's probably important to note here that while K&B had the word *pharmacy* in its title, it was actually a Medicare-certified DME supplier. And to own a DME supplier, you do not need special qualifications or even medical qualifications. A deliveryman, for example, can start a DME company.

Whack-A-Mole

Law enforcement and the federal government recognized the ease of DME supplier ownership and also the spikes in the number of DME companies operating out of South Florida and their respective Medicare reimbursements. A few years ago, the U.S. Department of Health and Human Services, Office of Inspector General (OIG) (the primary agency responsible for combating fraud, waste and abuse in the Medicare program) started Operation Whack-A-Mole. Named after the popular arcade game, the premise behind Whack-A-Mole was that as soon as Medicare shut down one DME company, another quickly popped up. This project consisted of conducting unannounced site visits to more than 1,500 DME suppliers in Miami-Dade and its neighboring counties, Broward and Palm Beach. Approximately 31 percent, or about 500 DME suppliers, didn't meet basic standards that required suppliers to maintain a business address and actually be open and staffed during business hours. As an auditor with OIG, I personally visited more than 100 suppliers in only a few days. Although K&B was not on my list, another auditor on my team did visit the store and found that Maria and Joe maintained the address that Medicare had on file and had staff present. K&B passed the first step of the Whack-A-Mole process, but Joe and Maria couldn't breathe easy yet. K&B was identified through Whack-A-Mole simply because it was a DME supplier operating in a zip code known for fraudulent Medicare activity. And although it passed the basic supplier standards, the store didn't have the appearance of an active Medicare business to the visiting investigator: There were no patients present, there was no one on the telephone taking prescriptions from doctors, there was no one filling prescriptions . . . there were just people loitering around.

At the time of this investigation, Medicare contracted with companies known as *program safeguard contractors* (now known as *zone program integrity contractors*) to assist in paying Medicare claims correctly by early detection of fraudulent claims, analyzing data and reviewing records. I routinely partnered with investigators from Florida's program safeguard contractor. One day I was speaking with an investigator about suspicious Medicare claims activity and the topic of nebulizers came up. She faxed me a list of DME suppliers that primarily billed for nebulizer-related drugs, and K&B was in the top ten. The companies that came before K&B were either national retailers or local DME suppliers we were also investigating. However, K&B was the only mom-and-pop business whose billings rivaled those of national retailers. We quickly identified K&B as a company deserving of a closer look.

Store Visit

Since we already had recorded observations of K&B from the Whack-A-Mole project, I decided that an audit was the next step to determine the appropriateness of K&B's payments. After receiving my manager's approval to audit, I prepared the necessary documentation and contacted Joe to schedule a meeting. This initial meeting was not unlike the countless others I had led. I brought two junior auditors with me, and we described the reason K&B was selected for audit and the objective, scope and reporting portions of the process. Maria and Joe were both at the meeting, along with a contracted pharmacist and a support person who ended up assisting us by making copies of medical records. Also present (in the background) were the dusty candy bars and medical equipment. At first glance, nothing during this visit seemed too strange. K&B had all of the necessary documentation I expected a legitimate business to have, including policy and procedure manuals and medical records documentation.

We requested supporting medical records for a sample of patients whom we had previously selected. One by one, we collected physician-signed prescriptions, equipment invoices and delivery tickets signed by Medicare patients. It wasn't until we started questioning Joe about his delivery policies and the day-to-day activities that cracks appeared. Joe was able to discuss the delivery process but allowed Maria any remaining business questions. This is common of nominee ownership cases, where a person allows his name to be used for recording legal ownership of a business yet has no actual decision-making capability over the business. A quick look at the billing records revealed that Joe was supposedly making 45 deliveries across three counties in a single day. Anyone familiar with traffic in a major metropolitan area would find this suspicious, yet Joe swore he made these trips. More important, these visits supposedly consisted of providing a patient with instructions on how to operate the equipment. When Joe's interview was complete, Maria excused him to walk her dog for the rest of the day. My audit team returned twice more to collect the remaining medical records, and both times the pharmacy was silent — there were no phone calls, no ringing fax machine and no patients. Throughout the audit process, Maria and Joe were very cordial, even offering to purchase us pizza from the pizzeria next door. They seemed very confident that the audit would result in their favor. I honestly don't think they expected what came next.

House Calls

Armed with documentation containing signatures of doctors and Medicare patients, we began visiting individuals to determine if they actually ordered or had received the equipment. One by one, doctors attested that the patients were not theirs, they did not have medical records for them and the signatures on K&B's files were not theirs. To ensure that no mistakes were made and to prevent relying solely on a doctor's memory, we sat with medical record clerks at the doctors' offices with lists of patient names for further confirmation that, in fact, they were not real patients. In total, we visited 12 doctors who supposedly ordered 100 nebulizers. Of these 100 claims, more than two-thirds were not actually authorized by the physician in K&B's documentation. One doctor in particular worked at an injury clinic that dealt primarily with workers' compensation, but he supposedly ordered 55 of the claims paid to K&B. Results from our visits to the patients also confirmed our suspicions. The majority of them had never heard of K&B nor did they have the nebulizers that had supposedly been delivered to them. After meeting with doctors and patients, we determined that 87 of the 100 sampled claims were errors, and we extrapolated these errors back to K&B's universe of paid claims. With our overpayment defined, I contacted Maria to schedule a meeting to discuss our results. At this meeting, I explained the additional verification steps we had taken and told Joe and Maria that we estimated K&B had been overpaid almost $2 million. Confused doesn't describe the looks on the couple's faces. I'm not sure if it was the bad news or a translation problem, but they requested that we explain our findings again in Spanish. And while they disagreed with our findings, all they could say is that they would appeal our results. They simply could not explain why a doctor would claim not to have ordered services supposedly rendered by K&B.

The Truth Comes Out

South Florida is teeming with so much Medicare fraud that it's usually difficult to get a law enforcement agent interested in your case. This case was different. We had strong evidence and physicians willing to testify that they had not ordered K&B's services; it was a slam dunk. It helped that the OIG has its own law enforcement subcomponent, the Office of Investigations, tasked with investigating Medicare fraud allegations.

We provided OIG special agents with boxes of medical records, physician attestation statements and a report of our findings. At times, I received calls from physicians wondering if their billing identifying numbers were being comprised and what was going on with the case. At other times, special agents would call for additional information, including updated Medicare claims data. It felt like the end would never come, but then I received a call from the case agent telling me that arrest warrants had been secured for Maria and Joe. Their arrests showed who the true owner of K&B Pharmacy was. Maria quickly hired a high-priced attorney for representation and bonded out of jail. Joe sat in jail for the weekend while waiting for his public defender. It was at this point that we learned Maria and Joe weren't actually married after all.

Maria and Joe were each charged with one count of conspiracy to commit healthcare fraud and five counts of healthcare fraud, each carrying maximum prison sentences of ten years. With the evidence mounting against them, Maria and Joe accepted plea agreements.

They eventually revealed that they accessed physician billing identifying information, such as a unique physician identification number (UPIN) or a national provider identifier (NPI), available publicly online. Once they had the ID numbers and the doctors' addresses, Maria and Joe took turns forging doctors' signatures. They took patient ID numbers from Maria's previous legitimate business, K&B Equipment.

Maria and Joe each ended up pleading guilty to one count of conspiracy to commit healthcare fraud, received 51 months of imprisonment and were ordered to repay the federal government more than $2.6 million. I remember feeling like Frank Wilson, the accountant who eventually brought down Al Capone. Finally, I hadn't just issued an audit report; I actually saw justice served.

Lessons Learned

This audit and eventual investigation taught me that the criminal mind is without limits and, in Medicare fraud, seems to always be one step ahead of the good guys. For example, the NPI system was created to standardize unique health identifiers for healthcare providers. In reality, it seems to have simplified access to information needed for Medicare and other healthcare fraud schemes.

I also learned that fraud examiners cannot simply perform an audit from behind a desk. We need boots on the ground and we have to talk to people. K&B had legitimate-looking documentation, yet talking to a handful of doctors proved that Joe and Maria had woven together an elaborate web of smoke screens and false documentation.

Recommendations to Prevent Future Occurrences

K&B was one small fish in the great ocean of Medicare fraud. Although $2.6 million sounds like a great judgment, investigators are drowning in schemes that plague South Florida. In fact, the approximate 500 DME suppliers found to be nonexistent during Operation Whack-A-Mole billed Medicare approximately $237 million in just one year. After multiple DME audits and law enforcement operations, the Centers for Medicare and Medicaid Services (CMS) implemented accreditation and additional supplier standards, the ultimate first step in preventing future occurrences of DME fraud. CMS now requires that suppliers seeking to obtain or maintain Medicare billing privileges become accredited through one of CMS's ten approved accreditation organizations. CMS also utilizes the National Supplier Clearinghouse to review DME Medicare applications and conduct site visits to verify compliance with DME supplier standards. During this investigation, there were 21 standards. As a direct result of the work conducted in Miami, these standards were increased to 30, adding requirements for maintaining minimum work hours per week and the prohibition against using beepers, answering machines, answering services or cell phones during posted business hours as the primary business telephone.

If you are dealing with an accredited supplier with a Medicare billing number, conduct proactive data analysis of the supplier's claims to identify patterns of aberrant or outlier billing activities. The claims data could reveal that one physician is approving all of a supplier's claims; that every patient is receiving the same package or bundle of equipment; or you may know that equipment should be billed as a group, yet the supplier billed for each component separately. Such analysis is not foolproof and should not be the sole determining factor in your investigation, but it should point you in the right direction.

Unfortunately, most fraud investigations are pay and chase — Medicare pays the claims and fraud is detected after the perpetrators receive the money, putting law enforcement in the position of chasing the funds. The best effort to combat pay and chase is to analyze data before claims are paid, through prepayment medical reviews or predictive modeling. Prepayment medical reviews are costly. Predictive modeling is used in other financial industries, yet it is difficult to predict a patient's healthcare needs. Through the government's Health Care Fraud Prevention and Enforcement Action Teams (HEAT), the public has been solicited for a data analysis system based on predictive modeling. CMS was "charged with developing a data system to facilitate the identification of illegitimate healthcare providers or suppliers when they apply for a Medicare provider number, before they receive the number and begin billing for services. The system, when implemented, should also be able to track billing patterns and identify aberrant patterns in a timelier manner than present systems."[1] CMS is currently using a system that builds profiles of providers, billing patterns and so on and then assigns a risk score to estimate the likelihood of fraud and flag possibly fraudulent claims.

(Continued)

---

[1]www.mintz.com/newsletter/2010/Advisories/0826-1210-NAT-HCED/0826-1210-NAT-HCED.pdf

Finally, if all else fails, get out from behind your desk and visit the individuals involved in the transaction: the doctor who supposedly ordered the service and the patient who supposedly received the service. Had we not visited the physicians and the patients K&B was billing for, we would not have identified a problem. I recommend these visits especially in cases were a supplier's documentation appears suspicious. Physicians are busy, and you may spend a lot of time in a waiting room. It helps if you are a law enforcement officer or a representative of a healthcare regulatory agency. Doctors, however, are concerned with protecting their billing privileges and professional integrity and therefore probably will assist in determining whether something was actually ordered. Speaking to patients is generally an easier task. If you are dealing with an elderly Medicare population, you might be the only person they've spoken with all day or all week. These visits are fairly straightforward; patients either have the equipment ordered or they do not. And with K&B, it gave me a chance to really determine if 45 deliveries were possible in one day. As I suspected, it was not.

About the Author

Mark Starinsky, CFE, AHFI, is a senior investigator with General Dynamics Information Technology, providing services to healthcare payers in the detection, investigation and disposition of cases of potential healthcare fraud, waste and abuse. Mr. Starinsky was a U.S. Department of Health and Human Services, Office of Inspector General criminal investigator and senior auditor. During more than ten years with the OIG, he was successful in identifying more than $1 billion of fraud, waste and abuse. He led various reviews of Medicare and Medicaid providers, including home health agencies, durable medical equipment suppliers, mental health centers and health maintenance organizations. Mr. Starinsky has received several awards for meritorious service and is an active Accredited Healthcare Fraud Investigator and Certified Fraud Examiner.

24

Rushing an Insurance Claim

PETER PARILLO

Most business owners spend a majority of their day thinking about how they can improve their business — how they can increase sales, increase productivity, be more efficient and pay the bills. However, for a small percentage of them, the thought process is very different. These individuals care more about how they can personally benefit from the least amount of effort, regardless of how many people are affected. Anthony Grau initially spent most of his time thinking about the right way to grow the business he inherited from his father. Anthony wanted to exceed his father's successes and expectations and was going to stop at nothing to preserve his family's legacy in the wholesale business. Unfortunately, Anthony's ability to grow the business did not match the demands of his lifestyle.

Anthony's parents, Victoria and Phillip Grau, were born and raised in Poland. Shortly after World War II began, they gathered a few of their personal possessions and left Europe for the United States. Soon after arriving in New York City, Phillip, barely 18 years old and with very little education, found a job polishing diamonds in New York City's jewelry district. This was a good job for Phillip since he only knew a few words of English. The weekly salary was low, but Phillip was happy that he was able to bring home some money and support himself and his wife. As the years passed, Phillip learned English well enough to interact with customers directly and build relationships. In 1946, after the owner of the company retired, Phillip used the professional relationships he had created to start his own company, Gold Rush, Inc. The business was modest and at first focused on polishing diamonds, but as Phillip's network grew, so did his business. He decided to begin importing gold and selling it to local retailers and manufacturers.

As Gold Rush grew, Victoria and Phillip welcomed their son Anthony. He began working for his father at a very early age and often spoke of his childhood memories involving the store, such as when he would visit his father and play with gold bracelets and rings. He would place the jewelry on his arms, neck and fingers, pretending he was the king of the world. Anthony's father thought it was so cute that he took a picture and placed it in a gold frame on his desk; it served as a conversation piece when customers came in. After Phillip passed away, the picture sat on Anthony's desk and served as a reminder that he wanted to be king of the world and would do anything to ensure his success.

Second Generation

Anthony did not have a college degree or take any business courses, but he was a businessman who loved to wheel and deal. Unlike his father, who established deep relationships with vendors and was comfortable that any deal presented to him was a fair one, Anthony almost always negotiated. He hardly ever took the first deal and frequently demanded better terms from vendors. The majority of the time, vendors did give him a better price. Anthony knew that a fortune could be made buying and selling gold and that the more gold he had, the more he could sell for a bigger fortune. Unfortunately, Anthony's credit limit prevented him from buying as much inventory as he wanted. But that would soon change.

For any business, it is not uncommon to have a line of credit with a financial institution for general business purposes. In the case of a jewelry wholesaler, a line of credit is used mostly to purchase gold or precious stones and on occasion for labor purposes (e.g., setting precious stones into prefabricated gold jewelry). In the wholesale jewelry industry, a line of credit is especially important during the holiday season. Purchasing gold for the holidays can begin as early as September, and a saying in the jewelry district during the holidays is "He who has the most gold is king."

Anthony realized that if he was to continue growing his business, he needed more gold. After speaking with advisors, he decided to take out a line of credit with a financial institution. This would allow him to purchase more gold and, better yet, secure the line of credit with the purchased gold. Anthony set up an appointment at a financial institution on the corner of Fifth Avenue and West 40th Street. Fortune Bank was a major creditor in the jewelry district and had the process down to a science. Anthony provided the bank with financial records and a business plan, and within a few days Gold Rush was approved for a $1 million line of credit. Anthony was excited and was eager to put it to good use. What he did not fully understand when he agreed to the line of credit was that Fortune Bank was going to hire an independent company to perform a monthly inventory count. In addition, Gold Rush would need to pay for that inventory count.

Within the first few days of receiving credit, Anthony purchased more than $500,000 worth of gold. He was buying from any supplier he could place an order with and selling the gold to retailers at a profit in just a few days. Anthony was finally running the business the way he envisioned.

Shortly after the loan was approved, the loan officer at Fortune Bank assigned the monthly inventory review to NewBridge CPAs, an independent firm specializing in gold inventory counts. NewBridge, where I was employed, was a small firm located near Fortune Bank, and the two companies had a long working history together.

Working at NewBridge had many positive points. Granted, the prestige did not compare with a Big Four company, but the diversified experience was second to none. As I began scheduling client visits for the weeks ahead, I saw an email asking the auditors if anyone could perform Gold Rush's monthly inventory counts. I recently had a new availability in my schedule, so I quickly volunteered. I obtained the contact information and account details and called Gold Rush.

"Gold Rush, what?!?" a man barked out.

"Hello, can I speak to Anthony?" I responded.

"Who is this? What do you need?"

I introduced myself and explained that I was calling on behalf of Fortune Bank and was scheduling an inventory count.

"Well, I'm Anthony, and I didn't agree to any inventory count!"

I explained that it was part of his agreement with Fortune Bank and that he should contact the bank directly to confirm.

"I will," Anthony snapped as he hung up.

I quickly thought that I might regret volunteering to take on this client.

Unwelcoming Client

After a few days I called my contact at Fortune Bank, Lori Rizzo. Lori was a no-nonsense loan officer who played by the rules. If a debt covenant failed on one of her loans, she acted immediately. I explained the situation to her, and she began to laugh.

"Yes, I know all about it. I explained the inventory clause to Anthony, and he was not happy. Regardless, I told him that if it does not get done, I will be forced to call the loan," Lori told me.

"What did he say?" I asked.

"Let's just say he had a change of heart. You should not have a problem scheduling a count, but if you do, call me immediately."

After I hung up with Lori, I called Anthony.

"Gold Rush, what do you need?"

Nervously I responded, "Hello, Anthony. It's Peter from NewBridge, how are—"

"Yeah, I know, you need to come in," Anthony interrupted. "Come in on Thursday before three o'clock," he said as he hung up.

As I sat at my desk with the phone to my head listening to a dial tone, I wondered if this was a joke.

Thursday arrived, and I prepared the documentation for the inventory count. The paperwork was straightforward and consisted of an Excel spreadsheet that automatically calculated gold value based on total weight and current market value. As I began my ten-block walk to Gold Rush, I practiced my introduction and explanation as to why the gold count was required. This would help me if Anthony began complaining that the count was taking too long. When I arrived at Gold Rush, I rang the bell and waited for a response.

Suddenly a voice yelled out, "Yes!"

"It's Peter from NewBridge," I replied.

A loud buzzer sounded and the door opened. I entered the office and was immediately greeted by Anthony. Not what I expected, Anthony stood about six foot six and was very thin. The clothing he wore looked five sizes too big; he reminded me of a kid playing in his father's wardrobe. In addition, he looked as if he had just woken up, with his hair in disarray and an unkempt beard.

"Hello, happy to meet you," Anthony said as he reached out to shake my hand.

"Hello, Anthony, happy to meet you in person too," I replied.

As I followed Anthony to the inventory bins, he stopped and asked, "So, how much gold do you need to count?"

Not sure what he meant, I just looked at him with a confused look.

He then continued, "What I meant is, you don't need to count everything, do you?"

Knowing that my response was not going to be what he wanted to hear, I decided to answer his question differently.

"Why do you ask; is there something you want to tell me before I begin?"

"No, not at all," Anthony quickly replied.

He then introduced me to the inventory clerk. "This is Ralph Joseph, RJ for short. He will be assisting you with the inventory count."

Anthony returned to his office, and RJ and I began the inventory count. Bin by bin, we documented and weighed each item by style number. Within the first hour Anthony checked in to see how it was going.

I told him it was fine so far and added, "The first time usually takes the longest since this is the initial documentation. It should be more efficient going forward."

I explained the process to Anthony, detailing that the two major drivers to the review were the cash balance at the bank as of the day of the inventory count and the amount of gold on hand.

We completed the count in three hours, and the initial calculation revealed that the inventory level was insufficient. I asked RJ if there was any additional inventory, but he just shrugged his shoulders.

"Let me ask Anthony," RJ replied.

After a few minutes, RJ returned with Anthony.

"How much are you short?" Anthony asked.

Knowing that he was looking for a specific amount, I responded, "The calculation does not work that way; it is based on outstanding balance on the day of the inventory count and total inventory level on hand."

"Well, I still have old gold that is being smelted. That is a few pounds and should be enough. I have to pick it up tomorrow. Come by first thing and I can show you."

Reluctantly I agreed. I noted the finding in the work papers and left the office. Early the next morning, I returned to Gold Rush. As I entered the office, Anthony greeted me with "Good morning, the stuff is behind you."

I turned and noticed a dolly with three large plastic containers on it.

I immediately asked, "I thought it was going to be smelted?"

"I have to return it to the smelter after you look at it," Anthony snapped.

I was expecting to count one-ounce gold bars, which would have made my visit easy, not three large containers. I took out my computer and opened the containers and began counting.

Almost immediately Anthony became enraged. "What are you doing!?"

"What do you mean?" I asked. "I have to document the inventory."

Rubbing his head, Anthony grumbled, "This is going to take forever."

After an hour, I was able to document the items in the containers and noticed that it did not match what I counted the previous day. This gave me peace of mind that Anthony had not tried to pull a fast one. Also, the calculation revealed that the inventory on hand was adequate in relation to the loan balance outstanding for the month.

I turned to Anthony. "Okay, all good, see you next month."

"Can't wait," Anthony responded sarcastically.

Spending Spree

The following month, I prepared for the second count. I noticed that Gold Rush's outstanding balance on the line of credit had doubled. I immediately thought: Great, I need to spend more time at Gold Rush counting gold. I scheduled the inventory count with RJ and arrived onsite. When I entered the office, I was greeted by Anthony, looking very different from when we first met. He was dressed as if he was preparing for a photo shoot, sporting an expensive suit, tie and shoes.

Taken aback, I shook Anthony's hand and said, "Hello, Anthony, special occasion?"

"No," he replied. "I decided to treat myself a little."

Anthony then screamed, "RJ, Pete is here. Let's get this thing over with."

RJ emerged from the back of the office smiling and led me to the inventory bins.

I couldn't help but ask, "Hey RJ, what's up with Anthony? When did he turn into a model?"

RJ laughed and said, "Two weeks ago he and his wife went out and spent over $25,000 on designer clothes."

"You must be kidding me," I said in disbelief.

"That's not all. Anthony went and bought himself a $200,000 car last week and is going on an expensive vacation next month."

"Is this normal for him?" I asked.

"No," RJ said. "I've known Anthony for seven years, and he is cheap. This is different."

When RJ and I finished counting the gold in the bins, again the inventory level was insufficient. Anthony immediately jumped in. "I know, you think we're short again. Come tomorrow and I'll pick up the rest from the smelter."

Reluctantly I left the office and returned the next day to find a dolly holding four plastic bins filled with gold pieces. After counting it, the inventory level was sufficient, but not by much.

December is one of the busiest months in Manhattan. Tourists flock to the city to take in all of the sights and sounds of the holiday season. Rockefeller Center is the epicenter of it all, and around the corner is the jewelry district. Both locals and tourists window shop for gifts in the jewelry district as store owners battle one another to attract patrons. As the holiday season hit its peak, so did the line of credit for Gold Rush — Anthony had nearly exhausted it. I had assumed that he would dip into the credit to get through the holidays, but I was not expecting him to use the entire amount. I called Gold Rush and, for the first time, RJ answered. I immediately thought, What a pleasant surprise.

"Hi, RJ, it's Pete. I need to come in to perform the monthly inventory count. When are you available?"

RJ informed me that Anthony was away and would not return until Monday. I pointed out that, in addition to the holiday madness, the news was tracking a nor'easter that was on target to hit us over the weekend. If the predictions were accurate, the city was going to come to a standstill come Monday. I was able to convince RJ to let me complete the count the next day rather than waiting for Anthony to return.

The next day, the newspaper headlines were focused on the nor'easter, each one with a witty comment on how the city would be affected. As people prepared for the storm, I prepared for the inventory count. When I arrived at Gold Rush, the snowfall was well under way. I greeted RJ and we quickly began the count. Again the inventory was short. I asked RJ if there was any other inventory elsewhere, but he said no. Looking at the calculation and then out the window, I noticed that the snow was intensifying.

"Are there any plastic bins with inventory?" I asked.

"No, Anthony didn't tell me to go get anything from the other place," said RJ.

Thinking that I miscalculated in my haste to complete the inventory count, I decided it would be best for us both to head home before we were snowed in.

The following day, New York City was covered with snow and ice. The storm crippled the city, and mass transit was at a standstill. It was impossible to get into or out of the city. Luckily it was a Friday, and most people were happy to turn the snow day into a three-day weekend. Shortly after realizing that there was nothing on the television during the daytime, I began to think about Gold Rush's inventory calculation. It was a calculation I performed several times, and the result always supported an adequate inventory level. This time it did not. I opened my laptop and began looking at the supporting documentation. Everything was in order, and my calculation was correct. Gold Rush did not have enough gold on hand to support the loan. I wondered why the inventory was so low and what RJ meant when he said, "Anthony didn't tell me to go get anything from the other place."

The Robbery

The following Monday, the city was slowly getting back to normal. Huge piles of snow lined the streets and covered cars. When I finally arrived at the office, I had three voicemails. The first message was from Anthony on Thursday evening. He sounded a little flustered and simply said, "Peter, please call me immediately."

The second message was also from Anthony, this one on Friday. "Peter, I called you yesterday, I guess you did not come in today because of the snow. I need to speak to you immediately regarding the gold count."

The third message was left at 6:00 a.m. Again, it was Anthony. "Peter, please come to my office as soon as you can."

I had not even removed my coat, so I picked up my computer bag and headed to Gold Rush. When I arrived, Anthony was speaking to RJ, and RJ did not look happy.

I overheard Anthony say "Stay here and let me handle this." Anthony, again dressed to the nines, walked toward me and said, "I was robbed."

"Good morning," I replied. "What do you mean, you were robbed?"

Anthony explained that someone must have entered the office during the storm and stolen the inventory that was stored in the plastic containers.

"I already called the insurance company and told them what happened. They are sending someone today to take a look."

Anthony grabbed my arm and walked me toward his office.

"Personally, I think RJ took it," he whispered.

Not knowing how to proceed, I told Anthony, "Let's see what the insurance company says first."

As I walked toward the exit, RJ came over and opened the door for me.

"See you later, RJ," I said walking by him.

"Okay, see you later," he replied.

Suddenly he handed me a piece of paper and walked away. As I made my way out of the building, I looked at the paper. It only had a telephone number on it. I walked into a nearby coffee shop and dialed the number.

"Hello, Pete?" a voice asked.

"Hello, who is this?" I replied.

"It's RJ. I need to talk to you. Can you meet me tonight at seven o'clock in the coffee shop on the corner? You know the one I am talking about?"

I laughed and said, "Yeah. I am standing in it right now."

I returned to my office and waited for seven o'clock. Fifteen minutes prior to seven, I left the office and made my way to the coffee shop. I was very nervous, speculating on what RJ would tell me. When I walked in to the coffee shop, RJ was waiting in the corner. I walked over and sat across from him.

"How are you, RJ? What's up?" I asked.

"Not good, Pete, not good," RJ responded. "The gold does not belong to Anthony," he added.

"What do you mean?"

"Well, when you come to do the inventory count, Anthony calls a friend of his up the street and asks to borrow gold from them. After the count is done, I would bring the inventory back," RJ explained.

At that point, many thoughts whirled through my mind. What should I do next? What if Anthony is right and RJ did steal the gold, and this was just a cover-up? What if somehow I was to blame if RJ is right?

"Where did you go get the gold?" I asked.

"The name of the company is Aztec," RJ replied.

Not knowing how to proceed, I told RJ not to tell anyone that we spoke and headed home.

The next morning, I called Lori and told her what transpired. She was not happy. I told her the name of the other company and she began to laugh.

"That's our client too," she said.

"Great, can I get the file?" I asked.

"I'll send it shortly."

Within a few hours, I had the Aztec file and immediately accessed the gold inventory spreadsheet. Since the format was identical to the Gold Rush spreadsheet, it was very easy to perform a search. I searched for the first inventory item I listed from the containers, a match. I immediately set up a spreadsheet listing the identical items. Almost all the items listed on Gold Rush's inventory were also on Aztec's inventory. Anthony lied about his inventory and, even worse, another client of Fortune Bank was involved.

I called Lori, who said, "Send me the file and I will call Anthony and have him come in for a meeting. I will let you know when."

A few days passed and all was quiet until one morning when I arrived at work and noticed I had a message. It was Anthony. "Hey, Pete buddy —"I wondered when I became his buddy. "I just deposited the check from the insurance company, so there should be no issue now. Please call Lori and tell her all is well now. Thanks."

I did call Lori, and I informed her that Anthony deposited a check that he received from the insurance company. "Well, that just made things a lot worse." Lori stated. "Anthony is avoiding me, but I have a way of getting his attention; I am freezing his account to protect the bank and I will let him know that if we do not meet with him this week, we are calling the loan."

The following day I received a call from Lori. "Anthony will be at my office in two hours; come by now to prepare." I gathered the paperwork and schedules I had prepared and reviewed with Lori and headed to the bank. Once I arrived, Lori greeted me and invited me into her office.

"Let me do all of the talking," Lori said.

After an hour of idle conversation, a voice echoed through the phone, "Lori, Anthony from Gold Rush is here."

"Let him in," Lori replied.

Lori stood up and greeted Anthony at the door. "Hello, Anthony, take a seat."

"I don't know why we are having this meeting; I have enough money in my account to meet your stupid requirements," Anthony said.

Lori leaned forward and looked Anthony in the face. "We have an issue, Anthony. An issue that has grown much larger since you filed a false insurance claim."

"What? Are you crazy? I am going to get my lawyer and —"

"And what, Anthony? We know about Aztec and we know that you borrowed the gold from them to meet the requirements of the loan."

Anthony's face grew pale as he leaned forward in his chair. "This has to be a lie," he muttered.

Lori then asked me to explain what I found. As I described my findings, I knew that he was not listening to a single word I was saying. Anthony stared at me, not at the spreadsheet I handed him.

He got up and quietly said, "I want to speak to my attorney before I say another word," and began walking out the door.

"Just so you know, Anthony, I called the insurance company and I have a meeting with them tomorrow morning," Lori said. "Also, your account with us is frozen as per the agreement."

Anthony did not say a word as he left the office.

The following day, Lori and I met with Matthew, a representative from the insurance company, and I explained the findings once again. Matthew reviewed the documentation but had very few questions. I wasn't sure if it was company policy or just shock. I forwarded the work papers to Matthew as requested, and that was the last I heard from him. I assumed that the insurance company interacted directly with Lori.

The Rush Ends

A few months later, I had a meeting at Fortune Bank and stopped by Lori's office to say hello. Lori was on the phone as I poked my head in. I could hear her voice clearly as she dictated precisely to the person on the other end what she wanted. Again I thought, This lady is no nonsense.

"Pete, come in," I heard her yell.

"Hello, Lori, how are you?" I asked.

"Good so far. I guess you want to see if I had an update on Gold Rush."

"Well, yes, but if you can't I understand."

"Pete, I am grateful that you brought this to my attention immediately. Let's just say that because of you we only lost $125,000. It could have been much worse if we waited another month or so."

"What happened to Anthony and RJ?"

"What I was told from the insurance company is that they interviewed Anthony and he came clean regarding how the money was being used. Anthony explained that he started out with buying new clothes for himself and then for his family. That then led into him spending money on a new car for himself and his wife. That was only the beginning," Lori said.

"I guess having that much money at your fingertips is tempting."

"After Gold Rush closed up shop, RJ went to work for another wholesaler, but he provided a lot of information before he left."

"How so?" I asked.

"RJ gave us insight into Anthony's spending habits. He explained that Anthony loved to brag about his luxurious vacations, membership in a country club, and impromptu gambling trips."

"Anthony felt as if the money was his personal piggy bank," I replied. "Any punishment for his actions?"

"Anthony has really good attorneys, and I am certain that he will spend every dollar he has left making sure he does not go to jail. Personally, Anthony losing his family business as well as the respect of his family and friends might be worse than any jail time," Lori replied.

As I started to get up out of the chair, Lori stopped me. "Pete, I have to say that if it wasn't for you continuing to ask questions and following up, we would be much worse off. Anthony panicked, and his only way out was to say the gold was stolen.

"His lifestyle got too big for his income to support, and unfortunately he thought Fortune Bank and the insurance company were going to subsidize his lifestyle," she added.

I nodded and continued to leave.

"As a reward, I am giving you first choice of all new accounts we get," Lori stated, smiling.

"Gee, thanks, Lori. I am honored," I replied sarcastically.

Lessons Learned

As I walked back to my office, I could not help but remember my interactions with Anthony and RJ. I replayed every meeting in my mind, thinking that I missed a clue or hint that would have exposed Anthony sooner. Regardless, I used Gold Rush as an example when training new members of the team.

From this case, I learned that people do not like to admit failure or admit that they are wrong. A true professional will admit shortcomings and provide a solution to remediate. Others will make excuses and possibly lie to cover up their shortcomings and buy time to resolve the issue or hope that the other party forgets about it. Anthony was just plain greedy and dreamed of a lifestyle that his income could not support. The line of credit was too tempting, and Anthony dug a hole too deep to get out of. Fortunately for the insurance company, the fraud was discovered before Anthony spent his claim reimbursement.

Recommendations to Prevent Future Occurrences

I made the following recommendations to Fortune Bank's review process to help prevent similar situations from happening in the future.

1. Require managers who obtain a line of credit to post a sign asking employees to contact the financial institution directly or a third-party hotline to report inappropriate financial behavior.
2. Implement surprise inventory counts.
3. Require additional insurance coverage and review of prior claims.
4. Implement a zero-tolerance procedure, and recall loans immediately when borrowers fall below required thresholds or fail established covenants.
5. Perform additional follow-up procedures such as:
   - Confirmations, if time allows, of offsite balances
   - Telephone inquiry, if time does not allow confirmation of offsite balances
   - Site visits, if time allows and logistically possible, to confirm offsite balances

About the Author

Peter Parillo, CFE, CPA, CBM, CFF, CGMA, currently leads the internal audit department for a publicly traded company in New Jersey. Mr. Parillo has more than 25 years of audit experience, including 15 years' experience conducting fraud investigations. He resides in Freehold, New Jersey, with his wife, Lori, and two children, Victoria and Peter.

CHAPTER 25

Ignorance Is Bliss, While It Lasts

REBECCA BUSCH

Wilfred E. Ernster II — known as Junior in his family — grew up in the family business of selling supplies to healthcare providers. His father, a recognized philanthropist and well-respected family man, started his original company in 1915. As the eldest son, Junior took over the family business and in 1965 started a new enterprise, Med Supplies R Us, to replace the flagging original company. He founded it with his two adult sons, Wilfred III and Earl.

Wilfred III and Earl grew up in the family business, like their father did, and they enjoyed the perks of being members of a wealthy family with a dynasty of sorts to preserve. They were used to seeing their parents get dressed up to go to fundraising events on the weekends, and they thought nothing of being featured in the society page of the local paper. They were raised to run a company that was the lifeline of a community and to be active in philanthropic causes. This was the norm in the Ernster family, and the sons knew they were expected to continue it.

Med Supplies R Us enjoyed progressive growth pretty much right out of the gate, which pleased Junior because he wanted to provide a solid, grounded business to secure the livelihood of future generations of Ernsters. He took the company public in 1979, but the goals of the public offering were not achieved and the company reverted to a privately held entity in 1984. In the same year Junior retired and passed his interest on to his sons: Wilfred III became president and Earl became chief executive officer. The pressure to manage growth while maintaining the family's reputation in the healthcare industry and the philanthropic community was now the responsibility of the third generation. To continue growing Med Supplies R Us, the brothers initiated a series of acquisitions.

Under the direction of the brothers, Med Supplies R Us became one of the leading manufacturers and distributors of healthcare products in the United States, and its inventory included medical and surgical supplies, durable medical equipment and other day-to-day items for patient care. The company's catalog offered more than 150,000 items. Med Supplies R Us had more than 3,500 employees, $1.9 billion in annual sales, 60 distribution sites, a new 200,000-square-foot corporate headquarters and a 250,000-square-foot warehouse in Utah. The company experienced a significant surge in sales of protective gear following the September 11, 2001, terrorist attacks.

During this time, employer- and government-sponsored healthcare incentive programs grew in popularity and offered rich benefits to employees and beneficiaries. Med Supplies R Us enjoyed growth from these wellness initiatives because they provided coverage for the products that the company sold. However, the political climate for healthcare continued to change and evolve, and pressure was placed on all market players to manage costs. Med Supplies R Us started to feel the weight of these ongoing and new rules.

No Experience Necessary

William Bering graduated from college in 1984 — a difficult year because many graduates were entering the workforce but there were not enough jobs for everyone. A family friend of the Berings reached out to the Ernsters and asked if Wilfred III or Earl could find an entry-level job for William. He landed an interview and was hired to work in the sales department. William, happy to have a job, was eager to please, worked exceptionally hard and did as he was told. He was fresh out of college with no healthcare experience, so Med Supplies R Us provided him with all of his training. Over the years he climbed up the company ladder and was eventually promoted to executive vice president of sales. His lifelong dedication to the Ernster family for giving him his opportunity created a blind spot in William's judgment. He never would have imagined that he could be ordered to do something wrong.

William eventually married and had three children. As his responsibilities at work increased, he started to relieve his stress after work with coworkers at the local pub. The pressure was nevertheless taking its toll on the home front. Out of concern, William's wife asked her brother, Timothy, a well-known local attorney, for advice and if he could reach out to her husband.

During a family gathering on Thanksgiving, Timothy pulled William aside and asked how everything was at work. William candidly discussed how he was finding it difficult to manage the multitude of client relationships on behalf of Med Supplies R Us. He discussed a pattern of commissions and rebates among various sets of parties to others and explained how some delays in third-party commissions were upsetting their support vendors, suppliers and providers. The process was simply becoming overwhelming.

"I always have to manually figure out what percentage of the income we received as a result of this buyer and that referral agent." Timothy quietly listened to his brother-in-law describe the problems at work. When William was finished, Timothy simply stated, "William, we gotta talk."

Timothy understood that William was unknowingly describing a series of illegal kickbacks. These occurred in the sale of medical supplies and equipment to providers who then billed Medicare, Medicaid and private insurance companies for the items — plus the cost of the various inducements they paid to the hospitals and other public officials. Understanding such inducements is critical in the complex world of healthcare, and if someone does not have past experience or proper training, they can easily become confused.

Unbeknownst to many individuals, hospital executives have to submit cost reports to Medicare, which must include all their sources of revenue and documentation of expenses. These reports affect the reimbursement rates received from the government. Inducements from suppliers like Med Supplies R Us become a problem if they are not documented as revenue. A second concern is the undue influence they can cause in the purchase of noncompetitive goods. These unnecessary or unjustified purchases can result in higher expenses submitted to Medicare and Medicaid.

As an attorney with experience in healthcare fraud cases, Timothy was able to see the red flags in William's story, even though William didn't. As a result of their conversation, Timothy initiated the appropriate representation for William as a relator (whistleblower) and had a relator action filed under seal against Med Supplies R Us.

Second Chance

My company specializes in investigating healthcare fraud cases and is located in the same town as Med Supplies R Us. I became involved with this case when the original complaint was about to be amended and refiled. The schemes proved to be much more complicated than anyone originally involved thought, and the investigators and experts had not been able to clearly identify and establish the processes that Med Supplies R Us's personnel were using to provide kickbacks to their customers. The Ernsters' lawyers had filed a motion to dismiss the healthcare fraud charges based on the plaintiff's failure "to allege the essential element of the materiality." Also at issue was proving that executives at Med Supplies R Us were "knowingly and willfully executing or attempting to execute a scheme or artifice to defraud any of the money or property owned by or under the custody or control of any healthcare benefit program." Therefore, I was contacted by William's attorneys and went to a meeting to get the full story.

I attended a formal interview with three different attorneys to help them understand how kickbacks are often paid and to get a clear picture of their case and needs. My terms were simple — I needed to interview William Bering myself, I needed to review all the original documents in the file and I had to be able to obtain critical documents as requested. The attorneys eagerly agreed, and I went straight to work.

My first step was to meet with William. During my interview with him, I focused on learning the business activities specific to Med Supplies R Us and the company's rebate process. William gave me insight into the financial transactions his employer had with hundreds of hospitals, skilled nursing facilities and hospices — basically any healthcare provider that might need to purchase medical and surgical supplies.

William was in a unique position to know how the individual transactions and rebates were processed for each entity, and I needed him to explain the processes as thoroughly as possible. The U.S. False Claims Act prohibits suppliers from providing remuneration to induce purchasing, and I hoped I could find a violation of the Act in Med Supplies R Us's history. The False Claims Act is specific in stating that if any insurance claim submitted by a healthcare provider to obtain reimbursement for medical and surgical supplies is tainted by unlawful remuneration, it is improper. I was going to dig for these improper transactions.

Med Supplies R Us had a huge inventory of items for sale, and, without a well-planned strategy, such an investigation could easily become daunting. Conveniently, the medical industry uses two coding systems for supplies, services and diagnoses — ICD (International Classification of Diseases) coding and CPT (Current Procedural Terminology) coding. Any supply billed to Medicare, Medicaid or a private payer must have an associated code. In this case, I ran reports of medical supplies and the list of codes, which provided a baseline for me to understand the actual dollars involved. A review of Med Supplies R Us, its respective clients and the volume of sales by a listing of products and their CPT codes, along with the dollars associated with rebates that Med Supplies R Us offered, demonstrated a shocking magnitude of products sold using illegal inducements.

Nitty-Gritty Fraud Examination

After my first meeting with William and a thorough review of the company's records, I held a series of extensive meetings with him and his team of lawyers. We reconstructed movements of the business operations, money flows, client communications, contract terms and employee and vendor compensation. The charts we created with these reconstructions clearly demonstrated that the Ernsters were providing monetary incentives during sales, contracts and product exchanges. However, I knew all of this movement needed to be translated for a jury to understand, with specific behaviors categorized. The illicit compensation I discovered fell into several categories, which I labeled *bribes, donations, rebates* and *consignment kickbacks*.

I applied the principles of fraud examinations during the course of this investigation, including conducting interviews, gathering and requesting documents, assembling evidence, writing up report findings and working with attorneys. My prediction was established when the documents provided sufficient evidence of kickbacks to a wide range of entities that Med Supplies R Us served. William was able to produce management reports that he both developed and distributed under the direction of the Ernster brothers. He provided copies of management memos with specific targets for sales and the budget for inducements to secure those sales. Further, he provided corporate memos with instructions on how to mask entertaining expenses as legitimate business expenses. I also interviewed other nontraditional industry experts, including headhunters who placed employees in the healthcare industry, to gain insight on employment practices.

The fraud theory I developed was "a complex set of kickback mechanisms that were developed to provide unwarranted illicit compensation to induce purchases that were not medically necessary." My meetings with William helped me understand and chart specific workflows of the kickback mechanisms, defined by job function and job title. The work patterns identified how the inducements were incorporated into normal business operations. Further, this allowed me to make subsequent requests for data to measure the extent of damages and illicit inducements that were used to solicit and pay the kickbacks. I compared the description of the payments and their purpose to the guidelines published by the Centers for Medicare and Medicaid Services (CMS). The processes in place at Med Supplies R Us directly conflicted with CMS guidelines.

Bribes, Donations, Rebates and Consignments

Although the basic principle of bribery ran through all of Med Supplies R Us's transactions, the kickbacks that materialized varied among the company's clients. One instance I uncovered involved a county official who influenced the purchase of inventory for a local public medical center. Med Supplies R Us sent "corporate rebates" to a corporation that then laundered the funds and paid them to the county commissioner.

Another mechanism for the kickbacks came in the form of "donations." The Ernster brothers created a foundation arm of Med Supplies R Us with the explicit purpose of providing contributions to charitable organizations and scholarships, but instead the foundation submitted donations to foundations of hospitals that purchased supplies from Med Supplies R Us. These hospitals filed pricing and data reports that did not show the offset donated funds from the foundation. A parallel to understand this practice would be an independent consultant who submits a bill for travel expenses. The client reimburses the consultant for expenses, but then the consultant submits his tax return with a deduction for the travel costs — not documenting that the expenses were actually reimbursed. It is a form of double dipping. After the exchange between the foundations, the hospitals' purchasing departments directed doctors and nurses to be partial toward Med Supplies R Us's products.

The third scheme the Ernsters employed was the rebate. Rebates done properly are completely legal and often occur in healthcare; a manufacturer issues rebates after the sale and distribution of one of its products. However, the executives at Med Supplies R Us used the rebate account to submit payments to hospitals as an inducement for additional sales. Then the hospitals and other medical providers reported the full, unrebated cost to the government or private insurers, thus giving the appearance of paying a higher price in their cost reports. The medical providers were awarded a higher rate of reimbursement because they were claiming higher operating costs. The reality is the rebates should have been treated as revenue to provide a realistic account of what the hospital or clinic actually paid for the medical supplies.

Finally, Med Supplies R Us had a program to grant consignment kickbacks to some customers. This involved a very layered and complex arrangement that in essence resulted in on-demand loans to clients. The Ernsters created open-ended loans or on-demand loans that equaled 8.5 percent of total amount of purchases a provider committed to make. Providers are required to disclose and record fixed prices so discounts or refunds like this can be recorded properly. In this case, again, the open agreements resulted in medical providers recording higher-than-actual prices.

All of these kickback schemes had the same result: The hospitals submitted inflated costs for their supplies to insurers. As a result, Med Supplies R Us provided hospitals a mechanism to receive inflated reimbursements from Medicare, Medicaid and private insurance companies. Med Supplies R Us benefited from higher sales activity from these providers.

William Bering no doubt had his hands full in managing such a complex set of relationships and accounting procedures. Working for a family that was accustomed to a lavish lifestyle and a philanthropic edge to contribute can be difficult. The amount of work William had to juggle could probably drive anyone to drink. I also learned from my interviews with industry headhunters that all of Med Supplies R Us's employees were handpicked and groomed to perform this type of work.

At the conclusion of my investigation, the plaintiff submitted an amended complaint that defined and outlined the kickback mechanisms in place at Med Supplies R Us. This allowed William's attorneys to properly allege the "essential element of the materiality" required to file healthcare fraud charges.

The final outcome was a civil settlement for $120 million and a five-year corporate integrity agreement (CIA) with Med Supplies R Us. A CIA is a public document that outlines the obligations that an entity agrees to as part of a civil settlement in exchange for the Office of Inspector General's (OIG) agreement not to exclude the entity from participation in Medicare, Medicaid or other federal healthcare programs. CIA settlements often include civil monetary penalties and subsequent reviews for ongoing compliance. Med Supplies R Us's participation in the CIA agreement helped both the company and the Ernsters avoid criminal prosecution. It is common to find healthcare organizations agreeing to CIAs in civil settlements.

Lessons Learned

I was hired to facilitate the second amended complaint after the first one had failed. The first lesson in this case was not for me but for the plaintiff's attorneys. They learned the importance of hiring the right type of expert for the case — and the consequences of overlooking this critical detail.

The second lesson was all for my benefit: Listen to your gut, follow the evidence, stay focused and be open-minded to outside perspectives. In this case, I needed to understand the corporate culture of Med Supplies R Us, so I interviewed headhunters who placed employees in medical professions. Their outside perspectives helped me understand why the mechanism of bribery was so easily achieved and integrated in Med Supplies R Us's day-to-day operations. As a Certified Fraud Examiner who has experience with healthcare compliance and risk management, I found the pervasive attitude about kickbacks throughout the company's entire sales division mind-boggling. William was very matter-of-fact in describing all of the transactions; he did not even know anything was illegal until his brother-in-law pointed it out to him.

When I reviewed my notes to prepare my report, I recalled concentrated moments of looking at William and thinking, "How could you not know for the past 20 years that this was illegal?" I tabled the question until I had a general discussion with a headhunter about her recruiting efforts for healthcare supply companies. I asked her how people get into the business. During the course of the conversation, she made one very enlightening comment: "Oh, and when I get a candidate who has *no* healthcare experience at all, I send them to Med Supplies R Us; they will only hire people with no experience." It was an aha! moment.

With my final report in hand, I called William's lead attorney and — after we discussed the 200-foot Ernster family yacht and their vacation homes throughout the country and abroad — I asked her, "Did you know that Med Supplies R Us will only hire employees who have no healthcare experience?" Her response was "Oh, really?" I replied, "Yeah, no wonder they had such a pervasive culture of people not knowing what a kickback was in healthcare."

Recommendations to Prevent Future Occurrences

The bottom line in this case — and unfortunately in many others like it — is that the leaders at Med Supplies R Us violated federal rules prohibiting kickbacks to induce sales. They provided their clients with rewards for purchasing products they otherwise would not have purchased, and those clients then submitted inflated reimbursement requests to the government and private insurers.

Inducements that adversely impact the costs associated with a government-sponsored program such as Medicare and Medicaid simply cannot be permitted. In this case, Med Supplies R Us negotiated a settlement that included repaying $120 million and obliged them to participate in a five-year CIA that allows for ongoing audits to ensure that the company no longer provides illegal inducements to customers. Further, the organization must have an active compliance program with oversight from a compliance officer. The key to any effective compliance program involves proper training of employees.

The OIG has general and specific guidelines for compliance within various segments of the healthcare industry. Overall, the OIG offers seven key elements for a comprehensive compliance program, and anyone working to prevent these sorts of abuses in the future should be aware of them:

> (1) The development and distribution of written standards of conduct, as well as written policies and procedures that promote the hospital's commitment to compliance (e.g., by including adherence to compliance as an element in evaluating managers and employees) and that address specific areas of potential fraud, such as claims development and submission processes, code gaming, and financial relationships with physicians and other health care professionals;
> (2) The designation of a chief compliance officer and other appropriate bodies (e.g., a corporate compliance committee) charged with the responsibility of operating and monitoring the compliance program, and who report directly to the CEO and the governing body;
> (3) The development and implementation of regular, effective education and training programs for all affected employees;
> (4) The maintenance of a process, such as a hotline, to receive complaints, and the adoption of procedures to protect the anonymity of complainants and to protect whistleblowers from retaliation;
> (5) The development of a system to respond to allegations of improper or illegal activities and the enforcement of appropriate disciplinary action against employees who have violated internal compliance policies, applicable statutes, regulations or Federal health care program requirements;
> (6) The use of audits and/or other evaluation techniques to monitor compliance and assist in the reduction of identified problem area; and

(7) The investigation and remediation of identified systemic problems and the development of policies addressing the non-employment or retention of sanctioned individuals.

The Office of Inspector General, Department of Health and Human Services (oig.hhs.gov/compliance) provides the most current publications on compliance, along with advisory opinions, open letters, special fraud alerts, bulletins and other general guidelines. This is an important resource to check to stay abreast of the latest initiatives involving Medicare fraud, waste and abuse.

About the Author

Rebecca S. Busch, R.N., M.B.A., CFE, CCM, CPC, CHS-III, CRMA, CICA, FIALCP, FHFMA, is CEO of Medical Business Associates and the author of *Healthcare Fraud Audit and Detection Guide,* 2nd edition (John Wiley & Sons, 2012); *Electronic Health Records: An Audit and Internal Control Guide* (John Wiley & Sons, 2008); and *Personal Healthcare Portfolio* (Author, 2010). Ms. Busch is an instructor at Florida Atlantic University in healthcare fraud examination, risk management and compliance. She is also an inventor and holds seven U.S. design patents focused on efficacy, risk and revenue management for the pharmaceutical industry, plus a U.S. patent on an electronic health record case management system focused on efficacy, risk and revenue management for direct and indirect providers of patient care.

CHAPTER

The Name Game

WILLIAM D. MEADER

Just about anyone who has owned or operated a small business has purchased an insurance policy. State and local regulations mandate that a business owner obtain an insurance policy to receive a license from the appropriate regulatory agency before doing business. Contractors, cab drivers, commercial truck drivers and others search for low-cost insurance policies that satisfy the regulators' minimum requirements.

The business of insurance is highly regulated to protect the solvency of the insurer, the content of the policy and the handling of claims. In the United States, this regulation falls primarily to the individual states. Each establishes a department of insurance and hires an insurance regulator to license the insurance companies, agents and brokers that market insurance products in their state. The ultimate goal of the regulatory agency is to protect the consumer.

In the United States, an insurer that wants to sell in a specific state obtains a certificate of authority or license from the state agency. This lets the consumer know that the insurer has met the minimum capital and surplus funds to operate and pay claims. This also gives the state insurance department the authority to examine the books and records of the insurer to see that it remains solvent.

If an insurer licensed in another country can meet the regulatory requirements set by an insurance department in the United States, that company may be allowed to sell insurance to consumers in that state as a *non-admitted company*. The state's department of insurance reviews the company's financials and determines whether the foreign-based insurer meets the minimum level of capitalization and surplus required to do business. Non-admitted companies primarily market policies to businesses that cannot easily obtain insurance coverage from the admitted market.

Imagine that you are a truck driver, a plumber or the owner of a taxicab or roofing company, and you purchase a commercial liability policy for your business. The premiums are reasonable and the insurer is a well-known and admitted company. You have an accident and submit your claim. When you receive a letter from the insurer, you are surprised to learn that your claim has been denied. How could this happen? You paid your premiums. You call the 800 number on your policy to speak to the third-party administrator, World Market Limited. You leave several voice messages for Eric Bell, the managing director of World Market, but he does not return your call. In fact, no one from World Market will talk with you. You contact the insurer named on the declaration page of your policy, Goodtime Indemnity and Casualty, and learn that they have no record of issuing you a policy. You have a loss, no insurance, no one to pay your claim and the premiums you paid have disappeared.

This was the type of consumer complaint that insurance regulators in western states began receiving frequently one spring. As the number of complaints grew, regulators began to ask questions. Where did the consumers' premiums go, why were legitimate claims denied and who controlled the business that marketed and issued the so-called insurance policies? Who was Eric Bell?

Not Just Another Case

As a senior criminal investigator at a state's department of insurance with more than 15 years of experience, I had handled major cases before. This one was going to be different. An investigation was ongoing, but the investigator had just been promoted to a supervisory position, so he wasn't going to be much help. He moved out of his cubicle to an office, and I moved into the cubicle full of boxes of documents. There were so many boxes that the cleaning staff refused to enter because they were afraid the boxes would fall over; there were even more boxes scattered throughout the state in our nine regional offices. To top it off, my department's upper management wanted the case submitted to a prosecuting attorney immediately. In other words, I was told to write a report, get the case filed with a prosecutor and move on to the next investigation. At a time when state budgets were strained, management was not going to put many resources into this investigation. I was a team of one.

My first step was to begin a review of my colleague's work product. Dale Williams was a senior criminal investigator, and I was confident that I could review his work and write up a report quickly. As I started to go through the documents he had collected, I realized this was not going to be an easy task after all.

Dale had focused his investigation on insurance brokers who specialized in selling liability insurance to taxi drivers. To pick up fares in a city or county jurisdiction, a taxi driver has to have liability insurance (anyone who has ridden in a taxi knows that many drivers are an accident waiting to happen). The profit margin for taxi drivers is so small that they have to look for ways to cut costs, such as with cheap insurance. It was a win for the broker and a win for the driver.

When Dale started receiving complaints from cab drivers, his first step was to go to several train stations in the area and inspect the insurance cards of various taxi drivers. Under state law, a certificate of insurance had to show the insurer's name, policy number, effective dates of the policy and the broker's name who sold the policy. Dale quickly noticed a pattern in certificates he inspected: In place of a policy number was the acronym "TBD." When Dale followed up with the insurance companies named on the certificates, representatives told him the company had not issued liability insurance to the drivers. In fact, none of the companies even sold liability insurance to taxi drivers. When Dale contacted the brokers who sold the policies and collected the premiums, they told him "TBD" stood for "to be determined"; they issued the certificates but were waiting for policy numbers to be assigned by the insurer.

The brokers told Dale that World Market Limited had marketed the taxi liability program to them and that Eric Bell was the manager for World Market. Dale learned that the claims for the taxi program were submitted to a company called United National Claims in Southern California.

The lack of a policy number and the fact that the insurance company never issued the policy was evidence that the insurance certificates were probably fraudulent. I knew I had a prosecutable case if I could determine that the brokers, Eric Bell or World Market knew the certificates were bogus. That was a big if. I still didn't know who Eric Bell was or where World Market was located. I could write up the case and submit it to a prosecutor, but without that information it would be rejected. I had more work to do. I went back to digging through the evidence in my cubicle.

In one of the boxes I found what I was looking for — a bio of Eric Bell — as part of his application for residency in a small Caribbean island. Bell had submitted the application so he could work for World Market, which was based on the island. According to Bell's bio, he was born in Massachusetts on February 22 and was 60 years old. He had lived in California, Nevada and Canada. He married Kathleen L. Rivera on July 11 in the State of Washington. Bell was hired to be the managing director of World Market, despite having no formal insurance experience. Prior to this, Bell worked as a paralegal. The personal statement also gave me Bell's Social Security, driver's license and passport numbers.

I pored over the documents and found a residency application for Rivera. She was born in Arizona on August 22 and was 55 years old. She had lived in Nevada and Canada and also had no insurance background but was hired by World Market. Eager to learn more about the couple, I ran their information through insurance licensing, motor vehicle licensing, criminal history and federal court records. The results from the Social Security Death Index stopped me in my tracks — both Bell and Rivera had been deceased for several years. Bell died in Nevada four years ago, and Rivera died in New Mexico two years ago. But that was impossible, as they were both alive and working at World Market. I could now add identity fraud to the list of charges.

Beware of Intentionally Complicated Structures

At a dead end with the identities of Bell and Rivera, I turned my attention to World Market. The company was a limited liability company that operated from the Caribbean and acted as a third-party administrator for a number of insurance companies. World Market used PO Boxes in two states to collect premiums, but policy documents were mailed from an island address. Claims were submitted to another PO Box or faxed to an 800 number and then forwarded to a claims adjuster in a western state.

World Market paid commissions to a network of insurance brokers across the United States (many of whom fell in my jurisdiction) to sell liability policies. The brokers sent liability policies. The brokers sent the insurance applications to a fax number in the islands, and then an agent at World Market would approve it and send it to an underwriter, again in my jurisdiction. To finalize the policy, the applicant sent a down payment premium and subsequent payments to a PO Box in another western state, where the box holder forwarded the funds to the islands. Someone at World Market had gone to a lot of trouble to create a convoluted system.

An insured with a claim submitted it to World Market, and it was forwarded to an adjuster in my state. After the claim investigation, the adjuster's report was sent to World Market, and the claim was usually denied. In one claim a helicopter had been damaged when it was towed across the airport parking lot; World Market denied the claim on the basis that the policy only insured the helicopter while it was parked and not moving or flying. Denials such as this forced claimants to hire an attorney to litigate the claim, delaying the process while World Market continued to collect premiums. Small claims were often paid to give the appearance that World Market was a legitimate insurer.

I conducted a search of state and national insurance licensing databases and failed to find evidence that World Market had a license to engage in the insurance business. The 25 different insurance company names that were on the policies issued by World Market were similar to the names of licensed U.S. companies. I knew from my experience that legitimate insurers collected their own premiums and underwrote and issued their own policies. They would not have used World Market in place of their own underwriting departments.

Repeat Offender

I expanded my research and found out that World Market and Bell were the defendants in a number of lawsuits alleging failure to pay covered claims. Two in particular caught my eye.

One lawsuit alleged that World Market used the name of an insurance company without authorization. World Market claimed that it had not used the insurer's name but had set up a company with a similar name. The lawsuit was settled when World Market agreed to not use the insurer's name or any similar name.

The second lawsuit alleged that Bell and World Market defrauded an insurance company by issuing policies in the company's name without authorization. The attorney for the insurer had tracked down Bell in another country and deposed him. Bell gave no information about his identity and declined to say where he lived. He said he traveled extensively and never stayed in the same place very long. He gave details about the operation of World Market that confirmed much of what I had already learned.

I found a total of ten states that filed actions against Bell and World Market and issued cease-and-desist orders. World Market's counsel responded that the company was licensed in the Caribbean and could sell insurance directly to anyone who wanted to purchase a policy. World Market denied any wrongdoing and did not stop the sale of insurance.

Piling Up Boxes

I traveled the state and interviewed policyholders and insurance brokers. The interviews confirmed the way World Market operated. The policyholders said they would not have purchased insurance from World Market if it had not been represented by top-rated U.S. companies.

Next, I secured search warrants for ten insurance offices throughout the state based on theft of premiums, material misrepresentations and aiding and abetting an unlicensed insurer to transact insurance. More boxes of evidence piled up in my cube.

I prepared an investigative summary report based on the evidence discovered so far and met with County District Attorney Larry Kubota, who told me his office did not have the resources to prosecute a case that crossed so many jurisdictions. Kubota told me to take it to the feds.

A week later I received a call from Special Agent Marge Ringer of the Federal Bureau of Investigation. Agent Ringer said she had been assigned to investigate the movement of a large amount of money from my state to the Caribbean and that she had received information that the money was from the sale of insurance. World Market was the recipient of the funds. I told Agent Ringer about my investigation and we agreed to meet at her office. I gave her a detailed summary of my findings and said the DA had declined to prosecute. Agent Ringer said she would assist me and arranged a meeting with Assistant United States Attorney (AUSA) Betty Rooney. Agent Ringer said, "You'll have 15 minutes to sell the case." Then she said, "Get a passport; we're going to the islands." I told her my department would never let me travel out of country, but I got a passport nevertheless.

Agent Ringer and I met with AUSA Rooney. I must have done a decent job selling the case, because after two hours of discussion, she agreed to prosecute Bell and World Market. Rooney asked Agents Chris Tiger and Jason Fitzhugh from the Criminal Division of the Internal Revenue Service (IRS) to help Ringer and me.

I brought my boxes of evidence to our new team headquarters near Rooney's office. The evidence was placed in a secure office with restricted access. We set up the room with computers, tables, chairs, a chalkboard and a copier; Agent Ringer named it the War Room. We began the laborious process of reviewing and organizing the evidence and maintaining chain-of-custody documents. We created a timeline of key events.

The IRS maintained a liaison agent in the Caribbean, and Agent Ringer contacted him for assistance. He was able to get help from the Financial Intelligence Unit (FIU) on the island. The liaison agent and the FIU investigators confirmed that World Market was on the island and sent us a physical description of the office.

Agent Ringer and I wrote a search warrant affidavit that detailed the fraud committed by Bell and Rivera and the misrepresentations made by the brokers who sold World Market policies. Agents Tiger and Fitzhugh added a description of the premium flow and how it reached World Market. Agent Rooney then reviewed the affidavit and forwarded it to the U.S. Attorney's Office and FBI Headquarters in Washington, DC. They sent it to the FIU investigators in the Caribbean, where a judge reviewed it and issued a warrant.

Agent Ringer and I made our travel plans but were held up at the last minute by a hurricane that tore across the island. Meanwhile the FIU investigators raided World Market, escorted the employees out of the office, secured the building and posted an armed guard.

Several days and 24 hours of travel later (not to mention the cajoling I had already done to get travel approval), we arrived on the island. We met with the local police and FIU agents, and they took us to World Market's headquarters. The office occupied three floors full of cubicles with desks, computers and files. It looked like a typical insurance company office. An IRS forensic computer expert collected the computer hard drives. We diagrammed the floors and listed the employees who occupied each cube. During the search we found files that showed Bell had formed more than 25 shell companies with names similar to top-rated U.S. insurers.

While on the island we interviewed some World Market employees to better understand how Bell and Rivera ran the operation. They said Bell traveled a lot and ran the company through phone calls and emails.

You Can't Plan for Everything

During our island search, Agent Ringer received information that Bell and Rivera were in Canada, so she quickly contacted the Canadian authorities and the couple was arrested. Bell maintained that the passport and identification found in his possession were his and that his true identity was Eric Bell. He was told he would remain in custody until he provided his true name. Rivera was more cooperative and explained that she was actually Pam Winkler, 55 years old and born in Florida. However, she refused to say how she obtained the deceased Rivera's identity. She was released to the United States and indicted on the fraudulent use of a passport and released on bail. She would not consent to an interview with me.

After a month in Canadian custody Bell finally gave in and identified himself as Jerome Flores, born in New Jersey. He was returned to the United States to be indicted and placed in custody without bail.

Next we began to research the background of Flores aka Bell. I discovered that he had assumed two other identities and had been married and divorced twice before meeting Winkler aka Rivera. I located and interviewed his ex-wives, who were stunned to hear he was still alive. In each case he had suddenly disappeared, leaving them with a string of debts and no money. I showed them each a current photo of Flores and they both identified him as their ex-husband.

AUSA Rooney prepared the federal indictments against World Market for selling thousands of worthless policies nationwide, amounting to lost premiums exceeding $23 million, in addition to several million dollars in unpaid claims. World Market's underwriter was indicted along with Flores and Winkler on charges that included conspiracy, wire fraud and money laundering.

A year after his arrest Flores remained in custody awaiting trial. He became ill and was transferred to a county hospital ward. Just weeks before he was scheduled to enter a guilty plea, he suffered a major heart attack and died. Our case died the same day. Flores was the key participant in the fraud, so when he died, the other defendants petitioned the court to dismiss their indictments. The court agreed and all charges were dropped.

After the indictments were dismissed, World Market filed for bankruptcy in the United States and the Caribbean. I maintained control of the evidence in the event it would be useful for the bankruptcy trustee. Three years later I received a call from AUSA Martin Beck in Alabama. He asked if I still had the evidence from the World Market case and, when I said yes, if we could meet so he could review my files. He was investigating a case involving a liability policy issued by Pam Winkler — going by the name of Angela Bixler — using the World Market office as a front for her insurance scam. She had issued a policy to a tour operator, and shortly afterward the operator had a tragic accident in which several elderly people were killed. When the tour operator submitted a claim to World Market, he was told that he did not have a policy. With the help of my evidence, Beck was able to indict the broker, along with others working for the company, on conspiracy, wire fraud and money laundering charges. I testified at a bail hearing for Pam Winkler and was finally able to present the evidence in court. The suspects in Beck's case later pleaded guilty.

Lessons Learned

The key to a successful prosecution is to focus on the legal elements of the crime from the beginning and to gather evidence that can prove these elements. When Bell intentionally formed 25 offshore companies with names strikingly similar to the names of top-rated U.S. insurers, he knew his customers would be deceived into believing that their policies were underwritten by a legitimate company. It mattered to consumers because they knew that the well-known company would pay for a loss. Bell knew that these were not real insurers when he set them up and that any representation made that they were was untrue. Without these material misrepresentations, there would not have been sufficient evidence to prove a criminal fraud.

During the course of the investigation I had to look at any civil and regulatory licensing issues with the brokers who sold the World Market policies. In a discussion with AUSA Rooney, we decided to focus on the criminal activities of Bell and World Market and not prosecute brokers for regulatory violations. Their cooperation and testimony against Bell was more important than proceeding with action against them.

When conducting an investigation that spans several states and even international boundaries, investigators should maintain a narrow focus. With hundreds of policies sold and thousands of claims unpaid, we focused on victims with large claim losses in the states where Rooney had jurisdiction.

When I began the investigation I knew that one person or a single agency could not address the case properly. A team approach was the only way to prepare a successful prosecution, and by joining forces with state, federal and international investigators, we were able to obtain the evidence needed for the indictments.

Evidence management was crucial, and we diligently documented the sources of everything. We kept chain-of-custody records and monitored the transfer of evidence from the Caribbean police to federal agents and into the United States. Any breakdown in the chain would have provided the defense with a way to attack the evidence at trial. The cost of transferring evidence was also a factor, and we had to gather funds from the agencies before moving anything.

Although my case was dismissed after Bell died, the evidence was used in a subsequent prosecution that brought Pam Winkler and four other perpetrators to justice. They were convicted in federal court, sentenced to lengthy jail terms and ordered to pay restitution. More important, consumers nationwide are no longer being victimized by this fraud scheme.

Recommendations to Prevent Future Occurrences

Educating the consumer is a key step in preventing insurance frauds of this type. Consumers need to read their insurance policy before they incur a loss. State regulators should encourage policyholders to be proactive when purchasing insurance and verify that their agent or broker is licensed. They should contact the state departments of insurance and determine if the insurer is authorized to do business in the state.

Law enforcement should develop close working relationships with regulatory agencies and insurers. When these relationships are in place, investigators can share red flags about fraud scams and work as teams to shut down the fraud while it is in the early developing stages.

The prosecutor must be brought in during the early stages of the investigation to give guidance regarding the evidence needed for prosecution. In addition, the investigator should educate the prosecutor about the insurance industry and regulations. For example, Title 18 United States Code §.1033 prohibits people convicted of a felony that involved dishonesty or a breach of trust from being engaged in insurance unless they have obtained a waiver from a state insurance commissioner. This is an excellent tool to keep repeat offenders out of the insurance business, but, even though it was enacted in 1994, it is not fully utilized by prosecutors.

About the Author

William D. Meader, an Associate CFE, was a detective for the California Department of Insurance Fraud Division and a criminal investigator for the department's Investigation Division. During a 20-year career he investigated premium fraud, broker-agent fraud, company fraud and claimant fraud. He is recently retired and lives in northeastern Indiana. His email is bookmdano125@yahoo.com.

CHAPTER 27

Woo, Wed, Insure, Murder

WILLIAM P. HIGHT

Lake Snoqualmish lies a few miles east of Puget Sound. A 500-acre legacy of the Ice Age, its eastern edge laps at the foothills of the Cascade Mountain range. To the south Interstate 90 skirts the lake and begins an initial climb on its path to Granville. Despite its rainy reputation, western Washington experiences a perennial summer drought, and temperatures can reach the high 90s in late July and August. The cool, refreshing water of Lake Snoqualmish then attracts boaters, skiers and swimmers . . . and others who enjoy rowing a raft east across the narrow lake to quieter coves. This latter activity appealed to Chance Cagney and his new wife, Darcy, but the temperature that late July afternoon had soared to 99 degrees, and the normally quiet cove was filled with people, some of whom would become witnesses.

Chance and Darcy had been married for about a year following only a month of intensive courting. They set out on this boating adventure alone, leaving Darcy's two sons, ages nine and 11, and Chance's son, age 14, in a supervised swimming area. Chance, 39, an automobile mechanic at a local dealership, had been married three previous times and had custody of his son from his first marriage. Darcy, 34, was a homemaker whose first husband and father of her children had died of cancer five years earlier. His foresight in purchasing life insurance provided financial security for Darcy and the boys. Chance and Darcy blended their families and purchased a house together, financed largely by proceeds from the sale of her old house.

Rowing the six-man raft back across Lake Snoqualmish from the cove to the beach where the boys were playing took about 20 minutes. Several witnesses observed the methodical, unhurried pace of the single rower. One witness noticed that he faced forward toward the bow, sacrificing efficiency and speed. Another remembered that the rower appeared "expressionless, dumbfounded." No one reported that the rower sought a swimmer's help or attempted to flag down a motorboat.

249

Upon landing Chance instructed Darcy's older son to summon a life-guard but cautioned the boy not to make a commotion. The lifeguard pulled Darcy's blue body from the raft and immediately started cardiopulmonary resuscitation (CPR). As a crowd gathered, a registered nurse rushed forward to help and 911 was called. All the while Chance stood aside and impassively watched the frantic efforts. According to several witnesses he displayed no emotion, made no inquiries about her condition and offered no comfort to the boys. After a few minutes Chance busied himself with deflating the raft and packing up the family's belongings.

Darcy's lifeless body was transported to a nearby hospital where she was pronounced dead. The county medical examiner would later attribute the death to "asphyxia due to fresh water drowning." The only evidence of exter-nal trauma came from "two obliquely directed scratches" on the left side of Darcy's neck. Death was certified as accidental.

We Have a History

I learned about the drowning from reading a newspaper article the follow-ing morning. The article contained few details, but the name of the victim's husband startled me. As counsel for Hearth & Home Insurance Company, I recently had led an investigation into a burglary loss reported by, apparently, this same Chance Cagney. The case was still fresh in my memory. In fact, we had settled the claim following mediation only about ten months before, after two years of investigation and litigation. The claim file had arrived in our office with a yardarm of red flags, and our efforts only strengthened the suspicion that fraud was at play.

Hearth & Home had issued Chance a homeowners' policy that required submission of a sworn proof-of-loss document detailing the date, cause and location of the property loss as well as a description of the items lost or dam-aged and their purchase dates, conditions and values. Chance's proof was a 25-page handwritten inventory of work tools, home tools, electronic enter-tainment items and miscellaneous personal property including $960 in cash (mostly $50 bills). The inventory listed 214 work tools and 190 home tools. Chance claimed he was in between jobs, which explained the storage of work tools at home. The garage window had been broken, the carpets torn and the walls scraped. The backyard revealed fresh truck tire tracks. It was a list from memory because he claimed a file cabinet with most of his receipts and related paperwork (manuals, guides, warranties) had also been stolen. The list of more than 400 tools was specific in description (e.g., "6 pt. ¾ – 2-inch-deep sockets") and identified the manufacturer's catalog number for each tool — all high-end manufacturers. For a memory list, it was a *tour de force*. This led the adjuster to retain outside counsel to investigate the matter. One of our first steps was to consult two experts, an auto mechanic instruc-tor at a local vocational college and an experienced owner of a car repair business. Both confirmed that mechanics at major car dealerships purchase and use their own work tools but never on so grand a scale. There was no question — it was a wish list.

Working with a field adjuster and a private investigator, we inspected the house and interviewed Chance on several occasions, gathering background information about friends, former wives and girlfriends, neighbors, coworkers and where he purchased tools. During my first meeting Chance seemed reserved, not particularly nervous and otherwise unremarkable. At 5 feet 8 inches tall and 170 pounds, he was lean, nice looking and apparently fit. His home was well maintained and landscaped. His son was a cute 11-year-old kid at the time. We interviewed his next-door neighbors, whose 13-year-old daughter babysat the boy on a regular basis, and learned that he was a respectful neighbor, friend and caring father. As our circle of interviews widened to include male friends and girlfriends, a more complex and disturbing portrait emerged. We learned from Chance that he was a former Marine and from his neighbors that he claimed to have been involved in covert military operations. A former live-in girlfriend reported that he occasionally headed out late at night dressed all in black for "adventures," apparently some form of civilian covert operations. He was also very controlling, sought to isolate her from friends and maintained tight, dictatorial control over finances. Male friends confided that Chance had a menacing side and could be violent at times.

A search of court records revealed an interesting civil lawsuit brought by Chance against the State of Washington seeking $500,000 for the wrongful death of his second wife, Beth, seven years previously. She fell to her death while they were hiking alone in Falcon Nest State Park, an ancient volcano overlooking Columbia River gorge. The complaint alleged that the state negligently failed to warn hikers not to take shortcuts off the established trail and sought damages on his own behalf as well as for Beth's eight-year-old daughter who lived with them. The case was dismissed on summary judgment by the trial judge based on statutory immunity, and Chance's appeal had fizzled on a technicality only ten months before the alleged burglary.

Poring over public court records can be a dull and fruitless task. Factually substantive, discovery documents such as interrogatory answers and deposition testimony are often exchanged by counsel with no docket entry or any public trace. Here, however, we found several bombshells.

First, Chance's pre-litigation notice described how Beth's foot slipped as she turned a 90-degree corner: "Unable to stop herself, she rolled and slid down the moderately steep slope and fell over the embankment. [Chance], following approximately five feet behind his wife, could not reach her in time to break her fall. She plunged off the embankment and landed on a rocky shelf approximately 300 feet below. [Chance] ran down the trail, trying to find a way over the rocks to reach her. He was unable to do so." Second, in response to a "canned" interrogatory asking the attorney general to "please state in detail each act or omission of the Plaintiff which Defendants are contending caused or contributed to the cause of the incident referred to in the complaint," the response cited failure "to maintain secure footing . . . to remain close enough," and so on, and then concluded: "[i]t is also believed [Chance Cagney] may have intentionally contributed to the cause of [Beth Cagney's] death. Investigation continuing in that regard." Finally, in a supplementary answer to an interrogatory Chance acknowledged, reluctantly, that there was a $100,000 insurance policy on Beth's life.

No criminal charges were filed against Chance for Beth's death. He obtained the life insurance proceeds and would later admit that he had not invested or managed his newfound wealth well and that most of it was gone.

Character Testimonials

The picture that emerged from our investigation substantiated early suspicions that the burglary loss was fraudulent. The "character" evidence we unearthed was certainly consistent with a disposition toward fraud, but we had little success in obtaining specific evidence of a secret storage locker, fake purchases or a suddenly reappearing air compressor. Chance's friends and neighbors generally extolled his friendliness and minimized his dark side. Hoping that subpoena power and sworn testimony would help us crack the case, we filed an action for declaratory judgment in federal court, seeking a legal ruling that the claim was fraudulent and that no insurance proceeds were owed. If we could show on a more-probable-than-not basis that any part of the claim was a misrepresentation, under state law the whole claim would be disallowed. (This may vary with jurisdiction; consult counsel.) As costs mounted and prospects for a breakthrough dimmed, however, Hearth & Home and Chance emerged from mediation with a settlement of the $58,000 claim for payment of $28,500. After paying his attorney's fees, Chance netted $16,500.

It is likely that some of these property insurance proceeds were used to pay premiums on life insurance policies that Chance and Darcy purchased. The couple took out new policies on Darcy worth a total of $275,000, and Chance convinced Darcy to change the beneficiary on an existing $100,000 policy from her two sons to him as sole beneficiary. This was part of an agreement to name her as sole beneficiary on an existing policy on his life (which listed his father as beneficiary), a promise Chance failed to keep. On the day of her drowning death, Darcy, an unemployed housewife, had $375,000 in life insurance coverage, and Chance was the sole beneficiary.

Ten years after Beth's tragic death, 12 months after marrying Darcy in Reno and ten months after settling the burglary claim, Chance again found himself at the center of an insurance investigation. In interviews with authorities, he described how Darcy had developed a leg cramp while swimming. While he was steadying the raft so Darcy could climb in, a boat went by and its wake turned the raft over on top of her. He then heard her cough "as if she unexpectedly got water in her mouth." After about 30 seconds he righted the raft. At that point Darcy was lying facedown in the water. Chance then "breathed into her a couple times," but there was no response. Chance reentered the raft and pulled her into it. Discovering that Darcy had no pulse, he rowed back to shore; the trip took approximately 20 minutes. Chance did not attempt to summon aid from other boats on the water, nor did he alert anyone on the shore as he approached. When Darcy's sons came to the raft, he told them to get a lifeguard but not to create a fuss. A lifeguard and a paramedic unsuccessfully attempted to revive Darcy. During the resuscitation attempt and afterward, Chance was seen calmly collecting the family's beach gear and loading it in the car.

Witness after witness commented on Chance's absence of emotion. Several concluded he must have been a mere bystander and were astonished to learn that he was the victim's husband. Others assumed his demeanor resulted from shock. Questions abounded. Why did Chase bother to collect the towels and clothing floating in the water before rowing his unconscious wife back to shore? Why did he bother to put on his sunglasses? While accompanying the paramedic to the hospital, Chance mentioned that he had training in CPR; why had he not used it? On the drive home with his children, Chance reportedly told Darcy's older son to "quit crying; it's over and done with."

The impressions we form from observing the behavior and demeanor of other human beings, as screened through our own life's experience, can lead to conjecture, suspicion and even insight but not necessarily evidence admissible in a court of law. Imagine the daunting task facing county investigators and prosecutors: One witness saw a man and a woman splashing around the raft, but there were no witnesses to any foul play between Chance and Darcy out in the lake. There was no crime scene to secure and examine for evidence, no weapon and no signs of serious trauma to her body. From this bleak beginning prosecutors would have to meet the burden of proving homicide beyond a reasonable doubt.

Prompted by the newspaper article, I immediately contacted the detectives and alerted them to the fact that we had recently handled an investigation of a burglary claim brought by Chance under his homeowners' policy that we believed to be fraudulent. I also pointed the detectives to the Falcon Nest death of his former wife, his $100,000 life insurance benefit and the related wrongful death lawsuit. Thus began a cooperative effort to bring to justice a man who always seemed to be in the vicinity of lucrative insurance claims, some under tragic circumstances.

Different Kinds of Evidence

Over the next few months, police investigators compiled 3,000 documents and elicited statements from 130 witnesses. Chance's friends and neighbors, whom we had interviewed with little success, opened up to the authorities with damning disclosures. Tools allegedly taken in the staged home burglary, along with files of related receipts, were seized by search warrant. Chance's attic and crawl spaces were stuffed with equipment and supplies pilfered from his workplace. Statements from friends implicated Chance in a prior staged burglary at a friend's house as well as planning sessions for his home burglary I had investigated. Material discrepancies in the facts surrounding Beth's death in Falcon Nest State Park came to light from interviews of family members. We also learned that, perhaps seeking to further benefit from Darcy's death, Chance had made false statements in his application for Social Security benefits for his son.

Coordinating with the police, we held off until the last moment, moving to set aside the dismissal of Hearth & Home's declaratory judgment lawsuit (and its settlement) until the day of Chance's arrest on first-degree murder charges. His arrest came exactly one year to the day after our stipulated dismissal had been entered. Under the federal rules, we had one year to file for relief from the dismissal order. Most important, taking Chance into custody protected the newly cooperating witnesses from any retribution. In vacating the dismissal, the federal judge relied on the "disturbing allegations" outlined by Hearth & Home and the county prosecutor regarding Chance's "pattern of insurance fraud." Eventually, Hearth & Home was able to claim some of the "stolen" tools and pursue salvage rights.

Chance's "pattern of insurance fraud," cited by the federal judge, became the centerpiece of the state's case. He was eventually tried on three counts — murder in the first degree (Darcy Cagney), theft in the first degree (Hearth & Home), and theft in the second degree (Social Security). As the trial approached, a range of motions was considered by the state court trial judge. Evidence of an earlier false automobile theft and the two staged burglaries was allowed in. The similarities in the deaths of Beth and Darcy were allowed in to rebut the defense of accident and to prove motive (life insurance proceeds), along with incriminating statements made to friends and neighbors. Excluded was evidence of Chance's brother's conviction of first-degree murder of a hitchhiker, Chance's grandiose misrepresentations of his military service, his harsh disciplinary measures taken against his natural and stepchildren, polygraph test results and "witnesses' testimony as to their opinion and personal reactions to the defendant's demeanor following the deaths of his wives."

Both the state and the defense offered videotaped reenactments of the scenarios involving motorboat waves affecting the raft, accompanied by testimony from aquatic accident experts. The state's expert had been a safety consultant for the actual raft's manufacturer. Based on the reenactments involving that very raft, he concluded that the circumstances described by Chance "simply could not reasonably have taken place."

Key to the prosecutor's case was her ability to prove a decade-long, common scheme involving the various acts of fraud against insurance companies. Backed by the evidence, including the testimony of 26 witnesses, the prosecutor was able to tell a compelling story she described as "woo, wed, insure, murder." A pattern emerged of a single father who groomed single or divorced women with young children; married them; advocated the security of life insurance; and, with a policy in force, became emotionally cold, distant, manipulative, menacing and finally murderous.

Chance was found guilty of all three charges and sentenced to 50 years in prison for the murder count, an exceptional sentence warranted by the planning involved and the motivating greed. The judge ruled that a sentence above the standard range was justified by choosing to murder Darcy "in such a way as to directly involve her children as witnesses." He was sentenced to 12 months in prison for the staged burglary and six months for the Social Security convictions.

Affirming the murder conviction, the court of appeals commented that Chance's "guilt was truly overwhelming."

In addition to approving the trial judge's evidentiary ruling on "common scheme," the court of appeals also approved admission of extensive evidence to counter the defense theory that Darcy's death was just an accident. The court concluded that "the marked similarities between the victims, the physical circumstances of the crimes, and the relatively complex nature of the crimes support a commonsense inference that the deaths of [Chance's] spouses were not mere fortuities." Both Beth and Darcy were single mothers, both married Chance after very short courtships, both obtained large life insurance policies after the marriage and both died within a year of marrying Chance. Each death occurred during a recreational outing that was planned by Chance so that he could be alone with the victim, and the location of each death was remote, with no witness nearby. "Each killing was an orchestrated plot, predesigned to ensure the availability of a large life insurance policy and to cloak the victim's death with the appearance of accident. We are convinced that these similarities are sufficiently unusual to ensure that a second recurrence would be objectively improbable."

By statute, of course, a slayer who is the beneficiary of a life insurance policy insuring his victim may not receive life insurance benefits. In subsequent state court proceedings, Chance's father was appointed guardian of his grandson, who received $88,000 in benefits. Darcy's best friend was appointed guardian for her two orphaned children, each of whom received $149,000 in benefits.

The murder conviction and institutional confinement did not diminish Chance's greed. He opposed Darcy's estate representative and sought an accounting and recovery of property (including some he had secreted), finally relinquishing his community property rights for $30,000 from sale of their house. This was deposited in his criminal counsel's trust account. He also filed a petition challenging the criminal trial judge's minimal award of $4,500 in restitution. He lost.

Lessons Learned

This investigation reminded me of how insurance fraud is viewed by some members of the general public as more of a sport than a criminal endeavor. Justification for bending this moral line rests on the false view that there is no victim or that insurance companies have earned a measure of retribution by virtue of vaguely perceived misconduct or bad faith. This case study demonstrates how passive acceptance by otherwise upstanding citizens can enable insurance fraudsters to reap gain from their deception and — in the case of the rare sociopath — escalate his greed to include murder. I remember visiting Chance's neighbor and good friend after Darcy's death and asking why he was not more forthcoming about his knowledge of the staged burglary during our investigation. He mentioned fear of retribution but also admitted candidly that it was "only" insurance fraud. Fear of retribution by the fraudster against witnesses or investigators might be valid or merely a rationalization for inaction, but coordination with law enforcement authorities might help allay those fears and can certainly enhance convictions and efforts at deterrence.

New findings in behavioral research offer simple, inexpensive ways to reduce fraud. This burgeoning field may hold great promise. For example, results of an experiment described in *The (Honest) Truth About Dishonesty*[1] shows that simply by rearranging a form to require a verifying signature at the beginning rather than at the end of the submitted information measurably reduces dishonesty. The standard proof-of-loss form (as well as recorded, sworn statements) used by Hearth & Home and most property insurers typically have the sworn signature line at the end. One might reasonably be skeptical as to whether this would have thwarted Chance or even stirred his conscience, but the same principle may have weakened the code of silence that prevailed among his friends and neighbors.

Another lesson from this case study is that intuitive observations are not necessarily admissible evidence, but they can help a case nevertheless. Intuition played an important role in investigating Chance Cagney's frauds. Witness accounts of his inappropriate demeanor and the inconsistencies in his stories about events immediately surrounding his wives' deaths were striking. They surely gave energy to investigators and might have been useful subjects to discuss with reluctant witnesses. For example, Cagney told one friend that Beth died from a rope accident on Mount Rainier and another that she fell as she was taking pictures on Falcon Nest. In some stories she was behind him; in others she was in front. People telling fictional cover stories often get the "facts" wrong, but people who retell a true story can introduce variations of memory. Even though the dramatic evidence of Chance's emotional detachment never made it to the jury, it helped uncover the hard evidence that did convict him.

---

[1]Dan Ariely, *The (Honest) Truth About Dishonesty* (New York: HarperCollins, 2012).

Finally, investigations of potentially fraudulent insurance claims can be expensive undertakings, but most insurance contracts allow specific, useful tools of discovery. Interviews and recorded statements can be conducted by special investigative unit members (in-house fraud examiners) or private investigators. Examinations under oath, which are permitted by contract, are usually conducted by counsel and follow the formalities of depositions, including the use of court reporters, sworn testimony and signed verbatim transcripts. The insured can be compelled to provide copies of financial records (bank statements, check registers, tax returns, business records), but this tool is not enforceable against friends, non-insured family members, neighbors or colleagues. Obtaining subpoena power for depositions or production of documents from others requires commencement of litigation. Care must be taken by the insurer and its representatives to avoid bad-faith acts or omissions in the course of investigations. Often the standard for bad faith is unreasonableness or lack of equal consideration, but the definition varies from state to state, and counsel should be consulted. An investigative misstep can risk imposition of tort damages, attorney's fees or even punitive damages, depending on the jurisdiction.

Well over 90 percent of all lawsuits end in a plea bargain (criminal) or settlement (civil), but lawyers assess the strength of the case based on what they believe will be *admissible* evidence. Early retention of counsel, even if just on a consulting basis, is often the wisest use of limited investigative dollars.

Recommendations to Prevent Future Occurrences

1. Cast a wide net of informal interviews of friends, coworkers and former spouses to maximize opportunities for tips and inconsistencies.
2. File a complaint for declaratory judgment to access subpoena power to depose key witnesses identified in informal interviews. At the outset of each deposition and later as warranted, obtain verbal acknowledgments of the deponent's legal obligation to testify fully and truthfully. Explore the deponent's understanding of and attitude toward insurance fraud. Exploit inconsistencies between prior statements and testimony.
3. Consider selective surveillance particularly in circumstances where allegedly stolen or fire-destroyed personal property may be stored offsite.
4. Calculate disposable income to evaluate purchasing capacity for the quantity and quality of damaged or lost personal property.
5. Focus on issues of soft fraud (exaggerated qualities, quantities or pricing) to establish misrepresentations because of fraudsters' typical failure to think through details.
6. Where the background investigation raises character issues, develop a psychological profile before deposing the insured(s).

About the Author

William P. Hight, J.D., CPCU, consults and provides expert testimony on insurance coverage and good-faith claim handling. A graduate of Duke University (B.A.) and the University of California, Davis (J.D.), he is a member of the Washington and California State Bar Associations and has more than 38 years' experience in private law practice. (Additional information can be found at www.HightLaw.com.)

Mystery Shopping for Fraud

STEPHEN PEDNEAULT

Sang Min Lee and his wife, Soo Jin Lee, both middle-age natives of South Korea, owned a small, single-location jewelry store, where Soo Jin was responsible for the day-to-day sales and operations. On many days when not in school, the Lees' three small children stayed at the store, sitting behind the counters coloring, playing with their electronic devices or running in and out of the back storage area. Sang Min's mother occasionally worked at the store when Soo Jin could not. However, Soo Jin almost always ran the store during operating hours.

Matthew Morrison was a property and casualty claims adjuster with National Insurance. Nearing the end of his professional career, Morrison counted 24 years with National. Another National investigator, John O'Connor, worked with Morrison. O'Connor was a retired police officer who served with a local police department for nearly 30 years and concluded his law enforcement career as a sergeant. Too young to permanently retire, O'Connor launched a second career with National and had already logged four years.

Silver Star

The Lees operated Silver Star Jewelers, a small, local jewelry store in a strip plaza on an edge of Westford known for problems. The store occupied fewer than 1,000 square feet, with a public entrance facing the parking lot and a private rear entrance accessible from behind the plaza. An alarm system protected the property, and it featured a panic robbery component as well as fire and burglary systems. Silver Star did not operate a website, nor would consumers likely expect to find one for this level of retail.

Silver Star's retail space included one long glass counter with jewelry on display, visible to customers from the top looking down as well as from the front, looking into the display case.

The design limited behind-the-counter access to its far end, toward the rear of the store. The walls behind the counter held pegboard displays with miscellaneous items not typically associated with jewelry stores, such as hair extensions and head scarves. On the showroom floor stood several round clothing racks — once again, items not necessarily associated with a jewelry store. The store operated weekdays from 9 a.m. to 9 p.m., Saturdays 9 a.m. to 6 p.m. and was closed on Sundays.

Independent Expertise

I was working as an independent fraud examiner within the firm I established three years earlier, focusing on fraud examination, forensic accounting and litigation support on financial matters. I received a call from Matthew Morrison at National about a claim to which he was assigned. Morrison explained that the claim involved a property loss related to a business known as Silver Star Jewelers, and that he had worked for some time with O'Connor to understand the claim details and assess its legitimacy. The Lees told O'Connor they did not maintain normal business records and therefore based their loss calculations on created spreadsheets and handwritten receipts. Morrison said O'Connor had monitored the store's operations on a few occasions while sitting out in the parking lot and noticed that an older Korean woman also worked at the store.

Morrison also told me that he and O'Connor struggled with two barriers in the claim. First, neither Sang Min nor Soo Jin spoke any English, and each time either Morrison or O'Connor sought to elicit information from them, they needed a Korean interpreter. Second, Sang Min and Soo Jin told Morrison and O'Connor, through their interpreter, that the store did not maintain any means to track sales, and therefore, they could not provide any documentation to support the daily, weekly or monthly sales amounts they used to calculate and support their claim.

Morrison — and the case — had certainly gained my interest.

I gave him my background and told him that, based on my training and experience, I could get to the heart and facts of the matter. I asked Morrison what information I could review, and he rattled off a brief list of documents received to date. He agreed to scan and email me the insurance claim and documents for review, and so began my involvement in the case.

I identified other financial documents the Lees likely possessed and asked Morrison to track them down for me.

I read through the Lee's insurance claim; according to their narrative:

> On Thursday night, Soo Jin closed the store as usual. She removed all the jewelry from the glass display case as she did every night and placed it in the safe in the locked storage closet in the rear of the store. She closed the store and set the alarm. At some time late Thursday night, a strong

thunderstorm set off the alarm at the store, and the police responded but found the store secure. At some point after the police left the plaza, someone cut Silver Star's alarm and phone cables at the rear of the plaza. Someone then kicked in the store's back door, smashed through the locked storage closet and accessed the jewelry in the safe. Soo Jin discovered the damage and theft when she opened the store on Friday morning, noting the alarm had been disabled. She contacted the police, who took a report and searched the scene for any evidence. Soo Jin called Sang Min, who came to the store to review the damage. Soo Jin told the police that hair products and clothing were also stolen during the break-in, although much of both items remained out on display and available for sale in the store.

Once the Lees repaired the physical damage, they reopened for business with very few jewelry items in the glass display case. However, by the middle of the following week, the glass case once again brimmed with jewelry and the store functioned as before.

Shopping Trip

I knew what my first step should be: I called Jeff Mandel, a colleague and fellow Certified Fraud Examiner, and when he picked up the phone I announced: "Road trip!"

I picked up Jeff two hours later, and together we drove off to go shopping . . . for jewelry. During the ride, I explained the case and what I wanted to accomplish during this mission. We arrived at the plaza with Silver Star, parked discreetly and sat in the car to observe the store's activity for a while. Scanning our surroundings, we quickly realized that we weren't in the best part of town, and perhaps other jewelry shoppers felt the same way — we didn't see a single customer enter or leave Silver Star.

After a while, we went inside the store, which was empty except for an Asian woman behind the counter. I scanned the jewelry in the glass case while Jeff looked around the premises. As he walked around the few racks of clothes on display, I sought to "find" an item not on display and focus my shopping efforts on that particular item.

I noticed the display case held no charms and thus "found" my item. The woman stood up from her stool and walked over to me. She asked if I sought anything in particular. I told her it was my anniversary, and I hoped to buy my wife a charm. She replied she didn't have any charms.

Acting disappointed, I explained I lived in another area of the state and asked her if she knew where I might find a charm today. She suggested I try the Buckland Mall and gave me directions from the store.

I thanked her and told her I wanted to poke around a bit more to see if anything else might catch my fancy. I spied an inexpensive pair of gold earrings, and, as she put them into a box for me, I turned to Jeff, who had finished looking around, and told him I found something for my wife. Jeff played along like an experienced wingman.

I followed the woman down the counter and pulled out my cash to pay her. She rang up my sale on a cash register, and I handed her my currency. She gave me a receipt, my change, and a small bag. I put the receipt in the bag and thanked her for her help. I then (intentionally) haphazardly repeated the directions to Buckland Mall that she provided and listened as she laboriously ran through them again, based on the puzzled look I had put on my face.

Jeff and I walked back to the car, and I told him I considered the mission a success. I had accomplished my two goals, both of which Morrison found to be barriers in the past. First, I demonstrated that the woman understood and spoke English, giving me *very* detailed directions to the mall. Second, I learned that the store possessed and used a means with which to track sales: a cash register that also prints receipts.

From another plaza about a mile away, I called Morrison and updated him. Then I drove back to drop Jeff at his firm and put the earrings, receipt and bag into evidence.

Broken Paper Trail

A few weeks later I received a call from Morrison. He had more information produced by the Lees and wanted me to review it. Within a day, I met up with him to get copies of the records. I quickly glanced through them and recognized copies of tax returns, along with handwritten schedules. I noted to Morrison that I didn't see any paid invoices, inventory details or anything else I had specified for him to request of the Lees.

He said the Lees claimed these constituted the entirety of their records and that nothing else existed. Disappointed at the level of information produced, I returned to my office with the copies and added them to the evidence collected.

The next day I sorted through their records and focused my initial efforts on the tax returns, something I almost always do to get acclimated to the nature of the entity's revenues, expenses and balance sheet.

The tax returns comprised corporate returns: S corporations, to be specific, or Form 1120S, and it appeared they had produced complete copies of their filed returns for the past three years (seldom received in complete form in *my* world).

As I reviewed the most recently filed return, I noted the entity's year-end was October 31, and the return covered the period up through the October prior to the claimed burglary event.

I flipped to page 4 of Form 1120S (the balance sheet) and looked to see how much inventory they reported as of the October just a few months prior to the robbery. The inventory line item was blank. I moved to page 2 (the cost of goods sold) and looked for the beginning and ending inventory amounts. Both lines were blank.

I looked at the two prior years' returns and found the same blanks regarding inventory. I smiled because I knew the Lees had a well-stocked store and a back room full of inventory, but for tax purposes, they had expensed their purchases rather than treating the items on hand as available for sale as inventory. Tax fraud! I knew the first question I would pose to the Lees once I had the opportunity: "How could you suffer losses due to a burglary at your store just a few short months after your year-end, when you reported to the Internal Revenue Service that the store did not have any inventory?"

I turned my attention to the remaining schedules the Lees provided. The handwritten, columned analyses described items in the first column, price in the second column, quantity in the third and an extension of the value they had calculated (price times quantity) in the fourth. Without corresponding inventory schedules, I determined these constituted nothing but unsupported client-created schedules.

Worse, I noted most of the line items referenced bulk purchases of gold and silver, listing the weight and cost per weight for each line, rather than specific items of jewelry. The Lees' claim specified individually identified items lost in the burglary, but the supporting purchase schedules reflected bulk purchases of gold and silver. Nothing would enable me to match their lost inventory to any other documentation. They also failed to produce paid invoices or supporting documentation.

I called Morrison and told him that unless the Lees produced paid invoices, canceled checks and other supporting documents, I could do little with our information. Morrison suggested we set up a meeting to ask the Lees some questions under oath, an available tool similar to a deposition.

Under Oath

A few days and several emails later, Morrison and I had a date and location for the meeting. Morrison told me the Lees had retained counsel, attorney Jung Hee Kim. He also told me a court reporter and a translator would participate in the meeting.

The morning of our meeting, I prepared the conference room in my office building. O'Connor arrived first. While he determined who would sit where during the meeting, I retrieved the tax returns and schedules the Lees had provided and lined them up in front of where I would sit — near the end, close to the Lees, across the table and facing the door. I then put the bag, receipt and pair of earrings on the table in front of me, in plain view as attendees arrived.

The court reporter and translator arrived next and set up their work areas for the meeting. The Lees arrived second to last, followed by their attorney.

I'll never forget the image of Soo Jin Lee as she entered the room. She looked right at me, as if she remembered me but couldn't place me. Then she looked at the table and saw the bag, receipt and earrings. I clearly saw the light go on as she suddenly connected me with the sale at the store. Then she quickly looked away and sat down. Sang Min Lee shook my hand and sat down, as did Attorney Kim.

I looked over at Soo Jin Lee and asked her if she remembered me. I told her I had visited the store to buy earrings and pointed to the jewelry on the table. She nodded but didn't say anything. The translator asked O'Connor when she should start interpreting for the Lees. O'Connor told her she could sit back for now, as the Lees understood and spoke English, and her services would be needed only if there was something they didn't understand. O'Connor told the Lees he would swear them in and then turned the questioning over to me.

I started by showing the Lees their most recent tax return. I asked Mr. Lee if he recognized the signature on the Form 1120S. He said he did. I asked him if he remembered signing the return, and again he said he did. I asked him if he understood the tax return he signed. He said an accountant had prepared it but that he basically understood the tax return.

I asked him to turn to page 2 and show us the inventory amount the store had on hand as of October 31. Mr. Lee turned to page 2 but could not identify any inventory. I pointed to the lines that called for beginning and ending inventory and asked why the lines were blank. He said there was no inventory for tax purposes.

Next I asked Mr. Lee to turn to page 4 and point out how much inventory Silver Star had at the beginning and end of the year. He struggled through the balance sheet but couldn't find where the inventory should have been listed. I pointed to the lines for inventory and asked why they were blank. He again said there was no inventory for tax purposes. I asked Mr. Lee what method of accounting he used to track his business and file the tax return, and he seemed confused by my question. I asked him if he filed on the cash or accrual basis. He said, "Cash basis, we filed on the cash basis." I asked him if he knew the difference, and he said he did not.

I asked Mr. Lee if he could provide copies of paid invoices reflecting the inventory purchased between October 31 and the date of the alleged burglary. He said he made few, if any, purchases between the dates. I asked him how that could be, reminding him that the store reported to the IRS that it had no inventory as of October 31, and yet just a few short months later the store lost its entire inventory as the result of a burglary. I said if the store had no inventory on October 31, he needed to buy inventory between October 31 and the date of the burglary, or the burglars would have found the store empty.

Mr. Lee stated, "You don't understand. It doesn't work like that. How we keep the records for the store are not the same as what is on the tax returns. Those are simply tax returns. There's no inventory on the tax returns — we don't track it like that."

I asked Mr. Lee how he tracked it. He said, "We buy the inventory for the store. It is an expense. We write it off because we paid for it. There is no inventory at the end of the year for the tax return. We keep track of what is in the store for sale in ledgers."

Hearing Mr. Lee describe and admit to tax fraud under oath with a court reporter taking it all down, I pressed on. "So let me make sure I understand what you are saying, Mr. Lee. You have inventory in the store and on your ledgers to keep track of things, but when it comes to filing your tax return, there is no inventory because you paid for it. Is that right?"

Attorney Kim piped up with "Mr. Pedneault, I don't think you understand the method of accounting he is describing. They have two methods of accounting for their inventory. It is expensed as they purchase it."

Not having expected Attorney Kim to speak under oath, I looked over to him, rolled my eyes and asked him if he really wanted to continue this line of questioning under oath in the presence of a court reporter. I asked him if he thought it might be better to move on to another subject. I saw the light go on over his head as well, and he agreed perhaps we should move to a new subject. I knew I had them for tax fraud, under oath, and on the record.

I turned back to Soo Jin Lee and asked her if she kept the register receipts and tapes from the daily sales activity. Before she could answer, I held up my receipt and told her I knew she had a means to track the daily sales. Mrs. Lee said she threw away the receipts and register tape each night. How convenient, I thought; no one could ever determine their actual sales.

I focused my next line of questioning on the Lees' schedules of bulk purchases. I asked Mr. Lee to explain how the schedules worked and how they related to the stolen jewelry. Mr. Lee said he didn't understand, so we asked the translator to repeat the question in Korean. She did, and he responded to her in Korean. She said that Mr. Lee said it didn't work like that. He buys gold and silver in bulk. For example, he may buy 36 ounces of gold bulk, which represented three gold chains.

I asked how the bulk purchases connected to the listed items, and Mr. Lee said it couldn't easily be done, which was why he provided schedules showing that the store bought more bulk than the combined weight of all the listed items. When I asked him where the receipts and invoices supporting his purchases were, he said he always paid cash and that the scale weight slip served as the receipt (multiplied by that day's price for gold or silver). Many similar handwritten slips existed.

I asked if all of the bulk purchases went into the store's inventory, and Mr. Lee said some went into their other store in Massachusetts. Other store? The Lees had a second jewelry store? That was a revelation to me.

I asked Mr. Lee what records he maintained and could produce for his second store and was informed that both stores shared one set of records, including inventory and bulk purchases. The Lees also said they moved inventory back and forth between the stores regularly, depending on what sold well at each store. Great, I thought, a commingled mess! When I asked them to show me how they tracked inventory transfers, neither of them could locate the information on their records.

I asked O'Connor if we could take a break and speak in the hall. He suspended the recording, and we adjourned to the hall. I told him I did not believe a burglary occurred but that the Lees moved their inventory from the first store to the second one and filed the insurance claim. After investigators visited the first store, I suspected that the Lees moved the inventory back, thus explaining how they were able to restock with minimal purchases.

Settlement Discussions

Already on the same page, O'Connor asked if we should include Attorney Kim in our conversation. I thought it made sense for him to know what we thought and to understand that his client had committed — and admitted to — tax fraud.

Kim joined us in the hall, and O'Connor brought him up to speed. Kim said the Lees were good people, and he believed they suffered a loss. He said he could see the difficulties they would have in documenting their loss, but that he felt they did suffer a loss and should be entitled to something from their policy. He said the insurance company should make them an offer to settle their claim. O'Connor told him that because the Lees could not articulate their claim according to their policy requirements, the insurance company should deny the claim, but he would ask Morrison to resolve the dispute.

We returned into the conference room, and O'Connor ended the meeting. Kim and the Lees left, followed by the translator and court reporter.

I later learned Kim continued to pressure Morrison into paying the Lees something toward their loss, arguing they needed cash to rebuild their business. Morrison ended up settling the Lees' claim by sending them a check as final payment, but only for a fraction of what they claimed to have lost. Their claim was for an excess of $200,000 in losses, and they received a payment for $20,000.

Lessons Learned

I learned too late into the investigation that the Lees owned a second store. Had I known this earlier, I could have requested the tax returns and records of that second location, possibly matching items "stolen" from the first as inventory at the second store. I would likely have shopped that store as well.

This case demonstrated the importance of creative thinking and techniques, such as visiting and shopping the store to prove that the Lees' spoke and understood English. The same applied to showing that they also tracked their sales, which they initially denied doing. The execution of creative investigative measures, coupled with experience in accounting and taxes, minimized this claim payment for the client.

Recommendations to Prevent Future Occurrences

Before delving into the details, remember the basics when conducting a new engagement. What easy measures can you complete before waging battle with the documents and supporting information? In the context of this particular case, the following questioned were helpful:

- Is the insured's claimed loss even plausible?
- Could the event have occurred as reported?
- Could any other explanations account for their loss?
- Do supporting records exist and, if not, *why* not?
- If supporting records do not exist, is their explanation plausible?
- Do they have copies of filed tax returns?
- Are their tax returns realistic?
- Could an individual outside of a direct relationship with the insured provide independent and objective information?
- If so, is that individual available and, if not, is the explanation plausible?
- Can you visit the site of the loss?
- Do videos or photos exist showing the claimed event?

After answering such questions during the triage portion of the new engagement, an examiner can review supporting documents to determine if they corroborate the reported loss. Creative thinking, coupled with the application of creative procedures, often successfully identifies fraud.

About the Author

Stephen Pedneault, CFE, CPA/CFF, is the principal in a local public accounting firm he established to focus solely on fraud investigation, fraud prevention, forensic accounting and litigation support. An established speaker, author and professor, Mr. Pedneault has 24 years of experience in public accounting and fraud investigations.

Index

Printed and bound by CPI Group (UK) Ltd, Croydon, CR0 4YY

23/04/2025

14660929-0002